MANUAL FOR
PLANETARY
LEADERSHIP

JOSHUA DAVID STONE, Ph.D.

MANUAL FOR PLANETARY LEADERSHIP

Dr. Joshua David Stone

THE EASY-TO-READ ENCYCLOPEDIA
of the SPIRITUAL PATH
✦ Volume IX ✦

Published by
Light Technology Publishing

Cover design by
Fay Richards

ISBN 1-891824-05-8

Light Technology Publishing
P.O. Box 1526
Sedona, AZ 86339
(800) 450-0985

Printed by

MI**SS**ION
PO**SS**IBLE
COMMERCIAL
PRINTING

P.O. Box 1495
Sedona, AZ 86339

Dedication

This book is dedicated to three of my very dear friends Dr. Mikio Sankey, Rev. Janna Shelley Parker and Wistancia. These three beautiful souls help me perform my leadership duties in the Melchizedek Synthesis Light Academy and Ashram, and in my overall global world service work.

Preface

The idea for this book came one day during a telephone conversation with a dear friend. We weren't even meditating, just chatting away, when Melchizedek, the Universal Logos, popped into our conversation on the inner-plane level. He said, "Joshua, this is going to be one of your next books."

As our conversation came to a quick halt, I asked him what he was referring to. It seems we had stumbled upon the word "leadership" during our talk, and Melchizedek then reaffirmed that the masters wanted me to write a book on this subject. Melchizedek rang my inner bell with this idea. Here was a subject I was very interested in but had never written about. The excitement I felt was overwhelming. I asked Melchizedek what I should entitle it and he said, *The Manual for Planetary Leadership*.

I immediately wrote this title down. My friend and I thanked Melchizedek and finished our conversation. It is with great excitement that I now begin this book.

A Note from the Author

It is my opinion that the information in this book can and will be extremely helpful and interesting to my readers; however, as with all channeled information, feel free to agree or disagree. Above all else, trust your own God connection. It is my most heartfelt prayer that the information in this book will help you, my beloved readers, to clarify your own leadership roles in the divine plan and your perspectives on the great philosophical, social and political issues of our time.

Contents

Introduction by Melchizedek

This book has been brought into three-dimensional reality because it had to be. The time has come where the energies and magnificence of the higher realms must find their rightful place upon Earth. It is no longer the time when the call of initiates is directed only to the hidden crevices of the cave or to the distant peak of the majestic mountain. This has been done by some of you in ages past and by many of you during this time of mass ascension and acceleration. You are now asked to bring that light frequency into the realm of humanity and civilization itself.

The information in this book is readily available to everyone. What this material does, however, is serve as a lens, refracting these issues from the generalized and vague awareness of disciples and initiates into crystalline thought forms that can be examined and acted upon. The need to ground the spiritual into the physical on a personal and planetary level has never been as essential as it is in the present.

The higher spiritual realms accessed by many are seeking an ever-deeper infusion into the life form of civilization itself. For this to occur, the action of disciples, initiates and embodied ascended masters is needed to make this manifest upon the physical realm and within the core, or fount, from which the governing forces of humanity spring forth.

The theme of this work is universal in the sense that the grounding and anchoring of the spiritual principle must be brought fully into the daily life and activity of every initiate. The way of manifestation, however, is distinctly personal and individual. No one is being asked to be who he/she is not, yet all are being called to bring forth and manifest the best of what they are as spiritually enlightened beings.

The full anchoring of the divine essence into whatever place and position in life you are now living or to which you feel called is the best and noblest way you can serve. All that is being asked is to expand your awareness into the greater scope of the planet as a whole and with this new awareness to act accordingly, ever remaining in harmony with your own individual and distinct God-self and divine blueprint.

1

Spiritual Leadership in the New Age

Self-Leadership

One of the first prerequisites to becoming a leader among people is to become a leader within your own self. Each person's own personality is a government that must be led in and of itself. The president of the United States is the leader of the Senate and House of Representatives and people of the United States. In a similar vein, each of us is the president of our inner constituency. Our inner constituency is comprised of our mental, emotional and physical bodies, personality, chakras, desires, instincts, feelings, thoughts, intuition, sensations, subpersonalities, past-life aspects, inner child and subconscious mind. If one does not know how to govern oneself, it is not possible to effectively govern another. If you are not a strong leader over yourself, your inner constituency is victimizing *you.*

The first key quality to becoming an effective inner and outer leader is the quality of personal power. This also might be called the integration of first-ray energy. El Morya is considered an expert on leadership and is one of the trainers of the world spiritual leadership community because he is *chohan,* or lord, of the first ray.

The first ray is the will, or power, aspect of God. Personal power is a most important quality in achieving psychospiritual health. Without personal power you will become completely victimized by your energies. Your personal power is your will. Personal power translates into self-mastery, self-discipline, and the ability to remain focused and committed at all times and being the cause rather than the effect of your reality. It translates into being master of your self and your life rather than victim. It also translates into having the spiritual-warrior archetype readily available at all times, being incredibly persevering and relentless in one's efforts.

In my opinion, personal power is the number-one key quality for becoming an effective leader. Most people own their power as long as they have physical energy, alertness and wakefulness. As their physical vitality goes, so goes their personal power. The key to understanding personal power is not to give it away to anyone or any aspect within yourself—ever. The key is to always remain in your power. This takes great mental discipline and training. You do not want to give your power to your thoughts, feelings, emotions, desires, physical-body appetites, sexuality, instincts, imagination, dreams, subpersonalities or any other inner qualities.

Once you have mastered this, work on never giving your power to other people no matter who they might be. True leaders maintain their personal power at all times no matter what the situation. This leads to even-mindedness, involved detachments, divine indifference, objectivity, ability to witness, equanimity, and mental and emotional stability.

The Second Key Leadership Quality

If personal power is the first key quality to being an effective leader, then love is the second most important quality. True spiritual leaders in whatever field always use their power in a loving way. Hitler, Stalin, Mussolini, Genghis Kahn and Napoleon all had personal power, but they didn't have love.

First ray blended with second ray is personal power blended with love. This is why the masters Djwhal Khul, Kuthumi and Lord Maitreya are wonderful teachers of leadership. All seven ray-masters are excellent teachers of leadership, though each has a slightly different focus in the way this leadership manifests.

The ideal leader has what might be called tough love. He/she is tough as nails in his focus and discipline but loving and harmless as the Virgin Mary. A true leader never attacks and is never negatively angry. He might have positive anger, an expression of the spiritual-warrior archetype, or great first-ray destructive energy used in a positive sense to destroy outdated form, but he is never negatively angry.

People we respect as leaders have this wonderful combination of personal power and unconditional love emanating from their being. Certain masters are more disciplinary than others—for instance, El Morya, Sananda and Yogananda's guru, Sri Yukteswar. Yogananda and Djwhal Khul, for example, are less disciplinary. Each master has a different style within this understanding. It would make sense that El Morya, being the head of the first ray, would have a little more first-ray energy. To say they are disciplinarians does not mean that they are not loving, for they are. They might just have a little more masculine energy in their personality makeup.

I relate to this myself, as I personally have a little more of the yogi, ascetic and Buddha-type energy than the average person does. This is nothing that I try to do; it is just there. I have a little more first-ray energy than the average person does, which is one aspect of my leadership ability. A lot of this has to do with the ray structure in one's monad, soul, personality, mind, emotions and physical body. It also has to do with how God built us! Even though I have a lot of first-ray energy, my actual soul- and monadic-ray structure is second ray. For me, this serves as a good balance since the second ray is the love-wisdom ray and that of spiritual educators of the world.

Leaders can come from all rays and ray configurations. I don't have any first-ray energy in my ray chart, yet that is one of my strongest qualities. So one should not limit him/herself to just that piece of the picture. One could say, however, that all leaders have tremendous first-ray energy as an underpinning of their program.

The need for leadership manifests in all people and all situations. First, it must begin with self, then in family, extended family, church, community, profession and spiritual life.

Spiritual vs. Egotistical Leadership

The next concept about leadership is that it has higher and lower aspects: spiritual leadership and egotistical leadership. Spiritual leadership we have already begun to introduce. Egotistical leadership is shown in those earthly people who have moved into positions of power without actualizing their personalities, souls and monads. They have become leaders in a physical sense, but not in a true spiritual sense. Hitler was the leader of Nazi Germany, but used his position to make himself and Germany superior and the Jews inferior. In truth, he was a leader serving the Dark Brotherhood. Djwhal Khul told me that Hitler was actually a walk-in of the Dark Brotherhood hierarchy.

When run by the negative ego, leadership is used for self-centered, selfish, misguided purposes. Instead of using this position of power to help and serve others, the position is used to help and serve one's own selfish goals and aims. Our history books are filled with such leaders. These examples are the result of individuals, usually men, who were given leadership and power, but were neither right with themselves nor with God. It is the misuse of power. Napoleon wanted to take over the world. The leaders of the crusades wanted to wipe out the infidels. Ayatollah Khomeini wanted to create a holy war. Saddam Hussein wanted to take over Kuwait. This is selfish power, greed and lack of true spirituality. The puzzling thing is that a lot of these people actually believe in God, or Allah, which makes what they have done that much more misguided. It is hard to believe that even Hitler dabbled in the occult.

Another key quality of true leadership is selflessness. A true spiritual leader is the servant of all and totally without ego in focus. Sai Baba comes to mind here. He is a being with such vast powers it is mind-boggling. There has never been a being of this spiritual magnitude physically incarnated. Yet there is no one on this planet more selfless. He is the embodiment of unconditional love and selfless service to humanity. There is no ego emanating from this glorious being.

The Bible says, "For what is a man profited if he gain the whole world and lose his own soul?" One of the great tests of the spiritual path as disciples and initiates move into leadership is the test of power. Will the power go to their heads and will it become abused? It will if they have not done their spiritual homework on learning how to control their negative egos within themselves.

Egotistical leadership promotes within the person the need for superiority and self-inflation. True spiritual leaders could care less about this. They are more interested in group consciousness. They recognize the leadership they have been given; however, they not only don't flaunt it but are also incredibly humble, grateful and honored to have the opportunity to serve—which is really the basis of leadership.

Psychological Clarity

In my opinion, the key to effective leadership is not really so much your level of initiation or light-quotient level as your level of psychological or psychospiritual clarity. You can have the most advanced light quotient on the planet or have passed all seven levels of initiation, but not have the necessary psychospiritual clarity to be a leader. If you are not in control of your negative ego, emotional body, subconscious mind and desire body and you have not learned how to parent your inner child, you will not be qualified to lead anything, for you have not learned how to lead yourself.

Clairvoyance or being a clairaudient voice channel does not qualify you for leadership in the slightest. If you want to come into true effective leadership at the highest possible level, then do your psychological homework. This means learn to own your power and never lose it.

Techniques for Owning Your Power

Learn to:

- Maintain unconditional love at all times.
- Never give in to your negative ego.
- Be focused at all times and never lose your commitment.
- Integrate all twelve archetypes, but do not allow one to outweigh another.
- Balance and integrate the twelve rays.
- Integrate and balance all twelve astrological signs.
- Parent your inner child properly with firmness and love.
- Control your astral, emotional and desire bodies.

- Maintain self-mastery and self-discipline at all times.
- Become the master of where you keep your attention.
- Have absolute mastery over your physical diet so that you are not run by lower-self appetites.
- Properly master and integrate your subpersonalities.
- Integrate your three minds.
- Balance your four bodies.
- Balance and integrate your seven chakras and each of their functions.
- Integrate all ten sephiroth on the Tree of Life.
- Always maintain a good mental diet.
- Stay attuned to your higher self and mighty I Am Presence at all times.
- Have preferences and never attachments.
- Look at everything that happens as teaching lessons, opportunities to grow and spiritual tests.
- Forgive at all times and do not be judgmental.
- Transcend duality and remain even-minded at all times.
- Be the cause of your life and not the effect.
- Be a master and never a victim.

These are the key qualities of leadership. Develop these qualities and even if your initiation level might not be as high as another's, you will be placed in a leadership role. You will be recognized as a leader by yourself, God and the masters because you are right with self, with God and with your brothers and sisters. This is the true foundation of spiritual life. Those who have gifts of channeling, clairvoyance, clairaudience and clairsentience are wonderful; however, if they do not develop these other key qualities, there is a cancer in their program.

The psychological level is the foundation of your entire spiritual life—never forget this. Many lightworkers spend much too much time focusing on the ephemeral and don't learn the basics; therefore, they are truly not qualified for leadership when the time comes. It is absolutely essential that all lightworkers attain mastery on the spiritual level, the psychological level and the earthly physical level. All three levels are separate and require a different level of mastery.

The psychological level is the most important level of all. It is like the first story of the house. The spiritual level is then the second story. The second story will ultimately be destroyed if the first floor is not built properly. Purify and refine your character with utmost precision and this will catapult your spiritual life a trillionfold. Removing the cancer of the negative ego from your psychology should be your utmost priority, even beyond building light quotient and focusing on initiation. As Sai Baba said, "God is hidden by the mountain range of ego."

One's Ego Structure

Another important aspect of leadership is to develop a healthy ego structure. When I use this term I am not using it in a negative sense as when I speak of the negative ego. I could just as easily use the term "spiritual psychology." Every person must learn to spiritualize his/her ego personality. In my opinion, this is the most difficult aspect of the spiritual path and the most complex.

The number of complexes that disciples and initiates get caught up in is enormous. The following story of Krishnamurti, as told by Djwhal Khul, is a classic example of what happens when there is no proper integration of the ego structure.

Krishnamurti, born to a Brahmin family in India in 1885 and trained by the Theosophical movement headed by C.W. Leadbeater, was scheduled to be overlighted by Lord Maitreya in a similar way that Jesus was 2000 years ago. Leadbeater was an incredible spiritual teacher and clairvoyant whom I admire, but he tended to be a bit patriarchal.

Krishnamurti was groomed by Leadbeater from childhood and was always a child in this patriarchal-psychology sense. When he was asked to move from the constant student and son role to being overlighted by Lord Maitreya, where again he would be losing his own identity (or so he thought), he refused. He was not taught how to integrate his own identity into the mix. His choice to reject theosophy and the masters was a complete pendulum swing. On his own he thought he could have his own identity, but this could be done only with no training from the Theosophical movement or any connection with the masters. His ego structure and psychology were askew.

One more example common among lightworkers who are mediums is the high priest/priestess and the inner-child complex in which the lightworker vacillates between these two archetypes. This creates subtle separation and ego sensitivity, and it must be cleared for effective leadership. In truth, any of the twelve archetypes can create complexes in which lightworkers might get stuck. My book *Soul Psychology* offers more in-depth studies of these complexes.

Transcendence

This has always been a subject dear to my heart. This training had to do with learning to help those on the inner plane who had been persecuted in concentration camps. This, of course, brings up strong emotions for everyone.

The lesson here was being able to have compassion, to be detached to deal with the atrocities and then to have transcendence. Helping the perpetrators of these atrocities was also important—yes, even the Nazis who committed these unspeakable crimes. A spiritual leader must learn to love his enemies. As Christ said, "One can hate only the act or behavior to separate between the evil and the son of God who consciously or unconsciously chose to do this."

The number of people on this planet who truly operate out of a transcendent psychology is so small it is mind-boggling. Most lightworkers operate to a great extent out of duality: being caught in profit or loss, pleasure or pain, victory or defeat, sickness or health. They function from their emotional bodies, without the ability to remain balanced in all circumstances. Transcending duality is the consciousness of the God-self.

One example of this duality is found in many of our modern-day police forces. Because officers often become polarized from the criminals, they feel inclined to lie, plant evidence or physically abuse prisoners. Police see themselves as good and criminals as bad. But in truth, criminals aren't bad; for how can a son or daughter of God be bad? They are unconscious souls who are in need of training, education and redemption. These officers are not acting from transcendent love, not practicing innocent perception and seeing the Christ in every person they incarcerate. Instead, they are angry, caught in duality. That is why there is often a fine line between police and criminals.

It causes them to be as run by negative egos as the criminals, except they are playing the top-dog role and the criminals, the underdog. Transcendence has to do with letting go of both sides of the negative-ego coin and seeing God in all, even when appearances tell us differently.

Three Classic Leadership Styles

Three classic styles are the dictatorial, democratic and laissez faire. The dictatorial is the authoritarian—for example, Hitler, Stalin or Mussolini. Communist countries such as China use this same method, but as a group of people holding the power. The democratic form of leadership is based on checks and balances with everyone having an equal vote. Laissez faire leadership just lets things flow with little control—it's like being too yin, with the dictatorial style too yang and the democratic in the middle.

Our New Planetary Logos

There is new leadership on our planet since April 1995, when a new Planetary Logos took command. I have received the following information: Gautama Buddha replaced Sanat Kumara as Planetary Logos in a transfer that began on 12:12 but became official at the Wesak, or Taurus full moon.

The Buddha prepared for this for one hundred years. Sanat Kumara said this event had been slated for the year 2000, but because the doorway was opening and so many lightworkers were ready, the timing was accelerated. This new Planetary Logos ensoulment brings the energy of peace through the Buddha and the Christ. This, the merging of heaven and Earth—as above, so below—for which we have waited so long is now upon us.

The Buddha and Lord Maitreya together bring the Christ energy to all men and women everywhere. The third dimension is moving into the fifth and the fifth into the third, and the Earth is ascending.

Those who cannot hold the new higher vibration are either leaving or remaining in struggle and learning how to hold it. We will see a larger mass exodus, and some children will leave too if they are not able to hold the vibration. The ones who stay must be prepared to take the third initiation and move into the fourth. They have until 2012. Those who are not ready to remain here will continue to evolve, but not on this planet (as we know it). These new energies will bring more clarity as well as more duality, disaster and electrical storms.

Sanat Kumara held the Planetary Logos position for 8.5 million years, so this shifting of responsibilities was a huge event. When Sanat Kumara first ensouled the planet there were many electrical disturbances as well as other anomalies. Currently, we are also seeing shifts: new solar activity, stars moving to new locations and a comet never seen before in the heavens. We need to develop the capacity to stay centered without reacting emotionally. As we take an objective stance we will see the whole picture and be able to provide stability for others.

There is a parallel planet where people who choose, or are not ready, will go. Scientists can't see it because of the way the universe folds in on itself. Sanat Kumara's responsibility will include overlighting Earth and ensouling two physical-plane planets where people who cannot continue here are going. One of these planets is a backup. The Hierarchy does not want to have an overpopulation such as what has taken place here. These two planets are not part of Earth's solar system but are in a parallel universe enfolded on this one, so they cannot be seen.

These two planets are for the laggards, so to speak, but then we too are laggards from a much earlier time. They are for those who are not ready to move on. Normally when one leaves, he/she goes through the bardo on the astral and mental planes and then comes back. But with these new energies, people can't reincarnate on Earth unless they have taken the fourth initiation. They can't just keep hanging out on the fourth-dimensional astral and mental planes, so these other planets are being prepared for them.

All the masters are working together in synchronicity to orchestrate this great work.

Sanat Kumara will operate from his base on Venus, where he has the kumaras to assist him in supervising these new reincarnation patterns for those who are unable to return to the ascending Earth.

Serapis Bey is overseeing the mass ascension of those going from the fifth to sixth level. This is why we do not have contact with Serapis Bey at this time.

Melchizedek has taken over the seventh-level initiates to work with the synthesis model for seventh-degree graduates, those completing their 98 percent light quotient.

Lord Maitreya is overseeing all service work and holding the planetary Christ light. Sananda holds the Christ archetype for the individual. All the masters are working in synchronicity to orchestrate this great work.

This crucial lineup working with this next phase of the divine plan includes: El Morya, Saint Germain, Buddha, Sananda, Sanat Kumara, Djwhal Khul, Kuthumi and Lord Maitreya.

Through the two representatives of deity upon our planet, the Buddha and the Christ, the world of the spiritual and the world of human affairs are being brought closer together.

The Mahatma, a group being and energy that recently connected directly with Earth, embodies all 352 levels of existence up to the godhead. The Mahatma overlights, incorporates and graces all levels of existence. Its incredible energy of synthesis pervades all.

The Nature of Leadership in the Spiritual Hierarchy

In the Spiritual Hierarchy, or spiritual government of our planet, the leader, or Planetary Logos, Lord Buddha, is being overlighted in his new job by Sanat Kumara. They have the final say on all decisions. Lord Buddha has great input from the seven chohans of the seven rays (El Morya, Kuthumi, Paul the Venetian, Serapis Bey, Hilarion, Sananda and Saint Germain). On a higher level, Lord Buddha has input from Lord Maitreya, Allah Gobi (the Manu) and the current Mahachohan (name not known). Surrounding the Buddha are the six kumaras, who are his main core council.

Lightworkers must understand that there is a spiritual hierarchical order to the universe, and to the way inner-plane ashrams are established. Every person who is a leader, no matter at what level, is also a student or team member. Buddha receives guidance from Sanat Kumara and Helios, our Solar Logos. They in turn receive direction from the Galactic Logos, Melchior. Melchior, who is the leader of the galaxy, is a team member in the universal scheme under the guidance of Melchizedek. Lord Melchizedek, as leader of the universe, is a team member in the multiuniversal team.

The multiuniversal team members and leaders take their orders from the Cosmic Council of Twelve. The Cosmic Council of Twelve takes its orders from God. And God is our ultimate leader. If you want the ultimate example of leadership, pattern yourself after God.

It is every person's destiny to move into leadership in some capacity. All are leaders and all are students and team members. This is why no one should let any leadership position go to his/her head, because on the next level, spiritually speaking, each person is back to being a student and team member. The grand master himself, Lord Melchizedek, is a team member of God's ultimate leadership. In this regard every person does not have an equal vote in the running of an inner-plane ashram. In our political system, we vote in senators, representatives and president, but once they are in, they vote for us. And our president, for example, has incredible executive powers.

Djwhal Khul told me an interesting thing about how decisions are made in the Spiritual Hierarchy. Even though there is a leader at each level, there are many committee meetings taking place and a consensus is always reached at these meetings. He said there is often much difference of opinion initially; however, at the end everyone always ends up voting the same way.

Beyond the fifth dimension the akashic records and all knowledge is available and the masters do not operate out of the negative ego. Therefore, things are seen in a much clearer and more lucid manner once all the differences of opinion are put on the table, so to speak.

Knowing Your Proper Puzzle Piece

It is very important for all lightworkers to be clear with themselves. I, for example, am in charge of writing certain books and being the main coordinator for the Wesak celebrations each year. My job is also to be in charge of marketing, advertising and networking our entire program around the globe.

I cannot emphasize enough the importance of finding the puzzle piece you are supposed to play. No one person has all abilities. Spiritual leadership has to do with working for the team or the ashram, not for yourself. The core group and I constantly make adjustments in the ashram in terms of people and personnel to achieve the greatest possible efficiency and effectiveness.

For example, in the Los Angeles ashram I have different high-level initiates who surround me and help me in my work. Mikio Sankey is truly a most wonderful spiritual brother and is my main assistant in my work. His primary job is to assist me in putting on the Wesak celebration each year in Mount Shasta. This is an enormous job and responsibility and I could not do it without his help. Zandria Fossa and Elana Marti Peace in New York help input my books on the computer and do my first-draft editing. They are a godsend, for their work allows me to hammer out more books.

Raney Alexandre is a very devoted initiate and is in charge of all the computer work for flyers, books, charts and computer graphics. She is very gifted at what she does. The ability to make the products one puts out of the highest caliber and reflective of the beauty of the inner-plane energies is another leadership quality. Alexandre is also in charge of sending out all of the audio tapes from Wesak and my series of meditation tapes.

Janna Parker is another person in the Los Angeles ashram who is a very devoted Djwhal Khul initiate. She is a very lovely, selfless servant who helps me with the enormous amount of work from all the letters, phone calls, correspondence, registration packets and mailings that I do. She is an absolute angel.

A good friend of Jan's and a new friend of mine is another high-level initiate named Julie Kuever. She is in charge of research. Melchizedek has told me that he wants me to write literally about everything in this set of books called *The Easy-to-Read Encyclopedia of the Spiritual Path*. It is one set of books that I feel offers everything lightworkers need to know to achieve ascension and to move into leadership and planetary world service. In this vein Julie helps me to do some of the research that I do not have time to do.

Mary Rosales has recently moved to the Los Angeles area to work in the ashram. She has many diverse talents, one of which is her technical computer expertise and genius. Mary is a computer angel. Ultimately all aspects of her multifaceted gifts and abilities will be utilized, but for now she helps with putting my books on the computer as well as proofing them. In addition, she takes care of e-mail, the Internet and Web sites and is a Wesak assistant.

Shanti conducts the weekly classes in Los Angeles that I used to do, but has now graduated to doing much larger events. Paul is a beautiful soul who just recently joined the synthesis ashram and is my Los Angeles book editor.

Wistancia is another incredibly beautiful soul who is my book agent for all my newly written books beyond the first five officially published books. She is a wonderful channel in her own right and has her own cable TV show. My sister, Judith, is in charge of the local psychological counseling wing of the ashram. She is a wonderful light and has taken over the individual counseling work in Los Angeles that I am now too busy to handle.

Deborah and Fran are my kitchen and cooking angels. These angels do the cutting and chopping of all the vegetables and help to keep the kitchen clean as well as do the shopping for the ashram. Everyone has his or her indispensable puzzle piece and the reason the ashram runs effectively is that we all cooperate, taking pride in the puzzle piece the masters have given us.

Charles Marcarelli is our new emcee for the Wesak celebration when I am not on stage. His puzzle piece takes an enormous amount of details off my back at the actual Wesak event.

The key lesson here is the importance, in becoming a leader, of delegating authority. Some of the worst business people I have ever met are control freaks. I do not mean this as a judgment, but rather as an example of what *not* to do. People who are moving into spiritual leadership must realize that there are enormous numbers of people who are dying for the opportunity to serve in a spiritual capacity. Now, some of these people I do pay in a financial sense. Others are being paid in a spiritual sense. I have hand-selected all these people regardless of the money factor because of their devotion to the masters and their great work. True pleasure is serving God. They have become a part of an ashram team. They really do not work for me but for Djwhal Khul, Lord Maitreya and Melchizedek, just as they work for God.

There are spiritual benefits of service that come to us, for the masters recognize the core group and move them along. The initiates who help me experience a great spiritual acceleration because of their selfless service. Initiations occur in waves, and those who serve selflessly—no matter if it is just opening letters or stapling and making registration packets—are moved along in that more advanced wave. It is not what you do that matters; it is the selfless service that you demonstrate in your consciousness that is most important.

Whether you are a leader or a helper, all are equal in the work, for the divine plan cannot be complete without each person doing his/her part. I say to all lightworkers, volunteer your services wherever you think they might be best served. Even though I have been given leadership responsibilities, I am really just a helper in the work of Djwhal Khul, Lord Maitreya and Lord Melchizedek. In becoming a helper, in truth you are becoming a leader.

In my work in Los Angeles I also have about twelve other people who are the core team for helping Sankey and me coordinate the logistics for the Wesak celebration. Again, these are hand-selected people who are high-level initiates with what I call saint consciousness and are dedicated to going to the Wesak celebration to serve. They are the people in charge of registration, parking, name tags, security and meeting the needs of the people in attendance. Service is really *the key* to accelerating the ascension process.

All the people who work in the ashram are working out of group consciousness and the team concept for the good of the divine plan and the good of the masters. We are all just small links in a great chain of command, with God being our ultimate commander-in-chief.

As a leader, I recognize all lightworkers as my brothers and sisters, regardless of what ashram, spiritual teacher and/or mystery school or spiritual path they are involved in. There is in truth only one ashram, one teacher and one spiritual path, which is God. All roads lead to the same place. In this regard, I see us all as part of the same team.

Such a simple service act of turning on someone to a book can be one of the most important single events that can occur in a person's life. As spiritual leaders, do not be afraid to ask for help. Every lightworker I have ever asked has been very gracious and happy to help in the great work. Too often we try to do everything on our own, which is not really a quality of the new age. The touchstone of the new age is group consciousness. So in this vein, I officially ask you for your help in this regard.

The spiritual service team can be looked at as a sports team. Even though on every team there are certain star players and even a leader, if the goal of the team is achieved, every person on that team, no matter what his/her function, receives the same championship ring. Too many lightworkers remain isolated and too separate in their focus and do not network and combine forces for the good of the whole.

One other last thought on leadership is in regard to delegating authority. It is possible to delegate too much authority. I think of presidents such as Ronald Reagan and Richard Nixon where this was the case, in my opinion. The opposite of this mentality is one who thinks that nothing will get done properly unless he/she does it. This is not good either. Both of these extremes fall short.

Autocratic vs. Consensus Leadership

In reality, a balance must be achieved between both of these leadership styles. The inner-plane ashrams and different levels would not have leaders if there were not a need for them. There is nothing worse than an organization in which everything is done completely by consensus. Nothing gets done because everything constantly has to get voted on. Here on Earth among nonactualized ascended beings, this is hardly ever achieved. On the other side of the coin, without some form of consensus or democratic process, there is the danger of authoritarianism. In my opinion, a balance or integration between the two of them is necessary. On the inner plane there is a leader, but there is also a core council of people that the leader works with, so both leadership principles can work simultaneously.

Constructive Criticism

Another skill that is essential for leadership is to develop the ability to receive constructive criticism. The two extremes of the polarity here are either being too hypersensitive to criticism, which makes the leader dysfunctional, or being too closed and walled-off from feedback. The ideal is to be open to feedback but not hypersensitive and/or victimized by it emotionally. A true spiritual leader, no matter what profession or field, must have detachment and a thick skin. In other words, he/she has the ability to let negative things slide off like water off a duck's back but can absorb information through her screening process if there is a kernel of truth that needs to be heard.

One other danger that I have noticed among some leaders in the spiritual movement is to get your feedback only from people with the same imbalances. In other words, if someone is overidentified with his/her emotional body, then he might have friends and key coworkers who are all the exact same type. As Jung might say, such an individual's feedback will always be through the same lens. This could be true for a mental type, a spiritual type or earthly sensation-function type. It is good to receive feedback from a wide variety of people. When a leader and an organization cannot receive feedback, this is known as a cult!

Impersonality

It is essential for every person in the leadership field to develop the ability to be impersonal. With leadership often comes fame and the need to deal with large numbers of people. One cannot make personal relationships with everyone. Being impersonal does not mean unloving. On the other side of the coin, some in the leadership field are too impersonal once they come into power and hence can come across as aloof, too detached or even harsh or impatient at times. This is not good either. There must be a balance that is achieved here. There is also a need to develop a quality that I term "impersonally personal."

My particular style of leadership is to be a little more personal than most in my position. I even have my phone number at the end of my books, which is rare for most authors. I also, however, have a phone service that can take calls whenever I have had enough. In addition, I have initiates in the ashram who sometimes help me return calls when I get overwhelmed. In being impersonal as a leader you can still be totally loving and warm, but can also take care of business efficiently.

Boundaries

An ideal spiritual leader must know how to set boundaries. Again, when one moves into leadership, one deals with a great many people. One must learn how to say no and not feel guilty. One must learn not to be a slave to the phone. One must sometimes set boundaries with one's time. Melchizedek one day told me that I would be dealing with a great many fourth-dimensional types of people who are well-meaning, but would be pulling on my energies a great deal both outwardly and on the inner plane. Often I receive some bizarre letters and phone calls from some disturbed people.

Part of setting boundaries as a leader is to make good decisions in terms of who I spend my time trying to help. This brings me to the next quality of being a good leader, which is the issue of termination. Whether running a business, a spiritual ashram or a political team, there are people who come into the organization who are disruptive. Djwhal Khul has asked me on a number of occasions to ask such a person to leave and not come back to class or to a given workshop. I have to admit that it was not my favorite thing to do, but I knew it had to be done. I tried to do it as tactfully and gracefully as I could, but I also did it with full personal power and I knew this was important. These are sons and daughters of God who need to go elsewhere for help.

Another example of this might be during a workshop where some strange and/or eccentric person is repeatedly causing problems for the rest of the group or hogging the discussion. I am sure you all know what I mean. It is essential for an effective leader to step forward and stop this. This might be called tough-love confrontation. The danger here is for this power not to go to the leader's head and manifest as impatience, negative anger or intolerance.

I remember one Wednesday night class where a woman brought her baby, and the baby was disrupting the whole group. I did not do anything, and later the group members told me that it was even more disruptive than I had assumed. I promised myself that I would never let something like that happen again. On the other side of the coin, I have also been at workshops where I came in with a tough-love stand and created a confrontation when I should have probably been a little more patient. I have learned from these experiences, which have taught me to find a balanced approach.

Another aspect of boundaries is the issue of the selfish and selfless balance when moving into leadership. There is a great demand upon one's energies when one moves into leadership. This can lead to burnout if one is too much the workaholic or if one does not know how to say no. It is also a danger if one does not know how to be spiritually selfish. There is what is known as egotistical selfishness and then there is spiritual selfishness. Spiritual selfishness is an essential quality for the spiritual leadership group to develop. Being selfless all the time is a prescription for burnout. At times one needs to be selfish and regenerate one's energies, sleep, eat and have fun.

The Know-It-All

One of the other dangers of moving into leadership is becoming over-identified with the "wise one" archetype. This is called being a know-it-all. It is essential for an effective leader to, first, be able to make mistakes and, second, not to feel a need to have all the answers. Even the masters on the inner plane do not claim to have all knowledge. As a matter of fact, the Mahatma told me that it was customary for ascended masters to pass on the answering of questions above one's level to the masters at the appropriate level, even if the ascended master *thinks* he/she knows the answer. This speaks just to this issue I am bringing up here. To try and be a know-it-all is a manifestation of the negative ego. I actually respect people when they say they don't know; I find it rather refreshing.

Mystics, Occultists and Manifesters

The ultimate ideal is for every leader to develop the ability to become a mystic, occultist and manifester. It is very rare for someone to be well-developed in all three areas. This principle, however, is one of the most important for running an effective organization. The mystics are the visionaries or channels. The occultists are the ones with a well-developed understanding of what the vision means and how to formulate a plan to achieve it. The manifesters know how to physically manifest and build the vision and plan. It is essential for every person in the leadership field to recognize his/her strengths and weaknesses in this regard and to gather around himself those people who can help embody these principles.

Another aspect of this leadership concept is to have a good balance in terms of ray development. The masters guided Sankey into my life to help me personally with the manifestation of the Wesak celebrations. It is not that I could not do it alone, for I have in previous years; however, knowing that Sankey had put on martial-arts events for 5000 people freed up my energies to do other things, as I was confident in his capabilities. When an occultist tries to do the job of a mystic, there are going to be problems. If the mystic tries to do the job of the occultist, there are going to be problems. If either one tries to do the work of the manifester and is not developed at this skill, there are going to be greater problems still. This is why a great many spiritual organizations do not work, for they do not have the proper balance of all three. Gather around you those people who are gifted in these areas. It is not a shortcoming to recognize this, but an asset. I think there are but a handful of people on Earth who are truly gifted in all three at the highest possible level. Many might think they are, but not at the highest potential of each. This is another example of the importance of group consciousness.

A Universal, Eclectic Focus

This is a subject dear to my heart. It has to do with the importance of the spiritual leaders developing a universal and eclectic focus in their work. I personally feel that one of the biggest reasons my books and workshops have been so successful is because of this approach. My books honor *all* spiritual teachers, religions, spiritual texts, mystery schools and spiritual paths and synthesize them into one spiritual path. I do this even though I work out of the ashrams of Djwhal Khul and Kuthumi.

I could be focused only on theosophy, Alice Bailey and the Tibetan Foundation information, but I am not. Instead, I am well-versed, well-studied and well-read in all of them. I represent all masters, both planetary and cosmic. This is also why Melchizedek and Lord Maitreya overlight me in my work. Thousands of people are attracted because of the feeling of *inclusiveness* that is created, not exclusiveness. The feeling and thought that we are all on the same team is created. The unity of diversity is celebrated.

All seven ashrams of the chohans of the seven rays are all the one ashram of Lord Maitreya. Every spiritual teacher and path in this universe is the one ashram of Melchizedek. It is essential for spiritual leaders not to get self-righteous or superior about their particular sliver of the pie, for this is illusion. For example, my ray configuration puts me in Djwhal Khul's and Kuthumi's ashrams. However, I am in love with El Morya, Saint Germain, Sananda, Ashtar and the Ashtar Command, the Lord of Arcturus and the Arcturians, Virgin Mary, Quan Yin, Krishna, Buddha, Lord Maitreya, Serapis Bey, Hilarion, Paul the Venetian, Vywamus, Lenduce, Archangel Michael, Metatron, Sanat Kumara, Sai Baba, Yogananda, Babaji, Sri Rama, Helios and Vesta, Melchior, the Lord of Sirius, Melchizedek, Ramakrishna, Ramana Maharshi, Gandhi, Mother Teresa and Isis. Who can choose among these beautiful beings? I have been devoted to them all in full force at different stages of this life and past lives.

I have been surprised in my networking to find many of the spiritual leaders to be very isolated, often self-centered and self-focused in this regard, even competitive. This is because clearing of the negative ego has not been completed on the personality, or psychological, level yet. This is not a judgment, but it is quite a paradox that spiritual groups often do not cooperate, network and help one another. Many of the major spiritual leaders in the field are highly developed spiritually but not as developed emotionally. Lightworkers must take this into account, not as judgment but as discernment. It is time that all in the spiritual leadership realm put aside our collective egos and come together in unison and cooperation for the great work of enlightenment, redemption, salvation and ascension.

Sexuality

It is very important to come to a proper relationship and understanding of one's own sexuality as one moves into spiritual leadership. If one has not done his/her work in this area, then one will probably end up sleeping with a great many of the people in his charge. This can apply, of course, to both men and women in leadership. The opposite extreme is if the person is not clear in this area, there can be unconscious energetic bonding taking place.

There is obviously nothing wrong with sexuality, for God created it. But with leadership comes power and projection upon you by others of the opposite sex. It is of the highest importance that this honor vested upon you by God to move into leadership not be misused in this manner. One must have the highest integrity. I am sure you can all think of spiritual groups where the leader has misused this privilege. This is a point that is not often thought of in relationship to leadership but should be.

Projection

If the person who is moving into leadership has not cleared his/her negative-ego thinking, which is unbelievably common, then projection will take place. Every person thinks with either his/her negative-ego mind or Christ mind in making choices. When the negative ego interprets one's reality, projection takes place. Fundamentalist leaders, for example, will say that everybody who does not believe what they say is of the devil. New Age leaders do the same thing, but use New Age terminology.

The prerequisites of a true leader in the new age include balance in feminine and masculine energies, balance in the four-body system and three minds, good inner parenting and use of the Christ mind instead of the negative-ego mind. Finally, he maintains leadership over himself at all times, never wavering or faltering in this regard, and hence achieves stability and consistency within himself, allowing him to focus on serving others.

Personal Reflections and Colin Powell on Leadership

The day after I started working on this book I happened to be watching a Barbara Walters' special one evening. She was interviewing Colin Powell on his political views, as he was considering running for president. I was thrilled to hear her at one point ask him for his definition of leadership. Powell said, "Leadership is the ability to motivate people to achieve a specified objective." I immediately ran to my typewriter and wrote this down. Thank you, Barbara Walters!

As I mentioned earlier in this book, I have always been a leader, beginning at an early age. Prior to writing this book, if someone had asked me what the qualities of a good leader were or how and why I have been as effective as I have, I honestly would not have been able to say much. In a sense, I have just done it, not really thinking about what I was doing. This is why I am enjoying writing this book so much. It is giving me the forum to clarify the theory of what I have been doing very effectively—something that can be termed "unconscious competence." My goal at the end of this book is to go backward in the learning process and achieve *conscious competence*.

This issue that Powell speaks of as motivation is a key to my success. From a certain perspective, I have always been a motivational speaker. This skill manifested through being a psychologist, a marriage, family and child counselor and a spiritual teacher. In school as a teenager I took tests for professional aptitudes. One career that came up was sales. This is something that I thought I would never do until I realized later in my life that I *was* in sales. I was selling God, the ascended masters and spiritual psychology. I am a salesman for the ultimate product.

I do not mean sales from an egotistical viewpoint of manipulating people, which is its normal stigma. Instead, it is spiritual sales in that I am selling a product that I truly believe in, which is Christ consciousness and everything that goes along with it. When I think about the personal key leadership qualities that have helped me achieve the position that I now hold, the following come to mind: personal power, self-mastery, self-discipline, focus, commitment and decisiveness. This is the enormous first-ray arsenal.

Another driving force is my love for God and for people. A third element is my understanding of self, which has allowed me to understand others. Fourth is my attunement to God, which I maintain with steadfast vigilance. This has been strengthened by the first-ray energy along with the spiritual-warrior archetype.

In addition, my social skills, psychological training and ability to motivate people and my unbounded enthusiasm for God in all God's aspects so that every day is like the first day of my spiritual path, have been invaluable resources in achieving my goals.

This is not something I try to do. I believe that it stems from an intense devotion and commitment to achieve cosmic ascension and to be of service to humanity. Healthy spiritual desire and ambition is enormously developed within me and is an all-consuming desire every moment of my life.

In a sense, my leadership began in my work as a spiritual counselor for individuals. Then I began counseling individuals in relationships, then families and then groups. Inevitably, I lectured for larger and larger groups, which culminated in workshops for 1200 people and now the Wesak festival. It was a gradual progression of getting involved with certain key people in my life in terms of relationships and friends who added to my leadership abilities, as I did for theirs. I would also add to this list of positive relationships my parents, who were my good role models. I do not speak of my earthly family very much, but I was very blessed this lifetime. My father, Hal Stone, was very helpful as my male role model. He is a well-known psychologist who has written many books.

Being brought up in an upper-middle-class and well-educated Jewish family with two psychotherapists as parents definitely helped. This is not to say that my upbringing did not have its dysfunctional aspects as well, which of course it did. But overall I consider myself to be very blessed.

There are many more qualities of leadership I will personally speak of as this book progresses; however, at this moment these are the ones that stand out the most. The last one on the top of my head would be what I consider my most important *sadhana* (spiritual practice), which is my commitment to try to the best of my ability to transcend negative-ego consciousness.

Leadership by Example

I personally feel one of the most important qualities of leadership is to practice what you preach. There is nothing that will command more respect among lightworkers than this. Anyone can give a good lecture or channeling. The real test is, can you demonstrate your message? This is where a great many leaders fall by the wayside. It usually is the personality level that does not match the professional persona. One of the hardest lessons to accomplish on the spiritual path is to allow the spiritual self to fully embody in all levels of your being so as to achieve consistency between the three minds and four-body system. When a leader doesn't practice what he/she preaches, the respect from fellow disciples and initiates begins to falter. One's leadership abilities become damaged because you do not command the needed respect.

The Cancer of Ego

The cancer of ego is the biggest danger to leadership that I have seen in the spiritual leadership of this world in all professions including spiritual teachers. This cannot be emphasized enough. I have seen leaders who have completed their ascension and seven levels of initiation and who are even working on their cosmic ascension, yet they are filled with the cancer of ego. This cancer, so to speak, has destroyed their program and damaged their credibility. Negative ego is the root cause of all the pitfalls that curtail true leadership.

Cooperation

This is another Christ quality that is essential to develop to become a true leader among men and women. I like working with other people and I find doing so to be one of the great accelerators of the ascension path. The first principle here is the importance of cooperating rather than competing. This is a hard lesson for many lightworkers to learn. People even compete over their level of initiation.

When you truly move into group consciousness, a great deal of this can be released. To cooperate with others one must have a thick skin and practice much patience. One must also be able to practice humility and turn the other cheek. In addition, one must be able to communicate clearly. One must hold the greater work of the ashram more important than the pettiness of the personal sensitivities of the ego and personality. This level cannot be completely ignored, but it can be given a lesser priority.

Another key quality for establishing group consciousness is detachment. Also, an understanding of the psychodynamics among team members allows one to not get his/her buttons pushed as often. The principle is the choosing of love and peace instead of conflict, fear, attack and war. I am a peacemaker and I choose to remain on good terms with everybody at all costs, not for them but for my own inner peace. I will confront people when I need to; however, I will always do it in the most loving and respectful way I can while still getting my point across. I also try to be a love-finder instead of a faultfinder, seeing the best within people rather than being intolerant of others' faults and my own.

Soul Extensions

Another aspect of leadership has to do with becoming a leader for your own soul extensions. Each person has twelve soul extensions that comprise his/her oversoul and 144 soul extensions, or personalities, that comprise his/her monad or mighty I Am Presence. The ideal here is to become a leader and teacher, somewhat like an oversoul, for your own twelve soul extensions, which is your soul family, so to speak. Most of this occurs on the inner plane at night while you sleep. Becoming a leader for your soul family is one of the beginning steps to becoming a leader in the world.

After achieving your personal ascension and taking your sixth initiation, the next step is then also to become a leader for all 144 soul extensions from your twelve oversouls, which are connected to your monad and mighty I Am Presence. Then you have become a true leader within yourself, and this then allows you to be a natural-born leader among humanity.

Initiation Level

Leadership really has nothing to do with initiation level. There are a great many individuals who have stepped into leadership beyond those at higher levels of initiation, but not all people who are at higher levels of initiation have stepped into leadership. Leadership and world service are, in fact, the next step *beyond* ascension, but can begin prior to taking one's ascension.

One of the mistakes that lightworkers often make is that they wait to step into leadership and service work until they feel comfortable or have no doubts or insecurities. The nature of this mindset is that one might end up waiting forever. Insecurities and doubts will still be there after you take your ascension. At some point you have to power it out, take the risk and just do it. Sometimes in the beginning it is just faking it until you make it.

The Pursuit of Excellence

Another important quality that a good leader instills in his/her team is the pursuit of excellence. This applies to all levels of manifestation, from the spiritual plane through the mental, emotional and physical earthly plane. This pursuit of excellence is conveyed without being a perfectionist or overcritical, understanding that mistakes are okay and not judged but rather seen as learning experiences.

Charisma

Most well-known leaders have charisma or some kind of magnetic and dynamic quality about them. Charisma is something one is born with, but also something that can be developed. As you learn to come fully into your personal power and first-ray energy, this greatly increases your charisma. As you move fully into unconditional love and self-love, this adds to it. Having self-mastery and being the cause of your reality adds to charisma. Devotion to God and being a channel and/or link with the ascended masters in some form adds to it. Becoming clearer psychologically, physically and spiritually also adds to your light and magnetic quality. Developing more self-confidence and becoming more well-studied adds to this as well.

Do not be afraid to display your natural charisma, not from an ego perspective, but from the natural love and enthusiasm you feel for God and the masters. Your focus, commitment, dedication, warmth, sincerity and excitement will exude from your aura in a most natural way as you find your perfect puzzle piece in the divine plan.

Intuition and Common Sense

An effective leader has developed a good balance between the right and left sides of his/her brain. Said in another way, an effective leader has developed a good balance between intuition and common sense. One is not better than the other is; both are needed.

Social Skills

Another quality that is a very good thing to practice and develop in terms of leadership is positive social skills. By this I mean simply the ability to talk to people and make them feel comfortable. One of my jobs in the ashram is to play host to all the people who come for classes or workshops. I consider this a very important job and go out of my way to make everyone feel comfortable and special. I know how I feel going to a strange house and meeting new people.

The idea here is to treat every person who walks in the door as God, or see him/her as the Christ. People do not usually expect to be greeted so warmly. This has to do with practicing what is called in *A Course in Miracles* the holy encounter and innocent perception. This also applies to how you treat people on the phone.

One of the things I always try to do is make a warm, personal connection with every person I talk to without necessarily having to spend a lot of time doing it. People who are successful know how to do this and because of this skill, often succeed beyond the level of people with greater genius and greater skills. Most people make decisions more on feelings than résumés or technical skills.

As an adolescent and even in my early college years, I hated parties where I was forced to do this. I have found this now to be one of my greatest assets. I just forced myself to do it and one day realized that I was quite good at it.

The Ability to Sell Self

Another very important ability for all leaders to develop is the ability to sell oneself. Djwhal Khul told me it was one of the most important archetypes to develop. Using myself, for example, I am not afraid to tell people to buy my books and tapes and to come to my workshops. I am not doing this in a manipulative way like the classic car salesman. This is the negative-ego use of this archetype.

The spiritual use of this archetype is really one of the super keys to being successful and being an instrument of the ascended masters. The purpose is not to make money or inflate one's ego, but to get the information that people need to ascend and move into leadership and world service.

I believe in my books and know their value from my own experience as well as from the feedback from others. I have no compunction about giving people a sales pitch. I know they will bless me if they come to the celebration, get the ascension tapes and get involved in the ashrams of Djwhal Khul, Lord Maitreya and Melchizedek. I actually enjoy doing this, and to be perfectly honest, I never even think that I am being a salesperson. It is honestly just coming from my natural enthusiasm, my tremendous spiritual desire and spiritual ambition to get the work out to as many people as possible. I know that these books are easy to read, practical, on the cutting edge, comprehensive and integrated and that people will be greatly accelerated by reading them.

Again, if you are not willing to sell yourself, how are people going to be interested in what you do? Once again I say that I am not talking about being negatively manipulating here. I am talking about using your persuasive abilities in the service of God and the Holy Spirit to spread the love and ascended-master information around the world. I am talking here about sharing your enthusiasm and belief in what you do, the skills you have and the products you produce in God's service.

In selling yourself you are selling God. The whole purpose of what we are speaking of here, once self-actualization or ascension has been achieved, is that they are one and the same. When your enthusiasm is sincere and not an ego manipulation, people get it and are incredibly grateful that you have turned them on to your service. I honestly look at it as if I am doing them a favor, not from a pompous point of view, but rather because I know the benefit they will receive, and I want this for them. Sincerity and true desire to help others separate from your personal desires is the key.

Money

This is one of the most difficult tests lightworkers must go through. Oftentimes lightworkers are willing to be very spiritual, but on a conditional basis. In such cases, if these individuals are not paid what they consider to be their full due, spirituality goes out the window.

I recently had a situation in which a project that I was involved in with another person looked like I was going to lose hundreds of thousands of dollars and possibly more. This was due to major sociopathic tendencies on this other person's part that were now coming to the surface. When I first found out about this situation, it hit me like a lead balloon. But I quickly recovered and talked to the masters about it to see if this extreme financial loss was indeed a potentiality. They said it was indeed going to take place, although possibly not to as great a degree as my worst-nightmare scenario.

Strangely enough, I took a detached philosophical attitude about the whole thing because there was basically nothing I could do about it. My fate was sealed by decisions that had been made in the distant past, which now could not be changed. I even surprised myself by the way I was taking it even though it came as a major shock to my program. I just took the attitude that God would provide for me and worked with myself to hold this person in a positive light even though the negative ego had completely taken over his personality.

This is a service that each one of you could help with also, and I encourage you to step forward into leadership to do so. Do not get caught up in the numbers game, thinking you need to serve thousands of people. Even if you help just one person, that is enough. If you can help five, then all the better. One of the vows I made to myself early on in my spiritual path is that I would make the same effort regardless whether I was dealing with one person or with five, fifty or a thousand people. I also made the same vow in terms of money. I would make the same effort whether I was paid nothing, five dollars or fifty thousand dollars. Money and numbers mean nothing. All that matters is serving God and humanity every moment of your life.

Fame

This is another one of the major tests of the spiritual path. The three big tests are probably power, money and fame. Fame is a natural byproduct of being successful in one's spiritual endeavors. There is nothing wrong with desiring fame as long as it is from the perspective of the soul, not the negative ego. The negative ego wants fame in order to inflate one's ego and to gain recognition, power and money. The soul in some cases (not all) desires fame for an individual for the purpose of expanding world service.

There is nothing wrong with fame as long as it does not change one's personality. The test is to remain exactly the same in the way you deal with people as you did before you received the fame, fortune and public recognition. I am glad that fame has come to me at a later stage of my life when maturity has had a chance to flourish first. The danger, of course, among some in the leadership field is to let fame go to one's head, to become aloof, holier than thou and treat others as peons. As the Bible says, "After pride cometh the fall."

I remember an experience I had when I was around twenty-seven years old and was working in a counseling center. I had gotten my marriage, family and child counseling license a number of months before. The woman who ran the front office said to me one day that I was one of the few people who worked there whose personality remained the same after receiving his/her license. I was very appreciative of this feedback, and I made a strong mental note and vow to myself to always make this my modus operandi, so to speak.

Rewarding Team Members

Another very important quality for a leader to develop is the importance of rewarding team members for their efforts. Sometimes this involves simply giving praise or recognition. This is not done in a manipulative way, but in an honest way for work well done. This can be done by simply giving thanks or by financial reward. Praise can be given by the sharing of inside core-member spiritual information. Thanks can also be shown by spiritual rewards of certain accelerations for selfless service, pep talks about the importance of their particular puzzle piece and public recognition at large events, thanking the people who worked behind the scenes.

In my opinion, the true leader is not just a great teacher or channel, but rather someone who does all the little things involved with right human relationships. This keeps the team morale high and enthusiastic.

Vision

Another quality of leadership is clear vision. This has to do with seeing the big picture and not getting lost in the little picture. In business you see people who are penny-pinching and pound-foolish. This concept applies to all facets of spiritual life. Part of this is being very clear about the goals and priorities of the particular ashram or organization.

The second phase is then conveying these beliefs clearly to the team members. This again involves the vision of the ascended masters, the plans to achieve this vision and the exact procedure to physically manifest it.

Another aspect of this vision is to be able to see one's own strengths and weaknesses and the strengths and weaknesses in one's team members in a nonjudgmental manner. The second step is then being able to cultivate the strengths of the ashramic group and minimize the weaknesses.

Organization

Good leadership also requires organization and attention to detail. I see so many lightworkers who neglect these important leadership qualities. When a leader is not organized, information does not get to the team members properly. The people in the community whom the leader is serving hence get mistreated. The customer, student, client, disciple should always come first. To be outwardly organized, one's mind and emotions must be properly organized. When details are not paid attention to, they come back to haunt you. It really is the little things on the spiritual path that are the most important.

Friendship

The ideal leader must learn to balance the functions of being a leader and a friend. A leader by definition is in a position of management, but must learn to cultivate the ability to be friends with team members or coworkers. Some leaders become too friendly and their leadership function is curtailed. Others take on the extreme role of a leader and isolate or separate too much from the team. An integration of these two stances is necessary.

Feedback

A leader must learn to be able to receive feedback in a non-ego-sensitive manner and also to offer feedback in an uplifting manner. There is a psychic nutritionist, Eileen Poole, who is a dear friend whom I have seen on and off for almost twenty years. One of the most remarkable qualities about her is that you could be on your deathbed, yet after receiving her feedback, you will feel on the top of the world.

This is the quality of a good leader. Such an individual can call a spade a spade and share what needs to be said, but it is done in such an uplifting spirit of love, respect and honor that the person goes away feeling good even though he/she has been given constructive criticism. Sometimes this involves praising the person first or being tactful or touching the person or just wording the feedback in a way that the person can hear it and be inspired to improve. As long as he/she does not feel attacked, threatened or rejected, he will be able to hear it properly.

The Ability to Change

A leader must be very flexible and willing to change gears at a moment's notice if things are not working as effectively as they could. Good leadership is a constant process of making adjustments and refining vision, plans and implementation for highest efficiency. It is taking advantage of the group mind that comprises the team. This involves constantly learning from mistakes and failures and making appropriate adjustments.

Communication

This might be the most important skill of a good leader: the ability to communicate effectively with both one's team members and the public. As Virginia Satir said, "Communication is to relationships what breathing is to living." Effective communication often begins with good communication with yourself, your four-body system, your three minds, your chakras and your mighty I Am Presence. This integrated communication within self then translates to effective communication with others in alignment with the soul.

Process and Goal Orientation

The effective leader is very clear about what the goals are and conveys this in no uncertain terms to the team members. He/she, however, also conveys the importance of feeling joy, happiness, bliss and pleasure, as well as having fun and smelling the flowers in the process.

Creativity

The ideal leader is very creative. Many lightworkers are waiting for God or the ascended masters to tell them what to do. This is a mistake. The idea is to find your own path in making yourself of service to humanity. Be creative. Where there is a need, fill it. If you wait for God or the ascended masters to conk you on the head with a hammer to find out what your mission is, you might just find yourself waiting forever. It is your job to figure this out and to take action.

God and the masters guide you as you are helping yourself. One of the biggest reasons I have been successful is that I have trusted myself. As stated in Shakespeare's *Hamlet*, "Above all else, to thine own self be true." I have trusted myself even above the guidance of the ascended masters. Ascended masters are just people also and they do not have all knowledge. Do not discount their guidance, but trust your own also.

My books, progressions of my path, new ascension techniques and so on have been mostly my own innate creativity, which is an adjunct to the advice from the masters. It is important to form an equal relationship with the masters as perhaps older brothers and sisters, but still equals.

It is because I have trusted my own inner guidance above all else that my life has unfolded as it has. The universe is full of infinite possibilities. Tap into the unlimited potentialities that are available to you. Necessity is the mother of invention.

Humor

An effective leader has the ability to be humorous, which is a sign of detachment. This breeds joy in the community of helpers. If there is not joy and happiness and fun on the team, then something is desperately wrong. There is nothing worse than a leader who is too serious and too much of a workaholic. The ideal is to be a fun-loving workaholic. Too many on the spiritual path are way too serious, and this is missing the whole point of God's plan.

I am always joking around, teasing and laughing with the masters as they are with me. People mistakenly picture them as solemn and serious beings. But they are people just like us who are a little more advanced spiritually and who have much greater leadership responsibilities. Other than that, they are exactly the same. They are always making little jokes and teasing in between work sessions.

Loyalty

An effective leader is also very loyal to his/her team members. I have seen this most demonstrated by Djwhal Khul in his ashram. He is very loyal to the disciples and initiates who have been in service to him. When he moves on to the Great White Lodge on Sirius he will be taking all the senior initiates in his ashram with him. This loyalty is something I have made a mental note of in watching Djwhal operate, as it is a very noble quality to cultivate.

Dealing with Egos

One of the other great lessons one must learn in coming into leadership is dealing with the egos of other people who are moving into leadership. It is often those people who have moved into spiritual leadership in a major way who have the biggest egos of all. The ideal spiritual leader, of course, has his/her negative ego under control and is able to cooperate and work with other egos in a very loving and supportive way. Many are not clear, however, on issues of power. They are competitive, want to do their own thing and need to be in the limelight. This is rampant in the spiritual movement. One must be cognizant of this or he/she will be hit unexpectedly by a tidal wave of negative ego.

In getting leaders together in a group setting, this must be considered and there must be the proper mix. Sometimes a certain leader should not be invited because of the destructive influence he/she might have. Tact is also a quality that must be developed. True spiritual leadership must be free of ego control, self-inflation, ego sensitivity and judgment. Sometimes tough love must be demonstrated and a given leader must be given feedback and put in his place when he gets too far out of control.

I have had to take action on occasion myself. It is also essential never to argue or create separation over philosophical differences. Always hold love as being more important than theoretical beliefs. This is usually where the spiritual leaders get caught. They put philosophy before love and one-ness. Cultivate the attitude of inclusiveness, universality, harmlessness, defenselessness, and this will have a very disarming effect upon others. They sense you are not in an underlying ego battle with them, something they are used to experiencing.

Sometimes beginning conversations with compliments and positive feedback can set the tone for the rest of the conversation and contact. This can be a very tricky lesson at times and one that no lightworker will be able to avoid.

2

Laying the Foundation

The chapter that follows this chapter is designed to go straight to the core of the misuse of power and the contamination that exists within these particular arenas of human life. It is meant to call to action all those who work within these structures in order that there may be as complete a rehabilitation and overhauling as possible. This entire book is, in fact, an exposé of the problems that exist within those structures that for all intents and purposes move and control society as a whole. This is vital for your understanding and consideration, for in order to heal that which is hiding in the shadows, it must first be brought forth into the light to be seen.

Bringing into the light certain contaminated aspects within the world's institutions is necessary both for those who are directly involved in these fields as well as for the general public, who must function within the domain of those fields. As the nature of some of this subject matter cannot help but leave the reader feeling a bit overwhelmed, I am writing the present chapter, "Laying the Foundation," to offer some valuable tools of protection until these problems find their ultimate solution in the light.

Be mindful, however, that the issues brought forth in the following pages are meant to inspire you to effect change. For those of you who are not so directly involved, do be aware that action can be taken on whatever level you are operating at to create a world that functions from an ascended master's state of consciousness. Therefore, to the workers in the arenas under discussion I say, do your work! For those who are more inclined to the meditative and internal path, to you I say, meditate, visualize and pray for change. Create an atmosphere and vibrational frequency for the more socially active lightworker to go and do his/her work. In this way all are brought into awareness and therefore participate in the healing of the world.

Realize that no matter what the problem is in any given area, by connecting with your higher self, monad, the Hierarchy and God you will not be a victim. You have the power, protection and intervention of the Hierarchy of masters and angelic beings who hold you within their lighted auras. You have the ability to hold your own mind steady in the light. In fact, just by virtue of being upon the path of initiation and ascension, everything that comes into your life comes to propel you further along this path. So do know from the outset that you cannot help but function as a being of grace no matter what the circumstance.

Each particular situation, however, does have specific tools that you can activate to serve as further protection. It is important for you also to know that by using these tools you are not only helping yourself, but are likewise helping to realign and correct the difficulties within the situation. This is so because the nature of the energies you will be invoking will activate frequencies of healing and change. Remember always, beloved ones: the healing of the world begins with the healing of yourselves.

Tools for Handling Political Issues

When you are reading about the specific areas of the political system that bespeak of various degrees of corruption and manipulation, it is most important that you invoke your own mighty I Am Presence and the presence of the ascended masters, the angelic kingdom and the positive extraterrestrials. When you do this you will then be able to look at the problem areas from the point of view of the Christ mind. This will free you from having your own buttons pushed and thus free you from reacting out of your own negative ego. This tool is obviously meant to be used not merely while reading about this subject, but while participating in its sphere of influence even if all that means in your case is reading the newspaper or watching the news on television.

The basic theme of all the tools I offer is to allow you to both explore and aid in the healing of any of these issues from the point of view of the Christ/Buddha mind. These insights are not meant to instill fear in any way, shape or form. Neither are the opinions as channeled by the author meant to be automatically accepted as fact simply because they are presented to you. The Hierarchy does not tell people what to do or how to think. Yet these insights are indeed meant to stimulate your awareness on the matters under discussion so that you have the ability to participate in healing them.

In dealing with political issues, the help of the positive extraterrestrials can be most beneficial. They are a diverse group of beings who have direct dealings with government and are therefore able to aid all who ask. They will be more than happy to lift you to their expanded vision so you can see things more clearly. They are also quite proficient in protecting all who ask for their aid, and should therefore be included as a wonderful tool for clarity, direct insight and divine detachment when dealing with this arena of life.

When you need to decide on a particular candidate or issue to vote on, call upon your own higher self and monad. This will automatically put you in direct attunement with the Hierarchy of ascended masters. Then from this divine lens examine what each of the various candidates and issues stands for in order to see if it matches up with the intent of the Hierarchy. Good indicators that the candidate or issue has a true foundation in God include: a platform of unity, a show of compassion, an ability to lead infused with a basic foundation and belief in God, a true consideration of the welfare of all concerned and a demonstration of these higher principles. The best way to discern the christed or spiritualized aspects of others is to view them from that lens yourself. That is why centering yourself in your highest spiritual nature remains the best tool for both guidance and protection when confronting any of these major issues under discussion.

One final word on the subject of politics is, do not allow yourself to be confused by the barrage of words and judgments that are often thrown back and forth from one party and/or candidate to another. Look for the essence of things and for the best possible choice within the choices at hand. Stay divinely detached and spiritually attuned and listen to the intent and content that is coming through, between and within the words being spoken. Remember, the more attuned you stay to your God-self and to the ascended masters, the clearer you will see into the heart of things. I repeat the injunction to hold the mind ever steady in the light and this will then light your own way clear through the miasma of words, accusations and deliberate confusions that only the most discerning can see through. Those who see with the Christ/Buddha mind have this ability of discernment, and the best tool I can offer in the political arena is to remain centered within the divine self, whose guidance cannot fail.

Tools for Handling the Business World

As with each and every aspect of the issues under discussion, attunement to your own soul, mighty I Am Presence, the inner-plane ascended masters, the angelic kingdom and the positive extraterrestrials remains the absolute key. This, simply stated, is attunement to God. Included in this is seeing through the Christ/Buddha mind and not through the negative ego. This applies equally to every single aspect of both your inner- and your outer-plane life. I ask you to commit this injunction to your mind and heart right now. This will then continue to serve as the foundation for all your work. It will give you all the needed strength, vision, clarity and protection that you will ever need.

Therefore, I will not repeat this most profound and basic advice in the sections that follow regarding the various tools. This attunement, however, should be done before and during your use of all other tools. In fact, this basic attunement should form the core of all your spiritual and meditative work. So, beloveds, please do make this centering a daily part of your lives.

One of the best things that you can possibly do in dealing with the business world is to stay in your own integrity. This is not how the business world is generally handled at this time; however, what better way to help turn things around than to hold to the highest ideal possible? I am by no means encouraging anyone to be naive and to behave as innocent in this wheeling-and-dealing world. What I do ask you to do is be "wise as the serpent and gentle as the dove," as beloved master Jesus said. In this way you will be aware of what is truly going on in this arena, but you yourself will not fall into the lower aspects of business. Your awareness will prevent you from being taken for a ride, so to speak, while your integrity will prevent you from falling into the corruption that is a potential of this world. In time and with enough lightworkers holding to their highest integrity, this realm, as all others, will eventually be lifted into the light and business itself will be elevated to a higher sphere.

Tools for Handling the Arts

In dealing with the world of art you must be extremely selective in what you allow yourself to take in. All the various artistic mediums have work ranging from the grossest to the most refined vibrations. It is up to the lightworker simply to be discerning in these matters and choose from the higher self what you will allow to enter your sphere of influence.

If you find yourself a captive audience in a shopping mall, elevator or as a moviegoer being shown films that you would not see in a million lifetimes, simply tell your subconscious mind that you will not allow this in. If certain music bothers you and you cannot immediately get away from it, chant the name of God to yourself. If you find yourself subjected to a movie scene of an unpleasant nature, simply close your eyes. As long as you use your discernment to make the best choice possible whenever possible, you are more than halfway there. The rest of the time just crowd out unwanted stimuli by filling your mind and heart with the divine stimulation of God.

Tools for Handling the Scientific and Medical World

Since science and medicine are areas where most people feel they have little control, I want to point out right now that from a spiritual level you do indeed have much control. The fact that most of science is limited and isolated from God and all metaphysical and higher psychological understanding by no means suggests that lightworkers must be cut off from

God when dealing with this world. In fact, just the opposite is true.

When entering the arena of science and medicine either as professional or patient, it is one of the most important times that you should put on your armor of God attunement and stay centered in that most holy of places. As stated earlier, there is no greater protection than that of being centered in your own mighty I Am God Presence and in being attuned to the inner-plane ascended masters.

If you find that you need to go through the traditional medical environment for whatever reason, remember that you do not have to venture there alone. Blessed Archangel Raphael and his various ministry of healing angels, Dr. Lorphan and his team of galactic healers as well as various hosts of other inner-plane healers are all there to assist you. Call upon them. Ask them to guide the earthly hands that heal, for in truth there is but *one* great healer, and that is God. All who work as true healers heal by His omnipotent power anyway.

Although it is a sad truth that the traditional healers and healing modalities usually do not make use of these wonderful inner-plane healers or their own attunement to God, that is certainly no reason why you should not. In fact, it becomes all the more imperative that you make use of more of the spiritual aspects of healing, as it is within everyone's power to do so. Whatever method of healing you are applying, it is quite a simple matter to invoke the healers on the inner planes to help in the process. It is likewise suggested that lightworkers help each other by holding the person going through a health lesson in the light of perfect health and in sending him/her energies of love and light as well as offering prayers on her behalf.

No one needs to be intimidated by the lack of godliness in any system. What needs to be done is the invocation of God into that system so that it may eventually be raised up.

In terms of side effects from certain medications that might have been used on you in the past or that you might indeed still be on, please be aware that there are several spiritual methods to counter any negative effects. There are those who can heal and eliminate toxins from the system via spiritual means. Others do this via a more holistic or metaphysically scientific approach.

It is most important to see that while much healing needs to be done in the traditionally scientific, psychological and medical community, there is no need whatsoever to feel like a victim. As spiritual beings, you can always find a way to transcend the lower, and that is through the implementation of the higher. Beloved readers, please do not allow fear to enter into your exploration of these matters. This information is disclosed so that you may participate in the healing of sociological, institutional and other governing forces in society. For it lies within the domain of lightworkers who are called to such work to go and be about the Father's business.

Even if you are not actively called to participate, your work in these areas is equally needed through prayer and meditation. Whether it is the forefront of any of these major arenas under discussion or just sitting upon your meditation cushion, it lies within the power of all lightworkers to be about the Father's business. This is the true meaning of spiritual science, and all are called to serve.

Tools for Handling the Judicial and Prison Systems

Most of humanity is pretty much detached from the prison and judicial system, or so most people think. In actuality, the spiritual and etheric threads that link all of humanity extend into every area. Exploring aspects of our society that we do not generally relate to on a daily basis can be less than appealing and a bit overwhelming. The judicial system along with its prisons can seem like a giant steamroller rolling downhill with the ability to crush everyone and everything in its path. It is essential therefore that lightworkers realize that their very being is already part of the solution for this as well as for all social issues under discussion.

Again the clarion call goes forth for lightworkers to stay centered in the light when different judicial cases are propelled into the home through the enormous power of media, such as during the O.J. Simpson trial. Since many cases have recently found their way into the more private and self-contained worlds of lightworkers, the best personal tool I can offer is not to buy into the gossip, the antics, the hysteria and general craziness that is thrust before you. Give the amount of attention to these issues that seems appropriate to your puzzle piece, no more, no less. Yet remember, beloveds, whether you find that your calling takes you into the heart of a courtroom or simply has you glancing at the news for a brief moment during the day, do not succumb to the mass hysteria, maya, glamour and illusion that surround these issues.

The second tool is, of course, to stay centered in the light and love of your God presence and to radiate only that energy into this difficult area. When I say that it is time for the world-servers to serve, I mean just that. I am not calling lightworkers into the midst of a battle in which it is not their destiny to be involved. I am, however, calling lightworkers forth to be spiritual warriors. Let each and every lightworker stay within the guidelines of his/her own mission and from there radiate and manifest the highest of divine frequencies into the world, becoming a community activist in those areas where he feels guided.

The third tool in this arena is to begin where you are now and in whatever line of work or activities you are involved to create a world truly founded on the precepts of the qualities, attributes and aspects of God.

That is, find your ascension mission and proper puzzle piece and begin to make it a physical, emotional and mental fact. If society is to change and ultimately heal, then a society built upon love and light and equality must be made *fact*.

In order to bring the problems with the judicial, prison and other such institutions to a grinding halt, the world's environment must be changed completely. The only way this can happen is if the lightworkers do their service work from whatever place on the ladder of evolution, ray, inner calling and immediate environment they (you, beloved ones) now find themselves. The problem of the judicial and prison systems will ultimately be solved when there is little need for them. In order to begin this process, the line of demarcation between the haves and have-nots must slowly but surely be eradicated. Manifesting God where you are, seeing every encounter as a holy one, is a major way that disciples, initiates and embodied ascended masters can begin this process right at this moment. This lies within the power of each and every one of you and likewise acts as a shield of divine protection from the miasma surrounding these aspects of Earth life.

Self-Forgiveness

All humans at one time or another have participated in at least one if not in several activities that they would no longer participate in now. It is vital that you use the tool of self-forgiveness. Even if you find that at this very moment you are caught within a given aspect of Earth life that you would rather not be, I tell you most emphatically to forgive yourself this very moment.

Earth life is a tough school, and in the movement of the very evolution of Earth it is inevitable that those evolving herein get caught in the lessons life must teach. The job of the lightworker is to move through these lessons and in so doing, heal both him/herself and the world at large. This cannot be done if one is carrying around the ball and chain of guilt, judgment and nonforgiveness. I therefore request from the essence of my being that as each of you moves forward into the exploration of certain major planetary issues, you do so as a son/daughter of God, free from any guilt or shame.

All inner and outer problems are being called to light so that they can be seen, cleansed, purified and healed. They are not being called to light for either the judgment of self or others. Remember this, beloved disciples and initiates, cast aside any blame, guilt, fear or shame that you might hold regarding these issues. By purifying yourself in the fire of divine forgiveness, you are likewise well on the way of purifying, clearing and healing humanity itself.

Conclusion

I would like to close this chapter by reemphasizing the point that before the world's institutions and structures can be healed, it must be thoroughly understood where the corruption and mismanagement lie. This can be likened to transcending the negative ego and realizing the Christ/Buddha consciousness on a personal level. You cannot fully realize the Christ consciousness without having a very full and complete understanding of the negative ego. This is true on a personal level as well as on a global level. Unfortunately, the negative ego is in control of most of the third-dimensional institutions that govern this planet.

Part of the purpose of the next chapter is to expose this cancer in our society from a transcendent, nondualistic and hierarchical perspective. Humanity cannot heal the cancer until it fully understands the scope of the problem and the global organs and glands it has infiltrated. The following chapter attempts to fulfill this purpose with divine will, decisiveness, clarity, passion and the sword of discernment. The problems and challenges that face humanity cannot be healed until they are fully seen through a Christ perspective.

Do not feel overwhelmed by this exposé but rather exhilarated that it is being brought to light, for this is half the spiritual battle. It is very rare that spiritual teachers have attempted to enter this realm; this is because there has been a certain schism and separation of heaven and Earth. With the ending of the sixth-ray influence on this planet and the incoming seventh-ray planetary influence, it is now time to ground spirituality and the ascension movement into third-dimensional Earth reality. This in truth has not really been done before. Third-dimensional reality seeks to separate church and state, the soul from our educational systems and spirituality from our prisons and political system. The next chapter is my attempt to heal this breach and expose our global institutions through the differentiation between the negative ego's methods and the Christ/Buddha methods of structuring society.

This book is not meant to be the ultimate solution to such a complicated and multifaceted issue; however, it most definitely is the first major step in the process. The reader is encouraged to use this information as a launching point for much greater exploration, healing and transformation that is so greatly needed at this most pivotal time in Earth's history.

This exposé is by no means meant to be judgmental or critical but rather incisive. My aim is to bring forth spiritual observation, discernment and discrimination on these most confusing and complex subjects. There is a danger among many lightworkers that involves unconsciously living in a type of fantasy world and pretending that these challenges and issues do not even exist, do not affect them and have no relationship or purpose whatsoever in their lives that requires their attention. This is in truth a false idealism and one of the reasons that third-dimensional reality does not change. One example of this mindset is exemplified by the number of people who actually vote.

The true purpose of all our spiritual paths is not to hide in a cave, a monastery or even in an inner-plane ashram or ascension seat. It is to attune to these higher energies and then ground them properly into the mind, emotions, etheric body, physical body and, finally, into the third-dimensional Earth life and society. The purpose of the divine plan is to bring heaven to Earth, not just to achieve liberation from the wheel of rebirth and then escape Earth existence. True ascension, as has been stated many times is *descension*. It is being the mighty I Am Presence on Earth, helping others to become their mighty I Am Presence and, eventually, helping to create a mighty I Am Presence in society.

Living only in the celestial realms is indeed pleasant, but it is not our true purpose. This book is meant, in a metaphorical sense, to get our hands a little bit dirty. For as his holiness Lord Sai Baba said, "Hands that help are holier than lips that pray." Mother Teresa is a shining example of this. The third-dimensional world and all its institutions need ascended masters, high-level initiates and disciples, whom I will collectively call here the new group of world servers.

This is not the work for the faint of heart but those with the heart of God. These are the noble souls of all rays, all ashrams, all spiritual paths, all gurus and all religions who, with the will of God, the love of God, the wisdom of God and the active intelligence of God, will truly bring heaven to Earth and to third-dimensional society.

One of the problems in our third-dimensional world and with those involved in politics, whose job it is to speak of societal issues, is that the really tough dilemmas are often skirted. This is because it is not politically correct and it is too politically dangerous for those politicians who seek reelection. They instead speak on those issues that their advisors say are more politically advantageous. Since I am not running for any office and the only bosses I have are God and the ascended masters, I am not under such a limitation. My only endeavor is to raise consciousness of the problems that exist in our society from my lens of a spiritual teacher, ascended-master channel, spiritual psychologist, spiritual physician and spiritual sociologist.

If a person comes to me for counseling as a spiritual psychologist, my first responsibility is to understand the psychodynamics of his/her individual, relationship and/or family problem before I can help facilitate a spiritual, attitudinal and emotional healing. In the next chapter, in a global sense, I am taking on worldly society and all its institutions as my client.

The next chapter is in a sense the first stage of the counseling process, which is to diagnose the psychodynamics of society's problems. These are seen where the negative ego has created corruption and mismanagement. Also in this stage I will offer the Christ/Buddha and ascended-master vision for restructuring society. Society's psychological makeup must be completely seen and understood in all its multifaceted corruption and delusion before it can be cleansed, healed and transformed.

This process can be likened to going to a medical doctor and getting checked out for some illness. The doctor, naturopath, homeopath or chiropractor must run all kinds of tests to diagnose the problem. The doctor cannot prescribe a cure until he/she knows what type of illness it is and how pervasively it has affected the different glands and organs. Once all the tests have been run and all observations and discernments have been made, then and only then can the right cure or medicine, herb or homeopathic remedy be prescribed.

This next chapter is meant to diagnose the worldly ills of society. I emphasize here that what is unique about this book is the transcendent, nondualistic and hierarchical and/or ascended-master perspective taken in making this diagnosis. To the contrary, in most forms of media these issues are broached from a dualistic and personality-level point of view rather than from the perspective of the soul and monad. Sometimes in life, medicine or herbal tea must be taken to heal a given illness. This medicine or herbal remedy might not always taste pleasant; however, to heal the problem, this is exactly what the doctor ordered and is what is needed.

Contradictory to this point of view, politicians vehemently avoid prescribing medicine that doesn't taste good, or often they are too interested in getting votes, pleasing lobbyists and raising money. In the next chapter, with the help of the ascended masters, God's medicine is being prescribed. And in facing these suggestions, sometimes it would be more pleasant not to have to look at the extent of the problems and challenges that humanity faces at this time.

Yet when the true spiritual leader has this information, he/she does not try to escape or deny the work that needs to be done. The true spiritual leader is willing to become totally and completely involved in Earth life and in all society's institutions, serving as a leader and a spiritual warrior in an attempt to enact change. If we as the spiritual leaders, initiates and disciples of God and the masters don't do it, who will?

Politicians are often unwilling to speak and take a stand on issues such as entitlement programs, gay rights, campaign-finance reform, truly balancing the deficit, fiscal and financial belt-tightening and health-care reform because it is medicine that might not taste good to the voters. The issues presented in this next chapter are meant to stir your consciousness and make you think, possibly even motivate you to act upon the particular puzzle piece that is your destiny.

A great many lightworkers avoid this subject and feel this is not the consciousness of a true spiritual leader or ascended master. I am not saying that you have to be a community activist if that is a role that does not feel right to you. However, I am saying that it is your responsibility to become as knowledgeable and aware as you can of earthly civilization's problems and, if nothing more, pray, meditate, make affirmations and visualizations and do consciousness-raising work. There will be others who will be in the front lines, so to speak, as community activists, working within these different institutions. It is not okay, however, for lightworkers to ignore the problem and take no responsibility for being part of the solution even if it is simply through inner-plane work.

This book has been written to help facilitate a change in this process and to promote the development of forgiveness and unconditional love free from judgment. Also it is my aim to inspire the lightworkers on Earth to ground their spirituality not only into the psychological level but also into earthly civilization itself. This is a large piece of the revelation of the ascension movement for the next millennium. It is our job, my beloved brothers and sisters, to help make this come about.

The following chapter is not meant to be negatively critical; however, it is meant to be devastatingly honest with first-ray power, enthusiasm, divine passion, the will-to-good and the sword of spiritual discernment and discrimination. I have tried to bring forth the Spiritual Hierarchy's views on a wide range of subjects that I'm sure you will find interesting and thought-provoking.

Feel free to agree or disagree, for this is just one channel and author's wisdom and approach. The true purpose of this book is not necessarily to have you agree with everything I have brought forth, but rather to get each of you, my beloved readers, to think, ponder, meditate, pray and take action on these issues as your inner guidance guides you.

3

The Political, Social and Philosophical Issues of Our Time

This chapter deals with the great political, social and philosophical issues of our time, many telepathically channeled views of the Spiritual Hierarchy and ascended masters are presented. I say here that these varying viewpoints have been received through my own personal channel and by no means are meant to be the definitive truth on this wide spectrum of subjects. This channeled information is *my* personal truth as I have received it from the various masters with whom I work.

Leadership As It Manifests through the Seven Rays

When I speak of leadership I am not just speaking about being a spiritual teacher who channels and/or teaches spiritual principles. I am speaking here of leadership in all areas of society and in all professions. The following shows how leadership manifests through the seven great rays.

Ray one: government, politics and international relations

Ray two: spiritual education, teachings, writing, speaking, radio, TV

Ray three: finance, trade, economics, communication

Ray four: the arts, sociology

Ray five: the sciences, including medicine and psychology

Ray six: religion, philosophy

Ray seven: business, government protocol

Leaders need to step forward in all these areas and their subcategories to take over the running of this world. God is not going to do it; we are going to do it as His representatives. We all are the externalization of the hierarchy that has been prophesied. Each of us needs to take hold of the rod of power and fulfill our destinies with our piece of the puzzle that God built us to fulfill.

I want to say here that all the social issues I write about are not from a Republican, a Democratic or an Independent point of view. This is what is so unique about this book. I am speaking from a transcendent, spiritual or ascended-master perspective.

Politics

In politics look for the clear distinction between egotistical leadership and spiritual leadership. In our society politics is almost a dirty word, and rightly so. Politics as practiced in the United States and in other countries of the world is an ugly business. It is leadership at its worst. Politicians lie, cheat, have affairs and are corrupt. Instead of serving their soul, they most often serve the Republican or Democratic parties. They are nasty and rude to each other to such an extent that it is amazing they can even sleep at night.

Spiritual leadership in politics would be a completely different story if politicians would follow the dictates of the mighty I Am Presence and the ascended masters, not the good-old-boys' party line. Spiritual leadership would manifest as incredible courtesy and respect for one's appointees, never judging or criticizing them. Politicians would have the highest integrity. Legalized bribery, or lobbying, would not be allowed as it is practiced today. Politicians would care more about their own souls than in gaining the whole world.

There might still be Democratic and Republican parties, but they would function under a greater umbrella of spirituality. There would never be any kind of negative campaigning or negative campaign ads, for if they did, the American public would not stand for it. Women would hold high positions in the government in equal numbers to men. This would apply to other ethnic groups as well. Issues of integrity would be valued as much as political views.

What we have in office now are brilliant minds and bankrupt souls who are run by the negative ego. It is the corruption of power, fame and greed. In the future, politicians will stand for something other than an underlying goal to get reelected. Eventually, the leaders of all countries will be high-level initiates beyond at least the third initiation (and, hopefully, even more advanced).

In politics as it is practiced today, arguing is seen as a healthy thing, rather than engaging in loving, respectful discussions. The United States is not alone in this. Have you ever seen what goes on in England during their parliamentary sessions? It is like a room full of children booing and hissing and raising havoc. In most countries of the world there are dictatorships and totalitarian regimes. In some countries the officials even have fistfights in the parliamentary halls.

Eventually, the word "united" will really mean something and have some power. Political leaders won't hide the existence of extraterrestrials from the public. The CIA and FBI will be more controlled and the secret government will not be allowed to operate as it does. Politics, in essence, will become soul-infused and monad-infused. Politicians will truly be there to serve the people, not just give lip service. In the future, politicians will truly be working for the good of the whole.

Politics will eventually operate under the auspices of the Christ consciousness, which will be an amazing thing to see. The leaders in politics now are afraid to tackle the big issues that might threaten their reelection. No one is willing to touch the corruption of the entitlement system, gay rights and racism in our society, to name just a few of the difficult issues.

Signs of how backward our society actually is are clear if one simply looks at the improbability, given the current system, of a black or minority person holding the office of president, the fact that women still don't have equal rights or equal pay and the prevalence of racism. Nowadays politicians will say anything to get elected and seldom if ever keep their campaign promises. True integrity is lacking. Politics is devoid of spirituality; that is why it is so corrupt.

Most politicians are lawyers, and we all know the bad reputation that surrounds this profession. Lawyers are basically trained to argue. Can you imagine what the profession of law will be like when it becomes soul-infused? The earthly world has attempted to separate the soul and/or spirituality from all aspects of earthly life. This is wrong and this is illusion.

There have been small changes. Women are allowed to vote and we have desegregation and affirmative action in most states; however, the truth is, things are still not equal. Women still do not get equal pay. Racism is as prevalent as ever even though people do not like to admit it. Women do not run our government and neither do minorities.

From the soul's perspective, the concept of racism and prejudice is absurd. Everyone is God, or the eternal self, simply incarnated into physical vehicles. It is just a byproduct of seeing through the negative-ego materialistic eyes and looking through physical vision instead of spiritual vision. Interracial marriages are still frowned upon. Every person has had lives of all races and both sexes. Yet look at the number of hate crimes we have. Look at the amount of sexual harassment there is. Women are looked at as sex objects rather than as goddesses in female bodies. Gays are looked at as though there is something wrong with them. A lot of these views are unconscious prejudice and some are more overt.

These inequities are all interrelated with the spiritual bankruptcy of our educational system. Since our educational system has no spiritual element, it is a prescription to teach people to be run by the negative-ego body. Minds are developed; emotions and souls are not.

We need to develop leaders in the political and legal professions who are high-level disciples, initiates and ascended beings. Our political system needs both a Green Party that honors the environment and a New Age Light Party that is run by people who are psychologically clear as well as high-level initiates. These parties will transcend the dogma of the Republican and Democratic parties.

One example of a more progressive concept within the legal profession began approximately twenty years ago with the introduction of no-fault divorce. Prior to this there had always been a winner and a loser, and fault always had to be found. Therefore, divorce proceedings were usually incredibly vicious. Every aspect of our society needs to be revamped with laws based on the guidance of the soul and the transcendence of negative-ego values. This is part of the function of first-ray energy, which is to function as a destroyer of old forms. The structures of the world are unfortunately very slow to change. I asked the masters about this recently and they said that the world was still not ready for a Light Party. Humanity had not progressed enough to embrace it fully. It will be the job of the first-ray souls and monads who are reading this book to be the leaders in this area.

I do want to reemphasize that there are spiritual politicians and politicians with great integrity. This might not be the norm or the general rule, but they do exist and should be applauded for their efforts.

Campaign Advertising

Watching the recent presidential primaries, I was absolutely disgusted to see how debased politics has become. It operates out of the lower self instead of what in the future will be called higher-self politics. One way in which this lower self presents itself is through attack ads on television. One of the basic premises of the spiritual path and Christ consciousness is that it is *never* appropriate to attack anyone, for to attack is not of God. This is the classic case of gaining the world and losing your soul. This also applies to comparative advertising.

Politicians should ideally be very respectful, polite and complimentary of their opponents at all times. When speaking in public they should focus on their message and treat their opponent with total kindness. When attacked they should not retaliate, but just stick to the issues and not make politics a personality issue.

Certain political candidates have made a great effort in this area and have stayed primarily focused on their own point of view rather than on attacking others. These efforts should be applauded, as they reveal the fact that these candidates are coming from a much more spiritually attuned level than those who rely solely on attack tactics.

Political Spin

Political spin is a polite word for manipulation of people's consciousness. If politicians spoke from their God-selves, they would not have to spin anything politically. They would just tell the truth as they saw it regardless of their party affiliation. In my opinion, political spinning is akin to lying to support your party at all costs. It stems from egotistical thinking and vying for power rather than coming from the Christ consciousness at all times.

Voter Apathy

It is amazing how few people actually vote in this country. If 50 percent of registered voters actually vote it is considered a high voter turnout. One of the things that could be done to change this is to allow people to vote by mail and not have to leave the comfort of their homes.

A second thing that might help is to allow people to be registered to vote automatically through the Department of Motor Vehicles in their state. This type of legislation is not passed because the powers that be in the Republican and/or Democratic parties do not want all people to vote, for this might hurt their chances at reelection.

Free Elections

Free elections is a great concept that we in America are privileged to enjoy. The problem with this concept as it applies to the national presidential elections held every four years is not free elections but rather the lack of free *selection*. Who really decides which candidates will represent the two major political parties?

The presidential primaries begin on the East Coast at a time when there are still a number of candidates to choose from. By the time the primary reaches California, the most populous state in the nation, the candidate for each of the two major political parties has already been chosen. It appears that the candidate for each major party had been decided upon before the primaries and that the primaries and national conventions for the two major political parties are merely ways to stir up national interest in the election.

It will be very difficult, if not impossible, for any candidate from a third party to get elected to the presidency of the United States. In the presidential election of 1996, the leading third-party candidate was not even allowed to debate on television with the Republican and Democratic nominees! Both the Republican and Democratic conventions are given plenty of airtime on television, presenting the illusion that there are only two candidates running for office. There are always more than two candidates running for the presidency, but only one of the two nominees from the two major political parties will become president of the United States of America.

In order to ensure that a third-party candidate does not make it into the White House, we have the Electoral College. In reality, the popular vote does not mean much unless the controlling families behind the scenes decide that the public voted for the correct candidate. Twice in our history, with the elections of Rutherford B. Hayes in 1876 and Benjamin Harrison in 1888, candidates with less popularity than their opponents became president through the Electoral College system. As stated in an *Encyclopedia Britannica* article, the framers of the United States Constitution originally planned for the electors to choose the president. But the word "electors" referred to the members of the Electoral College.

If a third-party candidate is to have any realistic chance of becoming president of the United States of America, then the Electoral College system must be reformed.

Reform of the Primaries

Another interesting idea I received was that in the Democratic and Republican primaries for president there should be a lottery as to what states hold their primaries first. Usually the decision about who becomes the candidate in each party is decided by the time the first ten primaries are over. Why should New Hampshire or southern states have this power? California, for example, has ten times as many delegates, yet their primary is toward the end. The way they have the system set up is not just. This should be reformed, with the fifty states taking turns at having this opportunity.

Polls

Another interesting social phenomenon is the effect that polls have on society's consciousness. In actuality, I think in many ways it is a good thing, for I feel it gives more power to the people. In past times when polls were not taken, people voted their conscience and no one knew what was going to happen. Scientific polling has become such a science now that most of the time the public knows the outcome of an election before it is actually completed. When polls are taken on certain issues in our present-day society, this has an enormous effect on politicians. In the past they could get away with murder, for they really didn't know what the public thought.

The danger in polling, however, is twofold. The first danger is that it allows politicians to change their minds on certain issues just to get more votes. They are again pleasing the public and not honoring their own integrity.

The second danger is that sometimes people will vote against the grain because it appears that a particular candidate is going to get into office anyway. If the poll reading is inaccurate or accurate only in a given space of time and people buy into this reading and change their votes, a given candidate might find him/herself in office who, without the influence of polling, would not have been elected.

The trick is to stay centered and in integrity with yourselves at all times. In that way you, the public, will vote with awareness yet not be influenced to go against the grain. The politician obviously must learn to be in integrity in the first place and stay with his/her true and honest convictions. For that to happen, however, a shift into spiritual consciousness must pervade the entire political arena.

Push Polling

One other vile negative-ego political tool is what is called push polling. People call voters at election time and ask questions, but state them in a very slanted, negative, attacking manner to try to poison the voters. It is lower-self politics and needs to be stopped.

Entitlement Programs

One of the biggest problems in our government is the massive amount of entitlement programs, which are offered to the American people and are simultaneously bankrupting our economy. The problem is that the self-centered politicians are more worried about being reelected than doing what is right. They are afraid to touch this issue because of the voter backlash. The only hope for our political system is when the time comes that politicians learn to operate from their soul and monad rather than from their personalities and egos.

Republicans vs. Democrats

I want to make it clear here that I am not taking a Republican or Democratic position in this book, but rather an ascended master's position. The masters don't align themselves with either party, for they go issue by issue.

Spiritual Education

It is now time for lightworkers everywhere who are on the second ray to step forward and be heard, whether it is through doing counseling, teaching classes, giving lectures, writing articles and/or books, public speaking, doing radio spots or appearing on television. There is no more time to wait; you have studied and meditated enough. As Sai Baba says, "Hands that help are holier than lips that pray." Stop focusing so much on your individual spiritual growth and focus on service and raising the consciousness of this planet.

I have already given you permission to use my books as part of your curriculum as long as you give credit where credit is due. I give you permission to copy chapters. Apply the best that you have learned from any and all spiritual paths that you have been on and make the esoteric precepts exoteric facts in your lives. Live the truth that you have studied and are studying!

I challenge each and every one of you second-ray souls and second-ray monads to stop listening to your fears, doubts and insecurities and to take a risk. Leadership is empowerment, and you have prepared yourself enough and moved far enough along in the initiation process where you are more than ready to take this leap of faith. Do not compare yourself with teachers or worry about numbers of people. The work just needs to get out. God isn't going to do it and the inner-plane masters are not going to do it. If the world is going to change, it is up to us, the common people.

Business, Finance, Trade and Economics

Lightworkers of the third and seventh ray are often guided to move into this area of spiritual work. This is another area where soul and monadic fusion has not taken place. Look at most people in business and look at whether they do business from soul economics or from materialistic economic principles. Materialistic business practices devoid of spirituality operate through control, poverty consciousness, competition, fear and ripping people off. The notorious car salesman or car repairman who takes advantage of unsuspecting customers exemplifies this mentality. Such people worship money, not God. They will do anything to make money, including selling their soul to the devil.

Spiritual business practices are based on the ideal of service. Service to the sons and daughters of God is the first priority, and through giving good service, money comes. This is based on the law of karma. What you sow you reap, and what you put out comes back to you. Spiritual business practices are based on the highest integrity. To rip off a customer in truth is to rip off both God and you.

Continuing in this vein, spiritual business practice is based on the law of tithing and seed money, of giving ten percent of one's salary to a noble spiritual cause, and by the law of the universe receiving a tenfold return. "Seek ye the kingdom of God and all things shall be given unto thee," including material wealth. Spiritual business practices means valuing money, but not putting it before God and your own soul. When you do good work at fair prices, your business will grow by leaps and bounds because of the godly energy with which you are infusing it. People will sense this and become loyal customers.

In essence, spiritual business leadership has to do with manifesting the Christ consciousness into the way you deal with money and material trade. What if you gain the whole world (money) yet lose your own soul? Those who put money first will find themselves bankrupt on the inner plane even if they were millionaires on the earthly plane. This is every person's fate if he/she puts money before God.

There is nothing wrong with becoming a millionaire, and as a matter of fact this is what God wants for every person in this world, as long as it is done through spiritually honest means. It is time for third- and seventh-ray souls to take the rod of power and step forward, becoming leaders in terms of their own business and teaching these principles to others.

Part of our world's problems is that too many lightworkers are taking leadership in a second-ray focus. More are needed in these other areas for true world change. Do business and deal with money as God or Christ would deal with it and see yourself grow rich both spiritually and materially.

I remember a client I had who was in real estate. She was not doing very well even though she worked sixteen hours a day and was very bright. I helped her to become more soul and monadically infused, instructing her to let go of her fear and control and instead rely more on God. I had her doing affirmations and prayers and working literally half as much. It was hard for her to let go, but I finally convinced her to do an experiment and try this new approach. The experiment worked; she worked half as much and made two to three times as much money.

The chapter in *Soul Psychology* titled "The Laws of Manifestation" is a good reference for tools on reprogramming your thoughts. When you are right with God, money just comes; your consciousness is properly balanced, integrated and soul-infused, so you have the Midas touch. Let the soul govern how you deal with money, not the negative ego. When you start to worry, pray and do affirmations and visualizations for prosperity instead of contracting and/or giving in to the negative-ego methods. Study books like *Think and Grow Rich* by Napoleon Hill and others like it. Become a leader in your community through example, and if you are inspired to do so, teach people what this means.

The Arts and Sociology

This is another area in which the soul and monad need to become more infused. Music, art, theater and the likes need to be honored more in our society as it is honored and recognized on the inner planes. Artists and musicians perform a wonderful service to humanity. More of these artists, however, need to learn to channel art from their soul and monad and higher dimensions.

Music and art affect us more profoundly than we realize. Take, for example, the work of Michelangelo, which stirs the very depth of one's soul. Certain pieces of music have the same effect. Art can be channeled from different levels and aspects of one's being. Some New Age artists and musicians are creating music and art pieces that can greatly accelerate one's ascension, open chakras and clear one's field simply by experiencing these works.

More money in our society needs to be allocated for the arts, and it needs to be honored more for its important function. It must be realized that there are both lower and higher expressions of the arts. Rock 'n' roll, for example, is often a lower expression. The cadence, the wording and the volume often, though not always, lower your vibration. The lyrics of many modern-day pop songs are pathetic, teaching codependency and victim consciousness.

In the future, art and music will be an expression of the soul, monad, angels and archangels of the arts and of spirit guides who were incredible artists in past lives. New-age artists will literally be channeling the music, art and theater of the spheres. People will be taught to channel art from higher dimensions. This type of music, art, theater and architecture will raise the entire society's consciousness.

Certain buildings like the Parthenon, the Sistine Chapel, the Taj Mahal and the Great Pyramid at Giza have an enormous effect on one's consciousness. The possibility of the arts is unlimited, and I encourage New Age artists to take up the rod of power and lead the way toward creating and teaching people about this kind of art.

In our Wesak celebration we have music, vocals, physical movement and visual-art displays adorning the auditorium. During the breaks individual healers offer their assistance in relieving some of the pent-up energy within the physical body. Do you see that ascension is not just taught through a book or channeling? It is taught through all professions and all fields of expression.

Another area is ascension poetry. Can you imagine a society where everyplace you traveled during your day would have architecture and spiritual statues? Imagine spiritual music playing in the office buildings, nature and waterfalls everywhere and beautiful, uplifting paintings in the buildings. Do you see how uplifting this would be to the spirit?

In order to enact change, all aspects of our surroundings must be considered. Even the clothing we wear and its various colors have an effect on consciousness. The Arcturians have a society where every aspect is geared to uplift and aid in the ascension process. It is now time for the leadership of lightworkers to step forward and fulfill their destiny in these areas.

In the field of sociology, people will be taught to honor the cultural heritage while simultaneously recognizing everybody's oneness on an essence level. Spirituality does not mean that everybody should be the same and that all cultural and ethnicity should be abolished. It just means that we should not be so attached to it and instead look at the bigger picture. The same applies to religion. Our future society will still have a multiplicity of religions for people to choose from, which is good and as it should be. We simply must not allow the negative ego to tell us that one is better than another.

Religion

The leaders of our religious institutions need to let go of the narrow focus of their particular form and see the universality of all religions. They need to see that all paths lead to the same place. Religious leaders must work together for the good of the whole and realize that Christ consciousness, Buddha consciousness, Krishna consciousness, Allah consciousness and Moses consciousness are truly the same thing. Religious leaders must free themselves from the dogma and contamination of negative ego that has infiltrated these institutions. This has taken place in all traditional religions. There is now a need for more New Age, spiritualistic and universalistic churches that honor all masters, all religions and all mystery schools.

The churches of tomorrow will recognize the existence of the ascended masters. The teachings of the path of ascension and seven levels of initiation will one day be taught in every church and temple around the world. The bridging of the world's religions has taken place to a certain degree with the teachings of people like the Dalai Lama and the Pope, who encourage greater openness and tolerance between religious leaders. But more work in this area is still needed.

Fundamentalist teachings are still serving the Dark Brotherhood in many ways. It is time for the church leaders to step forward into the ministry and begin to merge traditional and New Age understanding. The Fundamentalist religions see the New Age movement as Satan, and this must change. On the other hand, many of the New Age movements are just as judgmental.

The Edgar Cayce organization thinks that all channeling stopped with Cayce. The I Am Foundation believes that all channeling stopped with Godfre Ray King. Theosophists are stuck in the Theosophical movement. The Lucis Trust and Alice Bailey-material organization think that Bailey was the last great telepath. It seems that whenever an organization is formed around a great channel and teacher, the negative ego moves in along with self-righteousness and growth stops.

If you look from an inner-plane level at the people who are locked into these organizations, they are stuck in 1890, 1930 or 1942. I know, for I too have been caught in this mentality. Even the Paramahansa Yogananda organization (Self-Realization Fellowship) teaches that you should study nothing else but his books. In my opinion this is a very narrow-minded view. Bear in mind that the organization is not necessarily representative of the teacher who brought through a new dispensation. It is not the intrinsic nature of many of the aforementioned teachings that must be guarded against, for some of these teachings are incredibly enlightening. I myself hold the newer revelations in the highest regard, as they are pivotal in their own evolution and in moving the planet as a whole one step closer to God. It is the organizational structure that one must look out for and be discerning about.

Often the force of a great revelation gets locked in the confines of the organization built around it. This is even true in regard to the teaching and revelation of Jesus Christ. One must therefore separate the baby from the bath water and see what the core of a specific teaching has to offer, despite the limitation that a given organization has put around it.

Sai Baba is one spiritual teacher who has broken out of this more than any other. He says, "I have not come to create a new religion but to repair the ancient highways to God." Sai Baba teaches that whatever religion you are, keep it, for he says he is all of them. No matter which master you call, he will be there—quite refreshing.

The religion of the future is the path of universalism and eclecticism. It holds the greatest opportunity for advanced and accelerated growth. In my series of ascension books I have attempted to synthesize and integrate all religions, all masters, all schools of thoughts, all spiritual texts, all mystery schools, all philosophies and all forms of psychology under the umbrella and foundation of the teachings of the ascended masters. This has been gathered into one set of books that respects and honors the traditions of the past, updates and brings them into the present, then channels the future dispensation. This is why I have called these books *The Easy-to-Read Encyclopedia of the Spiritual Path,* for the goal has been to have them include everything one needs to know to achieve planetary and cosmic ascension and to realize God.

The Sciences

Science is another profession in which soul and monadic infusion is sadly lacking. Our modern definition of science states that all that exists is what can be experienced through our five senses. This is, of course, the height of ignorance. More accurately, it states what can be sensed with the five senses is one-tenth of God's creation. So science by its own definition is 90 percent inaccurate.

This philosophy pervades our scientific institutions. It is hard to believe people can actually live in this state of consciousness. The only truth they acknowledge is what can be obtained from running a "scientific" experiment. In my opinion, 90 percent of the tests that are run are so incredibly obvious in terms of the truth or validity that a person should not even waste his/her time. Science rejects the right-brain and all-brain sources of obtaining information, such as channeling, intuition, dreaming, imagination, psychic gifts, telepathy and so on. Science basically worships the concrete mind and doesn't really even have access to the higher mind. I think we can see why it is said that humans use only about six or seven percent of the brain's potential. It is only when you begin to use the brainpower of the soul, monad and/or mighty I Am Presence that this begins to change.

In psychology this absurd philosophy manifests as behaviorism. People are seen as equal to rats, with no free choice. All differences between humans are seen as a function of positive reinforcement, negative reinforcement and extinction. This is the philosophy that most of our colleges and universities operate from in all nonclinical areas.

The clinical areas are not much better, for most of the clinical work is godless also. It is studied entirely on a personality level and does not address the level of the soul or monadic self-actualization. At least personality-level self-actualization is addressed.

I have spoken of the field of psychology extensively in *Soul Psychology* in the chapter "Soul Psychology As Compared to Traditional Psychology," so I will not repeat myself here. It is sufficient to say that a massive dose of soul and monadic infusion is needed in this field. It is my ultimate vision that these books will get into the school systems because of their comprehensive yet easy-to-read nature. Any help that the leaders in the field can perform in making this possible would be greatly appreciated by both the second-ray department of the Spiritual Hierarchy and me.

Traditional Western Medicine

Medicine is for the most part as godless and soulless as the field of psychology and, in truth, probably worse. Western medicine does not acknowledge the existence of a soul. It has no understanding of the etheric body. Western medicine does not recognize hypnosis, the power of the mind over the body or autosuggestion. It has no understanding of the emotions and feelings and the havoc they play if not properly integrated. Western medicine does not acknowledge the existence of the negative ego, although in most cases it is run by it.

Western medicine has no understanding of diet and nutrition or of the astral body and the role it plays in disease. It has no understanding of alien implants, negative elementals, astral entities, negative imprints and the part these play in disease. Western medicine does not understand or use home-opathy, herbs or acupuncture. Testing procedures are often invasive and bar-baric and poison the body. Western medicine has no understanding of envi-ronmental poisons or how to clear such things as lead poisoning, aluminum poisoning, chemicals, metals, mercury fillings, pollution or parasites.

Western medicine has no cure for viruses, which homeopathic reme-dies can cure incredibly easily. It does not integrate any type of spiritual, psychic or psychological insight into the disease process. In essence, Western-medicine practitioners are missing 90 percent of what is really go-ing on with their patients.

These practitioners often make their patients wait an hour or two for an appointment even though the patient is on time. It certainly appears that they feel their time is more valuable than the patient's. This serves to lower the patient's already-depleted feelings about him/herself, which then cre-ates a more favorable environment for disease.

Patients in waiting rooms are either ill and/or nervous about their ap-pointments. This is a fact often overlooked. A warm smile from the recep-tionist rather than the all-too-common sign-in sheet could work wonders in this area. If even one moment were given to ask the patient how he/she is doing or if he/she would like a cup of water, the patient's fear and isolation could be instantly wiped away. The feeling of being cared for and nurtured would begin the healing process right in the waiting room!

Western medicine's method of cure is dru-grelated, which sometimes cures one thing while poisoning the kidneys and liver in the process. They generally hand out antibiotics like candy for problems that often have noth-ing to do with the antibiotic they are prescribing. This poisons the liver and kidneys, destroys the yeast-bacteria balance in the body and has subse-quently created a plague of yeast infections in the population of the United States. And to make matters worse, they don't even have the knowledge to recommend supplementing the diet with acidophilus. This imbalance wreaks havoc on the immune system and the doctor self-righteously walks away thinking he/she has done a good job.

For emotional problems the medical doctor or psychiatrist prescribes Valium, which is seen as the cure-all, or some other psychotropic drug. I am not saying here that psychotropic drugs should never be used. I am just saying that it is dealing with the symptom and not the cause.

If a woman has breast cancer, doctors cut out the breast without ever addressing the cause. All this means is that it will grow back in some other place. There have been no lessons learned.

Western medicine has little understanding of preventive medicine. The antibiotics that doctors prescribe could be replaced with homeopathic remedies, which work equally well and are generally not toxic to the body.

The tests they run are only on the grossest level and they miss the entire field of subclinical medicine, let alone the spiritual, mental and emotional realm.

Western medicine can be quite barbaric in many ways. This is often seen by its tendency to jump to the most radical of treatments when a disease can be handled in a much less traumatic way. Examples of this can be seen in the large number of hysterectomies, appendectomies and tonsillectomies that are performed on a perfunctory basis. Many of these are finally being acknowledged as having been unnecessary. Much, however, is still prevalent today.

Emergency surgery often can and does save lives. The terrible shame, and even crime, is that so much unnecessary surgery is being done. All too often medical practitioners run their profession as a business. It is true that doctors must make a living as well as anyone else. The imbalances in this regard are due to the way in which health care is set up in general. Society must change the way the medical profession is handled so that it is not geared for the rich and elite. A way must be found in which the business element of the medical profession is relegated to its rightful place and doctors are free to emerge as the true healers that God intended them to be. The focus would then shift from money to health, where it rightly belongs.

For this shift to take place, three major elements would need to be manifested. First, appropriate medical care would be available to everyone no matter what his/her financial status. This is urgent. The number of individuals who needlessly suffer and die in our society due to lack of funds for proper health care is staggering!

Second, the truths that the powers that be are hiding from both the medical professionals and the public must be revealed. The knowledge of how to turn crisis medicine into preventive medicine is there. The sad and horrific truth is that this knowledge is being withheld. Greed has triumphed over compassion and this must change. Both the medical community and its patients have suffered and continue to suffer because of this. Certain money-hungry conglomerates and individuals are holding back vital knowledge that, if made known to health professionals and patients alike, could create a relatively disease-free society.

The patient is not the only one suffering because of the selfishness of certain drug companies and food producers. Various other controlling agencies also have less than our best interest at heart. Recent scientific research reveals that the life span of the average Western medical doctor does not exceed the mid-fifties.

Third, all forms of holistic medicine would be fully integrated into the scientific community. This again would ultimately benefit both patient and Western medical practitioner alike. It is well to bear in mind that it is not just the patient but the medical community itself that is suffering from this shortsightedness. We must constantly bear in mind that the difficulties seen within the practice of Western medicine go far beyond the field of medicine. They can be traced to the heart of the secret controlling forces that set the basic rules for society in general. In this statement, dear readers, lies much to ponder upon.

It is well to bear in mind that there are many more refined forms of healing that are currently available today. These are readily seen in the more holistic approaches, including homeopathy, naturopathy, oriental medicine and nutrition. Other progressive healers and techniques are: Hanna Kroeger specialists, who use pendulum procedures to test; bioenergetic doctors who use Vega-type testing machines; the inner-plane healing masters; the Arcturians; channels and clairvoyants who read into the physical body for deeper understanding; my own radionics machine or others, which do radionics clearing work; and both my matrix-removal program and the golden cylinder program.

The leaders in the fields of medicine, psychiatry and psychology are going to have to wake up. I do not mean this in a judgmental sense, but that the lens they are seeing life through is so narrow, they are only seeing one-tenth of reality. This is why someone like Deepak Chopra is so refreshing—a medical doctor who recognizes and honors the soul. This will be the prototype doctor of the future. It is time for the medical profession to stop being self-righteous and ego-sensitive and instead to open up to the incredible new-age technologies that are now available in the field of medicine.

The current advances in the new-age field of medicine are mind-boggling. It is the job of the leaders in this area who have been practicing for a long time and those who are now coming into the field to step forward and break out of the dogma and limitations of traditional medicine.

I had to do this in my field as a marriage, family and child counselor and psychologist. In order to integrate spiritual psychology into my practice, I had to break from tradition. This is what all traditional medical doctors, psychiatrists, psychologists, marriage counselors and social workers must do. Holistic and preventive approaches must be embraced. Do not stay locked into the materialistic and personal level of practicing. Have the courage to be a forerunner and initiator of soul and monadic infusion into your given field.

Flu Vaccinations

One of the big scams in America is the flu vaccination given each year, which generates millions of dollars for the pharmaceutical industry. The generally accepted view is that the flu virus causes the flu. The basic concept behind the vaccination program is that by introducing a small amount of the virus into the body, your immune system will produce antibodies to protect you from the real flu virus. One basic flaw is that there are dozens of flu viruses, so how do the manufacturers of the flu vaccination know which virus will occur that year? The answer is that the manufacturers do not know. In fact, the flu vaccine for any given year is already manufactured at least seven to eight months in advance of the flu season.

A healthy person with a healthy diet and lifestyle will not come down with the flu even if exposed to the virus. Pathogens including viruses, bacteria, fungi and parasites need an environment conducive for their survival and proliferation. An unhealthy body with a weakened immune system provides the environment necessary for it to thrive in.

Processed sugars are detrimental to one's health, and when consumed they create the environment in the body that encourages viruses and bacteria to grow. Dr. Wiley, head of the Bureau of Chemistry (later renamed the Food and Drug Administration), was removed from office in 1912 when he opposed white sugar and processed flour being introduced to the American public.

An interesting observation is that the flu season occurs from October through the following February. Cold, damp weather definitely is a factor in one's health. In addition, most people don't exercise or go outdoors as much in cold weather as they would in warmer weather. But the flu season occurs at the same time that adults consume large amounts of sugar. In October, Halloween unofficially signals the beginning of office parties and sugar consumption. Come November, pumpkin pie and other sweets are often included in Thanksgiving celebrations. Also the seratonin in turkeys can trigger flulike symptoms in people who are sensitive to it. Christmas season is the time to bake all your favorite holiday sweets. New Year's Eve is a time when many people consume excessive amounts of alcohol, which is then quickly converted to sugar in the body. The Super Bowl occurs in January, which is another time to party and drink alcohol. The last chance for high doses of sugar during the flu season comes in February with Valentine's Day.

Viruses are involved in both the flu and common colds. Antibiotics treat bacteria. Yet medical doctors today still prescribe antibiotics to treat flus and colds. Viruses and bacteria are as different as night and day.

There was a vaccine administered to the American public in 1976 for the swine flu. Leaders in the hog industry had been noticing animals that were experiencing severe respiratory-tract swelling and infections during this period and had asked the pharmaceutical industry to come up with a drug to "cure" these problems. But hogs are placed in very crowded and confined areas and must stand in their own fecal matter, which produces ammonia and other toxic gases, resulting in the respiratory problems of the hogs. The particular drug offered to the hog industry proved to be ineffective and was rejected.

This might sound unbelievable, but without changing one molecule of the drug designed for pigs, this exact same drug was sold to the Public Health Service—but with a tremendous increase in price. And the American public had the swine flu vaccine. The flu vaccination program in 1976 lasted from only the end of October until the beginning of December due to the lawsuits brought against the people administering the shots. The main complaints stemming from the effects of the vaccinations consisted of numbness and weakness in the arms and legs and even paralysis of the limbs. To cover up this grave mistake, the medical industry said there was a mysterious outbreak of Guillain-Barré Syndrome.

This is a syndrome named after two French researchers and is believed to be caused by a virus. The main symptoms of Guillain-Barré are weakness of the limbs with both impaired movement and sensation. If you look up Guillain-Barré Syndrome in any medical text, it will mention that a strange outbreak of this syndrome occurred in 1976 around the time of the flu season.

Another small detail that the pharmaceutical industry forgot to mention is that the side effects from the flu vaccinations usually do not occur until years later. With the retired and elderly being targeted for the flu vaccinations each year, could these shots be a factor in Parkinson's disease, Alzheimer's disease and various other dementias striking the elders in America?

The best advice to combat the flu is to eat healthy organic foods, do some sort of physical exercise on a regular basis and practice the art of loving, giving and sharing with others. If you happen to come down with the flu, the body is merely reminding you that something is not harmonious in your energy field. You might need to do some cleansing and letting go in one or more of your body systems. Keeping your bodies, minds and spirits in perfect health is to create a strong environment, which will attract only the positive.

I want to make it clear here that I am not a medial doctor and any opinions given in this section or any other section in this book dealing with medical issues are nothing more than a layperson's opinion. I would not write this or any other information in this book if I did not believe it was true; however, for legal purposes I am guided by the masters to say that one should always consult a professional holistically oriented M.D. for guidance on such matters.

Self-Leadership As a Patient

Since just about all of us have health lessons, we have at one time or another experienced the medical profession. A great many lightworkers are choosing alternative ways of healing, yet some are being treated in the more traditional modality of Western medical science. If you find yourself one of these, know that it lies within your power to create your own leadership within this arena.

Work with the doctors you are seeing, but do not give them your power. Know that your oversoul, monad, the masters and God are ever with you as the ultimate source of healing. Invoke the ascended masters and the angels of healing to work through your attending physicians. Call on Dr. Lorphan with his team of galactic healers to work directly on your four-body system for a total overall healing, as well as on the specific area that ails you. Call for increased light during your meditation and relaxation periods and direct that light to clear away all disease.

The point I am making here is that even the most seemingly average patient has the power to help heal him/herself. All healing ultimately takes place within anyway. Whatever method of medicine you are using from the traditional Western mode to the newest and most innovative holistic approach, you do not have to be the victim of anyone else's methods. Realize that any means of healing you choose still leaves you at the center of the process. With the help of your higher self, monad, God and the masters, you can claim your true position as leader of your own healing process.

Scientific Research

Research is another area that needs to be addressed in the field of science. This has to do with the way animals are treated. Animals are in truth, as the Native Americans say, our younger brothers. We are their caretakers. What is going on in the research labs is absolutely barbaric and inhumane. I am not saying no experiments should ever be run on animals; however, what is going on now is no less than torture with ignorant scientists having no respect for the soul or God who lives in these animals.

In the future there might be a small number of animals that volunteer for such service on a soul level to serve humanity. However, that is not what is going on now. It is allowed to take place because humanity accepts this and is sadly lacking in meeting its spiritual responsibilities in this regard. Scientists in their ignorance see animals as nothing more than objects. This is similar to how the extraterrestrial Grays see us: cold science with no emotion and no soul. It's disgusting, inhumane and needs to be stopped on both levels.

Another aspect of science that needs to change is the amount of money, time and energy spent on experiments and research that is a waste of time, has no priority or is already obvious from a commonsense or intuitive point of view.

Science needs to be guided by the intelligence of the soul, mighty I Am Presence and the ascended masters as to what the world really needs. Science needs to learn to integrate the right brain and spiritual knowledge. This will then form a perfect marriage or a more complete marriage.

All knowledge does not have to come from scientific experiments. All knowledge is already known. All one has to do is ask God and He will give you the answer. Material science and the science of the soul must merge and work together.

Science must recognize that there are more senses than the five they acknowledge. They are seeing only an extremely small fraction of consciousness within the full spectrum of reality. The master Hilarion is a good and appropriate ascended master to call for guidance in this area.

Scientists must learn to do their work from the perspective of the Christ consciousness, seeing the unity of all things and seeing that they cannot properly separate themselves from the things they study. Scientists need more unconditional love, more compassion, integrity, humility, unity consciousness, intuition, realization, comprehension, channeling, higher-mind integration, inspiration and soul infusion, to name a few Christ qualities.

It is now time for the fifth-ray souls and monads on this planet to step forward and take leadership in the fields of science, medicine, psychiatry and psychology to break us out of this materialistic morass we have been stuck in for so long. Be courageous, for you will take some flack from the traditional establishment; however, know you are working for a higher authority and you have a most sacred duty, mission and destiny to fulfill in this regard. The force is with you, and the timing to make this move could never be more ripe than now.

Center for Disease Control

Here we have another one of the great government agencies that is supposed to protect us. I am here to tell you that the Center for Disease Control (CDC) does not even believe in the existence of Epstein-Barr, also known as chronic fatigue syndrome. The CDC emphasizes word control and not disease prevention. So think twice before you put your faith in such governmental agencies. They are controlled by traditional doctors whose understanding of true health care is so limited that such an agency serves little purpose.

There is, however, potential for the CDC. As it is currently structured, one of its biggest obstacles lies within the realm of integrity. Money and personal control take the priority that disease control should have. Add these factors to the closed minds that most of the people administering this center have, and what you come up with is an ineffective organization. Could you imagine how effective this group would be if diseases were studied from all vantage points: physical, emotional, mental and spiritual? The potential for this center if run by initiates is enormous. Disease could be studied, understood and obliterated entirely. When the outer and inner vision merges with integrity, the Center for Disease Control will emerge to fulfill its highest potential.

Our Judicial System

Our judicial system is another area that needs the influx of new-age soul and monadic infusion and leadership. In the past couple years my personal opinion of the judicial system has drastically changed. I know that the United States has one of the best systems in the world from a theoretical or philosophical perspective, but somehow the judicial system and true justice are not always on the same page.

In recent times we have all seen the Rodney King trial where twenty or thirty officers were videotaped beating Rodney King for no good reason other than racism. In their first trial they were found not guilty. This led to the riots in Los Angeles. It was one of the most outrageous miscarriages of justice ever seen.

After that we had the Menendez brothers who admitted to killing their parents and there was a hung jury. Even if there was child abuse, common sense tells us that killing one's parents is not the appropriate action. Now, I can see maybe a lesser charge, but a hung jury is mind-boggling.

Then there was the infamous O.J. Simpson trial. Needless to say, what a media circus! In my opinion, I do not think these trials should be allowed to be on television.

Moreover, in Germany there was one of the worst miscarriages of justice I have ever seen. On national television Monica Seles, the world-famous tennis player, was stabbed in the back with a knife by a deranged lunatic for no other reason than he wanted the German tennis player, Steffi Graff, to win. If you can believe this, he was set free. I am no hard-core conservative, but it doesn't take a brain scientist to conclude that this man should have gone to jail.

What is going on here? What is wrong with the judicial system? I am no expert in this area; however, I do have some observations from a layman's perspective. First, there is a need for greater soul and monadic integration among all who are involved in the judicial process. In the O.J. Simpson trial we saw how nasty the lawyers are with each other. They are not coming from the appropriate detached unconditional love that a true initiate who was a lawyer would come from. It is never right to attack others; I don't care what the reason.

Second, often the jurors are so overwhelmed with legal technicalities that they lose sight of the main issue of guilt or innocence.

Third, some of the laws on the books need reformation. One example involves the third-strike law. A man had two offenses and then took a slice of pizza from a kid and ate it, and because of this law, he had to be sent to prison for life (for taking one piece of pizza: life imprisonment). Rapists and murderers are released in two or three years because the prisons are too crowded. It's crazy.

Fourth, many of us know that if you have expensive lawyers, like in the case of O.J. Simpson or any other rich person, the chances of getting off are a trillion times better than if you have a court-appointed attorney, which is the only form of representation that most people on this planet can afford.

Then you have all the good-old-boy attorneys who are friends and who cut deals with one another, using no-contest arrangements and the likes for clients they want to help out. And one of the biggest contaminants in true justice is the jury itself. I would never want my life dependent on twelve unknown jurors. I do not mean this to sound judgmental, but the level of intelligence, consciousness, discernment, spiritual and psychological development might not be very high.

The average third-dimensional materialistic person who sits on a trial is not right with self or right with God. How can he/she be expected to see other people clearly when he is not clear himself?

I also saw a newsmagazine show about the high frequency of jury tampering that goes unchecked and oftentimes unnoticed. There is also the influence of the media in most trials. Often there are so many rules and technicalities in the court proceedings that common sense and clear intuition do not prevail. In the O.J. Simpson trial one woman was having a nervous breakdown and another was suicidal. We often don't realize that jurors are not objective machines.

From the O.J. Simpson trial and the Mark Fuhrman tapes we saw how the police department plants evidence and the degree of lying and racism that is involved. With cameras in the courtroom, lawyers often play to the cameras more than address the real concerns of the client.

Then you have the actual integrity and Christ-consciousness level of the lawyers, judge and jury. How many of these people do you really think have Christ consciousness rather than materialistic negative-ego consciousness? Do they really care about their client or are they seeking fame, money and power?

Then you can look at the judge in any given trial. All judges are not the same. Some are hard-core conservatives, some moderate and some liberal.

One's fate is often totally up to the type of judge who presides over one's case.

Do you think that the average attorney tries as hard and works as hard for his/her client if it isn't a high-profile case and if, for example, he is getting the salary of a court-appointed lawyer? Lawyers have different motivations depending on their level of integrity and true Christ consciousness. Often lawyers have so many different cases they are working on, they cannot possibly give every client the time he/she needs and deserves. I am sure there is great variability in the quality of court-appointed lawyers.

Then there are all the technicalities that allow some to go free. You also have a great many who are incarcerated because of racist, overzealous police departments that are out of control. The Fuhrman tapes gave us a bird's-eye view of the level of intelligence of many employees of the police department. Undoubtedly, Fuhrman was not alone in his views.

Going back to the jurors, everything in life is perception, and our thoughts create our reality. We see through our minds and belief systems, not our eyes. How many people sitting on these juries have clear mental bodies, clear emotional bodies and clear beliefs? Most lightworkers, disciples and initiates are not even clear on this level, and yet we are speaking here of putting your life in the hands of a third-dimensional jury.

Most lightworkers or people with money and education do not even sit on juries. Most people who sit on these juries do not want to be there. Five dollars a day is not a great motivation. I am not trying to put down juries or jury duty, for in truth it is a civic responsibility. I am trying to point out the often extremely low level of psychological and spiritual clarity of the people trying these cases. Many have heard of all the petty fighting and nastiness that goes on between jurors. If one juror comes in with a black or a white agenda, the case is doomed before it even begins. Then add to this the fact that people in our society are most definitely not considered innocent before proven guilty. With all these factors figured in, the system becomes a joke.

In our society if you want to destroy someone, all you have to do is bring up false charges against him/her and the media will have a heyday with it. The media is not interested in truth; they are interested in ratings or selling their publications.

The American people and people of the world—and I include myself in this also—are often gullible and nondiscerning. I hear stories on the news and in my mind think they are true, but later find out they were not. We all do this.

Look what happened to Michael Jackson. Regardless of your feelings about him, no one really knows for sure if the charges brought against him were true or not. The fact is, he was found not guilty. Look what he had to

go through and the public humiliation he had to endure. If he was ultimately found innocent, then why did he have to go through that? Most people do not follow the principle "innocent before proven guilty."

I used to have the naive belief that the judicial system in the United
States was fair. Nothing could be further from the truth. Going to court is a
total crapshoot depending on all the factors that I have listed in this section
(and many more that I haven't mentioned). The main thing needed to remedy this problem involves the lawyers, judges, jurors, reporters and police
officers. All have to become more soul-infused and more guided by God,
their higher self and mighty I Am Presence.

If all the people involved in the proceedings on all levels are run to a
large extent by their negative ego, then how can anyone get a fair trial?
Fairness would only come if all involved would see through the eyes of the
soul and the mighty I Am Presence, which in other terms is known as Christ
vision. So we see here that the problem is due less to the actual legal system and more to the need for clarity among people.

I do want to say here that our system of justice is probably the best in
the world. If you see what goes on in South America, Arab nations, communist China, the Asian world, even in Russia, you will thank your bottom
dollar that you live in the United States. As bad as it is here, this is as good
as it gets.

Imagine how our society would be if only ascended masters sat as
judges and you had ascended masters and high-level initiates sitting on juries. Imagine also having ascended-master lawyers who stated their cases
but were very polite, kind and respectful to one another and all concerned.
If all were ascended, guilt and innocence would be quite apparent and the
fog of glamour, maya and illusion would not cloud things as it does now. It
is time for the spiritual leadership to step forward into these professions
and to set this new example.

A few more examples of injustice concern the fact that people of fame
are treated differently than a common person. Another example is if a black
person murders a white person, he/she is treated much differently than if a
white person kills a black person. I realize this is an awful example to bring
up; however, we all know the truth of this. Most white people do not recognize the lens that they see life through. A great many white people will say
they are not racist when in truth their vision is enormously colored by being
white, but they just do not realize it. They are not racist in the classic
sense, but rather in an unconscious sense.

It is hard for white people to see their lens because being white is an
enormous advantage in our society. We have no pain and suffering that
forces us to confront it as people of others races do. Our justice system will
not be truly just until the contamination of negative ego has been removed,

which is quite an undertaking.

Another problem in the judicial system is the lawyer's motivation for winning his/her case. Is the lawyer really doing it out of love and service to his/her client in this holy commission he has been given? It is more likely for money, fame, power and career advancement. The reverse of not putting much energy, time or effort in trying to win happens because the rewards for putting in the effort and time are not high enough. Would Johnnie Cochran and Marsha Clark put forth the same effort if a case involved someone less well-known than O.J. Simpson?

An ascended master would put in the same effort for a person who had no money and was completely unknown as for the richest and most famous person in the world. Each is equally important in God's eyes. I doubt this is the case for a prosecuting team hired by the city or state. This is all obviously wrong and needs to be changed.

One other very dangerous aspect of our judicial system and police force has to do with the way our judicial system is based on an adversarial system. There is nothing wrong with this except for the fact that the prosecution and defense will often go to any length to win their case. The problem here stems from the fact that the individuals involved are often run by their negative ego and are not based in the Christ consciousness. They would often sell their own soul to win a case.

I saw a primetime special about how police are now going into prisons on a regular basis to find snitches. The problem is that the prisoners know that if they give information to the police on other prisoners, even if it is a lie, they can cut a deal to get out of jail.

The police are not as objective as they should be; instead of taking a transcendent perspective, they are polarized against the criminals. As a result, innocent people are being put in jail and criminals who are lying are being set free. Part of the problem here is that prosecutors are given a quota of cases they have to win, which is also totally corrupt. This is similar to police officers being given a quota of a certain number of tickets they have to write.

Overzealous prosecutors and police will collude to win a case. In extreme cases they will even plant evidence. As I said before, there is often a very fine line between the police and criminals. Even if O.J. Simpson (or anyone else, for that matter) was guilty of murder and got away with it, he will not escape the higher authority, which is God, and must ultimately experience the effects of his causes. The police and prosecutors are often short-sighted in this regard. As the saying goes, it is better to let a guilty person go free than put an innocent person in jail.

One other corrupted aspect of our judicial system deals with what I am going to call paid witnesses. For example, in a jury trial, if DNA evidence is introduced, there are paid witnesses you can hire to either support or deny your scientific claims. These people are supposed to be scientific medical experts. I do not mean to sound crass, but in truth, they are often medical and scientific prostitutes. I do not mean to sound judgmental in saying this, and this certainly does not apply to all medical witnesses, but there are a great many medical and scientific experts who are basically for hire and will support any position if they are paid for it. Of course, this is counteracted by the opposing prosecuting or defense team, which will then hire its own medical and scientific experts.

The upshot is, if you have money, there is always someone you can hire who will testify for your point of view. This might be a psychiatrist, pathologist or a shoe salesman. If you pay the person enough money, he/she will testify for your side of the case. If that person will not, you can always keep searching until you find someone who will.

What is the consequence of professional witnesses who make their living working for lawyers in court cases? If you as a client don't have the money to hire them, you are out of luck.

Unfortunately, the jury often bases its conclusions on such experts' testimony and believes that these people are acting out of integrity rather than greed and self-interest. The courtroom should ideally search for the truth rather than engage in adversarial psychological combat. There is nothing wrong with having a medical or scientific witness to support your claim, but that witness needs to be truly credible and not a professional witness for hire.

Our Criminal Justice System

One other aspect of the criminal justice system that is incredibly corrupted and mismanaged has to do with how long criminals actually remain in prison. I happened to be watching *PrimeTime* last night and I was totally flabbergasted at the exposé they did on this subject. Because of the enormous corruption, mismanagement, greed and disorganization of our government on local, state and federal levels, criminals in Los Angeles, for example, on average serve only 23 percent of their sentence.

The crimes I am speaking of here are very serious ones such as assault, robbery, auto theft, child abuse and molestation, to name a few. If a judge hands down a sentence of two years in prison, the average criminal will serve only four or five months. I am not speaking here of an isolated case, but of every single prisoner in Los Angeles in every prison in this range of criminal activity. Spiritually what is happening here is the karma is being removed. Public defenders are just telling their clients to plead guilty because they know the prisons are so overcrowded that they will have to serve little time. Being a spiritual teacher and person, I am into forgiveness and redemption, but for most hardened criminals there must be some karmic consequence, for the time of learning by grace in most of these cases is long gone.

Los Angeles happens to be the worst example of this mismanagement and corruption; however, it is happening all over the United States. When the head sheriff in Los Angeles, Sherman Block, was asked about why this was happening, he said that the prisons are so overcrowded that there are just not enough beds or money to keep people in jail that he has no choice but to let them go. Even the prisoners think it is a joke.

To take this incredible mismanagement and corruption one step further, there is a brand-new, state-of-the-art prison in Los Angeles that is fully operational and has room for 4000 inmates, but for the past several years has sat unoccupied because there is not enough money to run it. It does not take a brain scientist to ask the question, why did they build a three hundred million-dollar prison if they didn't have the funds to run it? The second question is, why does it cost a hundred million dollars to run a prison for 4000 people? Do you think corruption and greed could be a factor here?

This example is really just a metaphor for all our third-dimensional institutions on this planet. This is what happens when the negative ego rather than the soul and Christ consciousness run individuals and institutionalized organizations. You have a completely irrational, disorganized, noncohesive system with everyone involved out for their selfish interest and greed instead of creating a unified, spiritual divine blueprint for the criminal-justice system (or any other institutionalized system for that matter).

Police Departments

One must realize that there is often a fine line between a police officer and a criminal. This is because police officers are most often just the other side of the ego coin of good vs. bad. A highly qualified police officer must transcend the ego distinctions between good and bad, superior and inferior and positive and negative. A new-age police officer must come from a state of consciousness that transcends duality. In other words, he/she must come from unconditional love, forgiveness, seeing the Christ in every person, even though he must still perform his job.

Do you see what I am saying here? Too often there is an ego battle going on between police officers and criminals. This is not right. Criminals are sons and daughters of God who are confused. They need tough love. Police officers, often not having this more fourth- and fifth-dimensional consciousness, are soured by all the negativity they see. They are often angry and engage in the same ego battle that binds criminals. Police officers thus often react instead of respond.

They do not have the needed detachment, even-mindedness and equanimity that comes from realizing the Christ consciousness and being merged with the soul and monad. Without this transcendence they are caught in the negative ego's game. They often feel superior, self-righteous and angry and live in a war mentality.

Being caught in the negative-ego dichotomy, they are often corrupted themselves. They are often racist and usually materialistic and third-dimensional in spiritual development. In many cases, the power has gone to their heads. For the sake of what they see as justice, they will plant evidence or beat up people and play judge, jury and executioner. The crazy thing about this is that they see nothing wrong with it. They actually think they are good people doing the community a service. Mark Fuhrman actually thinks he is a good police officer. This is the delusion of the negative ego, and it is more pervasive than we realize.

How many people in this world in general and in all professions operate out of a more transcendent spiritual philosophy? Most lightworkers are not well-developed in this area. Their spiritual development is often more developed than their psychological development, the issue to which this speaks.

Imagine again how it would be if ascended masters served on the police force. They would have great power but also great wisdom, unconditional love and compassion. They would respond and not react. They would be detached and be able to turn the other cheek. They would see each criminal as God and use violence only as a last resort. There would be no racism and, of course, they would never plant or manufacture evidence. The community would love police officers.

As it is now, police officers carry an aura of power and intimidation. They are often not friendly and are very businesslike. Their uniforms and helmets make them look like storm troopers. They have power, but for the most part they clearly do not have love.

As for the people they affect, I personally feel incredibly sorry for black Americans because of the way they are generally treated by police officers. What goes on with black people and the police department is unbelievable. Black people and other minorities are presumed guilty and white people innocent.

Well-educated, rich, spiritual, famous black people are stopped by L.A. police officers all the time and humiliated because of the racist police force in Los Angeles. I am sure it is not that different in other cities. High-level disciples, initiates and ascended beings need to move into this law-enforcement field and spiritualize it. It is currently operating out of a third-dimensional reality and this needs to change. The Mark Fuhrman tapes and the Rodney King beating are just the tip of the iceberg. Because police officers are on the other side of the duality and do not transcend it, they are often involved in criminal activity themselves. Even though they have lists of rough and abusive police officers, the leaders in the police department have rules that do not allow them to fire these officers, or maybe they just won't.

Police officers are like a group of good-old boys who will never rat on another police officer even if he is indulging in criminal activity. It is an unspoken code to stick together. This is why it is such a joke for the police department to investigate itself. What I am saying here also applies to the FBI and CIA. We have all seen movies of police officers who tell the truth, like Serpico and others like him, and we see what happens to them. They become ostracized and often set themselves up. There is enormous corruption and unchristlike behavior going on. This is because, as usual, it is run by the negative ego's interpretation of law enforcement, not the Holy Spirit's and soul's interpretation.

So as we see, every institution and profession in our world really has the same problem. The institutions reflect the third-dimensional, materialistic negative-ego consciousness that runs most people. Fourth-dimensional consciousness is an improvement but it is still caught in duality. It is not until fifth-dimensional consciousness is attained that unity consciousness can be truly perceived. The problem is that we do not have enough high-level initiates and ascended beings in the world. It is our work to change this and integrate lightworkers into all the professions and institutions of this world.

The Prison System

Here again we have another nightmarish earthly institution that is completely corrupted by negative-ego thinking. Prison should be a place of rehabilitation of the soul and of the mental, emotional and physical bodies. In our society it is a place of punishment, which is not a spiritual concept. Prisoners, in my opinion, should be forced to take classes in morality.

Instead what we have is punishment consciousness rather than mental, emotional, spiritual or physical rehabilitation. The prisoners are not treated like sons and daughters of God but are humiliated, beaten and often tortured. The gangs run the prisons and the weaker prisoners are often sexually molested. This is obviously condoned by the prison officials or it would not be allowed to happen. The guards are often corrupt and prisoners are not treated equally. The food is terrible. I have had clients and students in prison, and they are not even allowed to receive books.

Where are the prison laws and officials coming from? If I send a prisoner a book for free to help in his/her rehabilitation, he is never allowed to receive it. I do not care if the prison officials open the package; that is fine. However, if all that is in the package is a book, what is the big deal? They have recently passed new laws to take away weight-training equipment such as barbells. God forbid they should even rehabilitate themselves physically!

The basic view is that prisoners should rot in prison. There is no counseling, classes or spiritual training. Any problems a prisoner had going in are going to get worse; this is why most prisoners end up back in prison. It is such a negative environment in prison that the prisoners inhabiting it are usually filled with extraterrestrial implants and negative parasites. In most cases there is no program in place to assist criminals when they are released, and since they often have no money or jobs, they are all but forced to go back to a life of crime.

The flip side of this is that hard-core criminals who should remain in jail because they are a danger to society are let out because the prisons are too crowded. People who have murdered and raped go right back out and do it again. Their stay in prison has done nothing more than make them more likely than ever to continue the same pattern. The prisoners are treated like dirt, which does little for their self-esteem.

The government wastes an incredible amount of money on bureaucracy and waste, such as conducting useless space experiments and the like, yet cannot build more prisons—what a nightmare of an institution! The people running these institutions are sometimes not that much more evolved than the criminals. Our penal system must be completely revamped from the perspective of the Holy Spirit and soul. Because of the corruption of the prison systems, prisoners can still even get drugs and contraband of all kinds, often because of the corruption of the prison guards.

To completely change the orientation of this system it is necessary for high-level initiates and ascended beings to move into governmental positions and into the highest levels of the prisons. Prisons should ideally be houses of God run in a supremely disciplined manner. Gangs, drugs, sexual molestation, criminal activity and corruption exist because prison officials at some level condone it.

If you haven't come to this conclusion yet, the negative ego is the cause of all problems in this world. It is the opposing philosophies and orientations, which manifest as hell and heaven. The Holy Spirit and soul create all solutions. Can you imagine if ascended masters ran prisons? Prisoners would be treated in a firm but loving and respectful manner. They would be forgiven.

Prison would become an ascetic spiritual retreat of physical, emotional, mental and spiritual redemption, training and discipline. No one would be let out before he/she deserved to be let out. Parole boards would operate fairly and justly. Prisoners would be reading spiritual books, meditating and working to support the finances of the prison, not rotting in a jail cell. They would go to classes—go to school, so to speak.

I am not speaking here of a regular school, although that is a possibility, too. I am speaking, more significantly, of a psychological and spiritual school that would have classes on criminal behavior and what causes it, classes on how to clear and control the negative ego and move into a more spiritual way of thinking. Criminals would have to go to counseling.

A lot of criminals want to change; they just do not know how. I am no expert in this field, but common sense and a generalized Christ consciousness shows the direction we need to move. High-level initiates and ascended beings who are inspired in this area need to move into this profession and make the needed changes. I am trying to do my part right now in writing about this, waking up humanity from its apathy and unconsciousness in this area.

The government does what we, the people, want. If we do not accept the status qou and take steps to change it, in a hundredth-monkey effect, the overall consciousness will begin to change. We who have been victims of crime must let go of our anger, move into forgiveness and Christ consciousness and let go of punishment consciousness. The clarion call has gone forth for the spiritual leaders to step forth in this area and make changes in these laws and institutions and in the consciousness that runs them.

Mass Media

This is another area of negative-ego corruption that humanity is incredibly influenced by. Most people on Earth are victims who are overemotional and hypersuggestible. In other words, they live in hypnosis or automatic pilot or in a state of nondiscernment most of the time. We are a society of mass media. Mass media plays an absolutely enormous influence on our lives, including television, newspapers, radio and magazines. We are inundated by it.

We cannot go to the grocery store without seeing all the headlines in *The National Enquirer, The Star* and the likes. It is the grist for the mill of a great deal of our conversations at work and among friends. By watching CNN, we view wars going on, and due to this modern technology, the world has become a much smaller place. In addition, we have cable TV, Internet, computers and fax machines.

Let's take a discerning look at the effect of all this and what is really going on. It must be seen clearly that the mass media is third-dimensional, unnatural, very materialistic and very much of the negative ego. We are inundated with images of the "beautiful people." Sex is used as a major tool and ploy of advertising. Subliminal advertising is used even though it is supposedly illegal. The media moguls are masters of hypnosis and much more calculating and manipulating than the general public realizes.

All these conscious and unconscious messages sink into our collective unconscious minds. Lucky Vanos takes off his shirt in a Coke commercial, after which Coke sales go up 30 percent in the country!

One cannot help but be affected by mass media because we are inundated by it. Even if you could not stand watching the O.J. Simpson trial, you could not avoid it. It was everywhere. Everyone talked about it—especially the mass media.

We are captives in many ways unless we want to live in a cave. Lightworkers are trained to have more spiritual discernment, but most people in the world do not. Television news is more concerned with ratings than objective news. News in our world is to list today's twenty-five worst catastrophes in the nation in terms of murders, accidents, train wrecks, plane crashes, indictments, corruption, political intrigue and gossip. It is the most negative institution one can possibly imagine. I have had fantasies about a news show that reported only good news for a change.

We must also realize that the power elite owns the major news networks and that there is enormous censorship. We are spoon-fed the type of news that the power elite wants us to hear. For example, we never hear about extraterrestrial activity on the major news networks, for that is not acceptable to the secret government. We are given our news through a very specific lens, and people think it is the *real* news. How would Lord Buddha or Sanat Kumara report the news going on this day? We do not realize how narrow the spectrum is through which we are taught to view life.

Then we have all the violence on television, including in the cartoons children watch. The House of Representatives and Senate make idle threats in the direction of the television industries, which mean nothing and have almost no effect. People have been programmed to enjoy violence and consider it a form of entertainment.

I have not even mentioned Hollywood and the movie industry and the enormous effect it has on humanity. I happen to like the movies, but have you ever noticed how few good movies there really are and how much crap comes out? People go to see these movies and it programs their consciousness. What if television and movies were truly used in service of the soul? There would be many more movies like *Gandhi*.

Television would be more like PBS and would be a vehicle for the ascended masters and true spiritual creativity. It would be a vehicle for the arts. Most American households have the television turned on for over six hours a day. Look at what is programming our children.

What are the values we are being taught by the shows we watch? Are they teaching ascended-master values, or third- and fourth-dimensional values? Wouldn't it be great if there were shows about ascended masters and how they dealt with relationships, families and life that filled our movie screens and televisions? What if there were an ascended-master station that was run by the Buddha, Sanat Kumara and Lord Maitreya?

More and more our television news and magazine shows are becoming like *Hard Copy, Current Affair* and *Entertainment Tonight*. The mass media is caught up in glamour. Its values are shallow and materialistic. This is what we are bombarded with all day and all night long. For those who do not have a strong sense of self, great focus, self-mastery, self-discipline, psychological and spiritual clarity, it affects us and creates subtle temptations from the lower self.

On the Internet even a child can tap into pornography. The news programs and magazine shows, really the entire media, pander to sensationalism and gossip rather than quality journalism. A lot of this is also the public's fault because, unfortunately, this is what it seems to be satisfied with and this is what piques its interest. This is the glamour of the astral body, which is not transcended until fifth-dimensional consciousness is achieved.

The mass media makes heroes out of killers, rapists and prostitutes. The journalists of this day and age have very little ethics or morals. It is a dog-eat-dog world and they will do anything for a story. Whether it is true or not does not matter, or the effect it might have on other people's lives.

One of the worst qualities of mass-media journalism is its criticism. An ideal target of this negativity is anyone running for public office. I feel incredibly sorry for candidates. If God ran for president, within nine months' time He would be destroyed by the media. Those in the political arena tend to be an incredibly judgmental, cynical bunch and go for the jugular at every opportunity. Their idea of journalism is to find dirty laundry and skeletons in the closet. They will go to incredible lengths to find this dirty laundry. They are often extremely rude in their questioning and the goal is to "get you," which in truth is serving to inflate their egos by trying to embarrass the political official or candidate. It is the height of ego and is rampant.

This is what happens when third-dimensional, materialistic, unconscious people who are run by the negative ego are our reporters, journalists and media moguls. They are vicious and pompous, and to make themselves feel better, they love to tear down anyone of any true spiritual stature.

You also see this on the television in regard to the different political television shows, the names of which I will not mention. This is why many of the good people in politics who are spiritual and more sensitive leave.

God forbid you should have ever made a mistake in your life, for the media will jump on it with vengeance. All the players in this game of media really care about is making a name for themselves.

Now let us move to the talk shows, which have such an enormous effect on humanity. The producers of these shows search for the lowest element in our society. God forbid they should have a show that is actually meaningful.

Oprah Winfrey is the one exception in this arena, although I am often disappointed that many of the topics each week are very petty. But some of her shows are really phenomenal. Most talk shows have lower-class, third-dimensional, unconscious, negative-ego-run people fighting with each other. And the people who come and watch these shows are not much better. They cheer and scream, and the feedback they give is most often as judgmental as the people on the show.

Then there are a number of the talk shows that pander to the eccentric fringe element. I am absolutely amazed at the topics they choose for these shows. The level of unconsciousness is mind-boggling. People must watch these shows, however, or they would not be on—and this is another sad commentary. If the collective consciousness demanded better quality, I am sure we would get it.

Some of the shows that Oprah Winfrey has done exemplify the quality and meaningful programming that can be achieved. Oprah is a much more conscientious soul than many of the others and this is why she is so popular. The impact that she can and does have on humanity is enormous. It is such a shame that the other shows don't follow her lead.

On the opposite end of the media spectrum are tabloids like *The National Enquirer* and *The Star* and shows like *Hard Copy* and *Current Affair*. You would be amazed by how many people read these magazines and watch these shows. This of course is the cesspool of journalism. They will print stories that they know are not true to sell newspapers. The effect it has on the lives of people they tell these lies about does not matter. It is gossip, which is the negative ego's interpretation of free speech.

Another sad commentary on our society is that these shows and magazines are making tons of money. *The National Enquirer, Hard Copy* and now more mainstream newspapers and magazine shows will pay enormous sums of money to corrupt individuals to get a story. It comes down to greed, a willingness to do anything to make money, sell magazines and get high ratings. I have seen this trend in recent times of more of the news shows, mainstream magazine shows and regular news programs becoming more and more sensationalist. This is very disturbing.

The other thing I really do not like is how nasty these reporters can be in their interviews. One example is *60 Minutes*. I happen to like that show, but Mike Wallace is often incredibly nasty to the people he interviews. I have the same feedback for Sam Donaldson of *PrimeTime Live* and David Brinkley. I don't mean this as judgmental but rather as a point of observation and spiritual discernment. I don't mind a tough, incisive interview, and often the people they interview don't deserve to be coddled; however, it is not necessary to be rude and nasty and to put others down to make your point. This demonstrates a lack of soul, heart and spirit connection.

Again, what if you gain the whole world but lose your soul? The world needs the high-level disciples and initiates in this field to step forward and demonstrate a new example. This would be ascended-master or fifth-dimensional journalism. The mass media in all its forms and ramifications needs massive soul and spirit infusion to begin serving the purposes of the higher self and ascended masters rather than the purposes of lower self, negative ego, glamour and materiality.

The Education System

Spiritual leadership is needed in our educational system, for this bankrupt institution is probably the largest problem in our society. When I use the word "bankrupt" I am not speaking here of financial bankruptcy but rather spiritual bankruptcy. The third-dimensional, materialistic powers that be have cut the soul and spirit out of education, calling it the separation of church and state. The result is that we have coming out of our school systems brilliant minds and relatively healthy physical bodies, but highly deficient souls and emotional or psychological bodies, for this area is not addressed either.

Reading, writing and arithmetic are stressed, yet God, the soul, conscience, morals, values, how to be right with self, unconditional love, how to transcend negative-ego thinking, and balancing the four bodies and three minds are not. Is it any wonder that so many people are so screwed up?

The separation of church and state is a ploy of the Dark Brotherhood. It is possible to teach spirituality without proselytizing Fundamentalist Christianity. It could be taught in a universalistic and eclectic manner, and much could be taught from a psychospiritual point of view. Classes could be taught, such as an overview of the world's religions, romantic relationships from a spiritual perspective, parenting from a spiritual perspective, how to become self-actualized, how to think properly and how to balance the three minds and four bodies.

Is it any wonder our lawyers, politicians and doctors, to name a few, tend to be so egotistical? It is no judgment, for they have never been trained. These are people with brilliant minds but no soul training. I do not mean to pick on just them, for the cancer of negative ego pervades all professions and all institutions. I have chosen these because they are classic (but oftentimes truthful) stereotypes in our society.

In our present educational system, the soul, the emotional or psychological self and the right brain are not addressed. Our educational system breeds imbalance. It is literally a training to cut out spiritual development, psychic sensitivity and meaning in life and replace it with science. Nothing in our society will ever change until we alter how we educate our children, young people and young adults. This problem applies from kindergarten through all college training.

The earthly world leaders have attempted to extract the soul from all aspects of material life, and the whole purpose of life is to do just the opposite by infusing the soul and monad on Earth. For more information on this subject, read *Soul Psychology*, chapter 21, "Children in the World Today."

In closing, the world spiritual leaders of all rays who are involved or destined to be involved in our educational system need to step forward and take a leadership role in making this change in our society. It is possible to teach spirituality without teaching religion. One can focus on conscience, values, the lower self and the higher self. In other words, it can be taught from a psychological point of view. This, I believe, is the key to making new inroads.

The worldwide spiritual attitude could be replaced by developing a positive mental attitude. Instead of saying that God is teaching you a lesson, you can say *life* is teaching you a lesson. Do you see what I mean? This is a way for the leadership to teach spirituality and not get in trouble as the world goes through this transition phase to the golden age of this planet. Every profession on this planet is going to have to take this leap and be pioneers. I had to do it in the field of psychology, which was my initial chosen profession. These institutions will not change unless we change.

Government Workers

There are a great many people who work in governmental agencies such as post offices, welfare departments, social-service agencies and the like. These agencies also need to change. The first one that comes to mind is the U.S. Postal Service. It seems like every week a postal worker flips out and kills someone. There is obviously something wrong in terms of the pressure they are under or in the way supervisors deal with the workers.

Another area that needs great improvement involves agencies that deal with welfare, food stamps and the impoverished of our society. The people who come for help are often treated in a most degrading manner by the people who work there. Instead of coming from unconditional love and compassion, they are often incredibly judgmental, arrogant and curt.

By the grace of God I have not experienced this firsthand, but many clients and friends have told me how awful they feel going there. There is no excuse for this. Did not Jesus say, "We are our brother's keeper"?

Care for the Elderly

This is another travesty in our society and an area I have firsthand experience with, for I worked in a home for the elderly at one point in my life. It is a nightmare. At best the elderly residents get custodial care, and in most cases not even that. The nurses are often rude and uncaring. There is an overwhelming lack of caring and respect for old people. In Japan the elderly are revered. This is not the case in the United States.

Environments need to be created for elderly people that feed their souls and bring life back into their bodies instead of having them sit around in a wheelchair or in a bed all day long. Spiritual leaders need to step forward and create a new prototype system of excellent custodial care for not only the physical bodies but also the emotional and mental bodies and souls. The way we care for the elderly in our society is soulless.

What would an old-age home look like if ascended masters were running it? The elderly would be honored, loved, respected and treated like gods. The staff would be warm, friendly, patient and there to be of service. There would be lots of volunteers and family and friends to visit the patients. There would be more physical exercise programs, plants, flowers, paintings and an uplifting environment. There would be music, dance and entertainment, social hours, bingo and card games. There would be all kinds of recreational activities, political or current-events discussion groups, books, taped books and mental stimulation. There could be church services, meditation groups, prayer groups, spiritual study groups, sharing, group television and discussions. The list is endless.

The elderly people might teach classes themselves on subjects they have expertise in. They might perform during mealtime if they have talents in poetry, singing and/or dance. There would be programs for creativity such as playing musical instruments, painting and sculpting, maybe even singles events.

A future new-age home for the elderly would be a thriving city unto itself—almost like a summer camp, which they so richly deserve—where spiritual growth and joy, learning and growth can still take place with the care of a loving, service-oriented staff.

The problem in our society is that people often don't care. They are too self-centered and lacking in spiritual development to get beyond themselves and the idea of working for money rather than working for the joy of service and loving God, who exists in every person, animal, plant and mineral.

If people only realized that every person they are dealing with at work, whatever the job, is God visiting them in physical form, then they might change their attitude. No matter what job you do, do it with the attitude of service even if you are a garbage collector. Be the best garbage collector on the planet and see your job as cleaning up the Earth Mother. It is not what you do, it is the attitude you bring toward what you do. Bring the Christ attitude of love, service, compassion and godliness into being a secretary, into serving your customers at the post office or market. Work can be made much more enjoyable if every encounter with another human being is a holy encounter of Christ meeting Christ, Buddha meeting Buddha, the eternal self meeting another eternal self.

It all comes down to whether you are seeing life through God's eyes or the ego's eyes. This is the axis shift this world really needs. It is now time for the spiritual leadership to step forward in the field of the care of the elderly and help to revolutionize the health-care system. As Christ said, "Do unto others as you would have them do unto you."

Something else to consider in dealing with the elderly is that from one point of view they represent what many of us will face in our own futures. They also represent what all of us have experienced in the past, as we have all had to deal with old age and illness in previous incarnations. At some point we will all learn how to program ourselves for eternal youth, but this is obviously not an option for those currently in old-age homes.

We must learn how to see through the lens of oneness. We are all inextricably woven together and bonded in unity. The span of a few decades that seems to separate us from the elderly is but a façade of separation. This illusion of division that the passage of time casts over our eyes puts us in the position to be of service to those who are dependent on us now. In truth, we are not just our brother's keeper, but we *are* our brothers and sisters, for we are all aspects of the one God.

The Welfare System

Let me begin by saying that from the ascended masters' perspective, the welfare system is a wonderful thing. It provides emergency help for those in need who are impoverished and destitute. It would be inhumane not to have such a fallback system.

Some kind of welfare system is most definitely needed; however, there need to be improvements and refinements in how it is run. First, there is too much fraud and corruption. There have been many exposés on television about this. A great many people are getting more than one check under different names.

Second, often a person can make more on welfare than they can make working a full-time job, and this is not right either. How is a person supposed to be motivated to work? This might speak to the issue of the minimum wage.

Third, welfare should not be a long-term lifestyle, but a stopgap measure to help between jobs. There needs to be better job training and job placement for these individuals. Having more children should not be looked at by mothers as a way of obtaining more money from the government. A balance is needed between compassion and helping those in need. In addition, those who are taking advantage of the system and not being responsible should be forced to work. I have no easy answers, for it is a complex problem.

One should not be ashamed to have to go on welfare, as many are often made to feel. Many do not have family support and as positive a past-life karma as those reading this book. These people should he honored and respected, not judged. Like the story of Job, all of us could be put in that position with a stroke of God's hand, if that was the lesson needed to teach us humility.

The spiritual leadership of this world needs to confront this political hot potato in a fair but humane manner. The input is needed from the disciples and initiates who are leaders in this area to step forward and help clarify these types of agencies from the soul's perspective. The soul and the Holy Spirit have the answers to all questions. It is really just a matter of getting disciples and initiates into key positions to influence policy.

President Bill Clinton, for example, when he came into office, was a third-degree initiate, which means he was just going through his soul-merge initiation. The world is changing and now we need to get disciples and initiates into all institutions of earthly life.

The Health-Care System

This is another area where enormous greed and problems exist. I honor Bill and Hillary Clinton for bringing this issue to the public's attention. The problem is that because of partisan politics and petty partisan bickering, true change is slow to come. The problem with politicians is that they're more interested in party politics and getting reelected than they are in the good of the whole. In many ways we have emotional, psychological and spiritual children who live in adult physical and mental bodies running our country—quite an interesting discrepancy.

I think Republicans and Democrats will agree that our health-care system is not working. I already mentioned in a previous section how backward traditional medicine is from an ascended-master perspective, seeing only ten percent of what is really going on and having real expertise only in emergency medicine. That is just one problem.

The next is the enormous cost of getting sick. It can cost $20,000 a day in a hospital. Who can afford this? Anyone who has a serious accident or a catastrophic illness, no matter how much money he/she has, is going to go bankrupt. This is not right.

This brings the discussion to health insurance. People who are impoverished in the lower middle class cannot afford health insurance. They are more focused on putting food on the table and paying the rent. We need a system where all have health insurance. In our present system, if you lose your job you can lose your insurance. Every person in our society should have an equal right to proper health care. It is inhumane from an ascended-master perspective to provide anything less.

We also know how much traditional health care costs. Part of the problem is that health-care providers spend money on expensive tests that could be tested with new-age measures that cost nothing. The other thing, which is quite obvious, is the greed of hospital corporations. If you look at your hospital bill, they charge you fifty dollars for each pair of gloves the doctor puts on. I don't know where they shop for their supplies, but greedy hospitals and doctors are gouging the hell out of the consumer. It is absolutely absurd to be charged $20,000 for one night in a hospital. Common sense will tell you that someone is greedy.

Then you have the greed of insurance companies. I have Blue Cross, which has raised my premium every year for the past ten years. Doctors and hospitals bill insurance companies for all kinds of services that they either haven't done or don't need, just to make money. Greed seems to be the only word that covers the whole field.

What would the health-care system look like if ascended masters ran it? Doctors and hospital officials would be less focused on greed and instead give true service to their patients. The patients would be more important than money. Health-care providers would have integrity and know that to rip off others in truth is to rip off yourself. Every person would have health insurance, which could not be taken away under any circumstance.

The burden of paying for this would not be placed on the impoverished. Doctors and hospitals would charge fair and reasonable prices for their services and would have integrity and honesty in dealing with insurance companies. Patients would not be treated according to their wealth or fame, but equally, as all are innately godly. Ideally, all in the field would be soul- and monad-infused, where the good of the whole was foremost, not just the good of self.

New-age medical practices would be employed, which would probably pay for the cost of all medical insurance from the savings gained from energetic testing rather than mechanical, invasive testing. Preventive medicine would be emphasized and a more holistic approach would be implemented to save billions of future dollars in health care. In the distant future, hospital staff will include not just doctors and nurses, but also healers, clairvoyants, psychics, nutritionists, chiropractors, channels, pendulum workers, spiritual counselors, acupuncturists, herbalists, naturopaths, homeopaths and holistic health-care specialists, marriage and family counselors, social workers, hypnotists and implant and elemental removers, who will all form a team.

Classes might be provided in the hospitals to teach prayer, meditation, yoga, nutrition, preventive medicine and the like. Every hospital will have a universal chapel for family and patients. Staff will be ordered to train in these disciplines and hospitals will become more like spiritual retreats for the whole person, not just treating the physical vehicle.

Psychics and channels will psychically cleanse hospitals in the future. Rooms will be painted different colors depending on the need. There will be many more paintings on the walls instead of the cold, sterile, prisonlike atmosphere that most hospitals have. Aromatherapy will be used to get rid of the chemical odors most hospitals have and the aromas will be scientifically selected for healing purposes.

Normal hospital food will be destroyed and replaced with vegetarian and wholesome nonvegetarian natural dishes, prepared not only for the patients but for the public. Scientifically designed music will be played softly in the background at certain times for healing purposes. Doctors and nurses and other practitioners will pray together before doing any dangerous procedures and nurses will be trained in the science of prayer and meditation so they can teach their patients.

During all operations and anesthetic procedures, a hypnotherapist will be present or else nurses and doctors will be trained in this procedure in order to give suggestions to the patient to accelerate healing and reprogram the subconscious mind. Subliminal healing tapes that accelerate recovery will be played at night while patients sleep.

Are you starting to get the picture? Do you see how backward and behind the times our health-care system is? There would be no more invasive testing by using dyes or radiation or sticking needles in the spine. New-age subclinical equipment would replace all these barbaric practices. Love would be seen as the most important healing factor that all practitioners and hospital officials would practice. For love is truly the x factor in healing. Patients would be trained in affirmations and visualizations to help their healing process along. They would be taught how to continue these practices after they leave the hospital. Spiritual and health-related books would be in every room and in the library for patients to learn more. Hospitals would become true temples of healing as they were in ancient Atlantis.

The traditional medical world thinks it is so advanced when in truth it is in its infancy in terms of what true health and healing is all about. In the future, nurses and doctors will be trained to call in the inner-plane healing masters to help in every procedure. The Arcturians would be considered honored members of every hospital staff. Etheric healing teams will be called in to heal each person's etheric body. Radionics specialists will work in every hospital to treat each person energetically to accelerate healing.

Do you see how closed-minded traditional medicine is? The lens it operates out of is so narrow it is mind-boggling. This is because it is for the most part not open to the soul, the spirit and ascended-master consciousness. They are operating out of a third-dimensional paradigm.

In the future, doctors will not be allowed to make patients wait, and the patient's time will be respected as much as the doctor's. Hospitals will truly become a place of love, healing, and godliness. Nurses and doctors will be of the Christ consciousness, not arrogant, closed-minded and holier than thou. The responsibility for health will be in the hands of the patients, not the doctors. Euthanasia will be practiced when appropriate. Retaining the physical vehicle will not be seen as the ultimate goal from the perspective of the soul.

It is time for the spiritual leadership in all aspects of the health-care profession to step forward in full empowerment and make the needed changes to revolutionize our health-care system from a third-dimensional system to a fifth-dimensional system, from a negative-ego or personality lens to a soul-, Holy Spirit- and ascended-master-directed lens.

The clarion call is now going forth from Lord Buddha, Lord Maitreya and Sanat Kumara, the spiritual leaders of this planet, to lightworkers whose destinies lie in these professions to claim the rod of power and do your part to create this shift of consciousness.

Another aspect of the medical system that has become completely corrupt is the drug-manufacturing industry. These people are some of the greediest people on planet Earth. The prices they charge for drugs are outrageous. I saw one of the newsmagazine shows that disclosed that a drug company was charging an outrageous amount of money, approximately $250 per month, for the same drug that is given to animals for half a cent. They make up all kinds of excuses for this fraud, including the necessity of spending excessive amounts of money doing research. That is rubbish. It is greed—nothing more and nothing less. Unfortunately, it is the elderly who suffer the most, as they are living on a fixed income and literally have to skip meals to afford their medication. The system is so corrupt it is unbelievable.

Then you have the drug lobby paying our corrupt political officials enormous sums of money to ignore this problem, which of course, as with all lobbying, is nothing more than legalized bribery and which the political officials will do nothing about because of their lack of integrity and good-old-boy system.

This brings us to the pharmacy, which we mistakenly trust so naively. I saw another one of those investigative-news programs in which they did massive nationwide testing of the accuracy of pharmacies in filling prescriptions. They found that nationwide at least five percent, if not more, of all prescriptions filled contained the wrong medication, with the wrong written instructions on the bottle.

Then add to this the incompetence of both medical doctors and pharmacists, who tell you nothing about the dangers of mixing drugs. For example, I bet you didn't know that when women take birth control pills and antibiotics at the same time, it makes the birth control pills ineffective. Did your medical doctor or pharmacist tell you this? This is only one of thousands of examples of this. There are even certain foods that when mixed with drugs can actually be fatal. It is just more of the ignorance and incompetence of the traditional medical profession and our entire health-care system.

This then leads us to the discussion of blood transfusions. From the ascended masters' perspective this is another barbaric practice. The traditional medical establishment does not even consider the spiritual implications of this.

One must realize that one of the main ways that karma is balanced from life to life is through the glands that disseminate hormones into the bloodstream. Can you imagine being a high-level initiate and having a doctor give you a blood transfusion from a person you don't even know and who might not be that physically healthy (which is usually the case)? Even worse is receiving blood from someone who has not yet even stepped on the path of initiation. Do you have any conception of how incompatible this is spiritually? You are actually taking on the donor's karma.

If this is bad, organ transplants are even worse, and for the same reasons. The worst thing of all is that medical professionals are actually proud that they are putting pigs' and baboons' hearts and livers into human beings. Can you imagine? The medical profession is actually proud of this.

Getting back to antibiotics for a second, I saw a report yesterday that one of the medical watchdog organizations has sent out reports to doctors to stop giving out antibiotics like candy because they have found that patients have now begun to develop an immunity to a small number of antibiotics that doctors use. This organization is actually fearful of a plague of bacteria that traditional medicine will be unable to stop because antibiotics have been overused. Western medicine is already completely incapable of dealing with all types of viruses and now they are in danger of doing the same thing with bacteria. If they were open to homeopathic remedies or herbs this would not be a problem, but their ignorance makes these options unavailable to them.

One more interesting tidbit in this regard is that there is an absolutely brilliant doctor of oriental medicine in Los Angeles who is also an expert in bioenergetic medicine. This allows him to check things energetically without having to do the gross tests that traditional medical doctors use, which miss 90 percent of what is going on anyway. (As one medical doctor told me, a person could be dying of cancer and it might not even show up in the blood. This is the level of health care that most people rely on when they trust traditional medicine.)

Anyway, this brilliant doctor of oriental medicine, considered to be the finest doctor in Los Angeles, has found that one of the biggest causes of health problems in his patients stems from dairy products. It is not so much the fact that most people develop intolerance to dairy products after the age of twelve, which is bad enough. The main reason, he says, is the poisons they are filled with, such as tetracycline, pesticides and bovine growth hormones. In his research he has found that dairy products are causing heart disease, diabetes, Epstein-Barr, allergies, asthma, antibiotic-resistant bacterial infections, arthritis, bleeding in the digestive tract, childhood anemia, chronic ear infections, colic, hyperactivity, lung cancer, lymphoma, migraine headaches, osteoporosis, bone loss, ovarian cancer and vitamin D toxicity.

It is bad enough that in our society we are told by the traditional medical establishment to eat the wrong foods in the wrong amounts and in the wrong combinations. To make matters worse, there are shots and growth hormones in the meat we eat, pesticides and radiation on our vegetables and fruit, preservatives and chemicals put in just about everything. Even the produce is often waxed to make it look better, which is also poisonous to the body. Add to this dairy-product contaminants, environmental pollution and the poisoning from electromagnetic exposure, chemicals, radiation, mercury in amalgam fillings, psychic, emotional and mental poisoning, implants and elementals from negative extraterrestrials, and you have the major health problems facing most people—ones that the traditional medical community neither acknowledges nor addresses.

My recommendation is to have a traditional medical doctor, but go to him/her only if you absolutely have to, instead relying on your homeopath, naturopath and holistic health practitioners for the rest of your needs most of the time. Be sure to find good qualified people in the holistic health-care profession, for there can be a very wide discrepancy in terms of quality and reliability here also. It is the job of the spiritual leadership on this planet to begin educating the masses about these things, especially those who have been indoctrinated to trust their traditional medical doctors like God.

The same discernment is needed about psychiatrists, psychologists, social workers and marriage counselors. Most of these individuals are operating on a personality level at best, and most of the time not even very effectively on that level, so great discernment and discrimination is needed in finding proper help for self, friends and clients.

Another nightmare of traditional medicine that more people should be aware of is the number of mistakes that are made. In one case I saw on a nightly news broadcast, a woman was told that she had cancer and needed emergency surgery to save her life. She immediately went into surgery and they removed her breast. A week later after more x-rays, the surgeon told her that they had made a mistake and she really did not have cancer after all.

The surgeon took no responsibility and blamed the laboratory. The woman, needless to say, was psychologically and emotionally destroyed. The report went on to say that six out of every hundred lab results are completely inaccurate. The lesson here is, never trust anything your doctor or lab results say without getting a second or even third opinion.

In another case I saw on television about two weeks ago, a man had a severe problem with his leg and foot that forced him to have that leg amputated. He was not happy about this, but finally agreed to go into surgery, and when he did, the surgeon cut off the right foot by mistake. How much do you trust the medical profession? The lesson again is *never blindly put your life in the hands of a doctor.* Ask all the questions you need, and if he/she gives you a hard time, get a new doctor.

Another scary aspect of our health-care system is the FDA (Food and Drug Administration). It is supposed to be our protector, but it is often the vehicle of the Dark Brotherhood. It is completely drug-oriented, as are most medical doctors. The FDA tells us that pesticides do not bother us and that vaccines are okay. The malathion being sprayed in California to get rid of the Medfly will take the paint off your car, but according to them it does not affect humans. They tell us that it is okay to radiate our vegetables and produce. They tell us amalgam (mercury) fillings are safe. They also tell us our drinking water is safe.

Then they spend their time trying to outlaw herbs, vitamins, minerals and homeopathic remedies from our health-food stores and new-age pharmacies. This is one of the most disturbing, corrupt and ignorant agencies that has ever been created. If you think you can take a drug and feel safe because something has been FDA-approved, think again. The FDA even okayed AZT for AIDS patients, which is worse than the AIDS virus itself. The traditional doctors, drug companies and FDA are jointly killing people off faster than the AIDS virus. If you want to know the key principle that is driving this debacle, it is greed.

One other area of the health-care system is HMOs (health maintenance organizations). It does not have to be corrupt, but I'll tell you what the danger is here. When doctors contract with an HMO, they are paid a certain amount of money for each patient. The HMO monitors all the doctor's procedures. If they feel a certain doctor is costing them too much money by prescribing costly procedures to his/her patients, the HMO can fine the doctor large amounts of money and exert enormous pressure. They also give financial bonuses and incentives to doctors who keep costs down.

Do you see what the problem is here? The HMOs are more concerned about making money than proper health care. The doctors no longer have the say over what tests and procedures are needed; the HMOs do. A doctor might want to refer a patient to a specialist, but this costs money. He doesn't want to get in trouble with the HMO and get fined, so he doesn't make the referral. The bonus system forces them to think about making money instead of properly treating their patients.

Do you trust these HMOs to be soul-inspired and not negative-ego-inspired? In other words, do you trust these HMOs to be fifth-dimensional in their administration rather than third-dimensional, or spiritual rather than materialistic? I don't.

You can see the bind this puts doctors in. If they speak out, they can get in major trouble and even get sanctioned. These are some of the things going on behind the scenes in our health-care system that most people are not aware of.

If, however, you find yourself in the predicament of using an HMO for certain medical needs, do remember that it always lies within your choice to be either leader or victim. As the available medical care in this country is so limited at this time, you may very well find that the only treatment you can afford or the company you work for provides you with is an HMO. If that is the case, please do not allow any fear or other negative feelings to interfere with your healing process.

It is up to you to work with your doctors and invoke the highest healing forces of God. Ask for right guidance and ask that your physicians work at the highest level of integrity. Make sure to call upon the divine healers and remember you are a son/daughter of God. Affirm over and over again that all those attending to your physical needs are acting out of their highest integrity and are divinely guided at all times.

While doing this, beloved readers, do investigate any and every means of alternative holistic healing available. Take as much control and play as active a part in your own healing process as possible. All that I have said regarding HMOs is general fact. We each, however, have the ability to alter any given situation by what we bring to it. If you are an HMO patient, then alter that system by bringing God to it. We must never lose sight of the fact that we have the ability to assume leadership in all situations that we might be in. If we choose to leave, we can leave. If we choose to stay, we can alter the currents of a given situation by staying focused within our individual God presence. It is in our conscious unity with our higher self, monad and God that we become powerful leaders in any and every circumstance. This, my beloved readers, even includes HMOs.

Medicare

Another area in the health-care system where there is massive corruption is the Medicare program. The following piece of information I am about to share with you I learned from watching *20/20*. I like to watch some of these newsmagazine shows like *20/20, 60 Minutes, PrimeTime Live* and *Dateline*. Not always, but often they have some very interesting investigations and exposés on a wide variety of topics.

Since my job is to write about every aspect of Earth life as it relates to bringing heaven to Earth, I often get useful information and ideas from watching these shows, which I often build upon from the information received from the masters.

Recently I was watching an investigation of Medicare. Currently in our government there is a big vote to raise the cost of Medicare for the elderly. The Republican Party is saying that if they do not do something, the program is going to go bankrupt. As usual, Congress in its enormous unconsciousness has missed the point. Instead of passing the cost on to the elderly, they should be stopping the corruption that was a product of Congress' own ignorance.

This has to do with how the Medicare program buys all its medical supplies. Because of some stupid law that Congress passed twenty or thirty years ago, the Medicare program has to pay whatever the medical suppliers charge them.

The television show must have given twenty or thirty examples. Over a four-month period, one man was charged over $44,000 for bandages for one wound on his body. Medicare paid $1000 a pop for a back brace worth $50. A Band-Aid that the Veterans Administration (VA) hospital paid four cents for, Medicare paid $25 for.

Now, guess who is paying for this? *You* are! It is our tax dollars. Price-gouging by medical suppliers is too soft a word. When the members of the Republican Congress recently voted on this travesty of fraud, how do you think they cast their votes? They voted to *keep the laws the way they are*. This is the level of intelligence and corruption of our elected officials. The VA hospital does not have to pay these prices and doesn't. Medicare pays something like fifty-eight times as much for medical supplies as the VA hospitals.

How could our Congress possibly vote to continue such waste? We are talking about 30 billion dollars that could be saved and maybe much more if Medicare would just pay for medical supplies what the VA hospitals pay. How could they possibly vote this way? The medical-supplier lobby is probably bribing them with legalized large-scale campaign contributions. For what other reason could they let such corruption and waste continue?

Do you ever wonder why your health-insurance premiums keep rising each year? And this is not just occurring in the realm of Medicare.

Care for Veterans

While it is true that VA hospitals pay far less for supplies, the treatment of the average patient at the VA hospital is atrocious. These men and women have sacrificed life and limb to fight under the leadership of this nation for this nation and should be treated with decency, if not respect, for this service. Unfortunately, this not the case. Although there are always exceptions to every rule, in most cases the veterans of this great country are treated like second-class citizens when seeking medical attention.

While it is true that the patient in the average medical office must wait two to three hours, the VA patient must plan to spend the day at the hospital. I happen to have a close friend who is a veteran and I have gone with her to the VA hospital on occasion. We once spent three-quarters of a day there for a simple eye exam. I've gone there with her when she had the flu, and we literally had to spend the entire day there.

There seems to be a general attitude that those patients are being treated for free. The care I have seen administered seems severely lacking in any trace of heart or compassion.

Veterans are not being treated for free. The medical care that they receive has been earned. In some cases they have paid in advance by sacrificing any chance of living a normal, healthy life. It all comes back again to money and greed.

The system that is currently in operation rewards those who can afford to pay large health-insurance fees with the best medical care that traditional Western medicine can supply. These fortunate individuals get plush waiting rooms to wait in for a shorter amount of time than most. They have access to the best diagnostic equipment available. They are treated with all the respect that money can buy.

Now, I am not saying that these opportunities should be taken away from the wealthier individuals. What I am saying is that the best care available should be offered to *everyone*. It is a sad statement indeed that the nation and its institutions for which veterans have risked their lives and health cannot treat them with dignity and respect.

The Homeless

It is a travesty in our society that we should have people who are homeless. If we truly followed Christ's admonition that we are our brother's keeper, this would not be allowed to happen. Thank God for the spiritual and religious people who do provide homes, shelter and food for the needy.

In our present society it is incredibly expensive to get an apartment. With first and last months' rent and cleaning deposit, phone, gas and electricity and all the other moving expenses, it is not surprising that so many people are homeless.

I was blessed to have a very supportive family this lifetime. However, if I did not have my family, I would have been in big trouble, as I am sure most of you would be if you did not have families to help out in times of trouble or crisis. If you look at how much money we spend on the military or meaningless pork-belly projects in our government, clearly our priorities are wrong in many ways.

We each have a personal responsibility in this regard and we must become more politically active to channel our tax dollars to help people rather than allow politicians to waste it. There is so much corruption and waste in our government. If we just got rid of the corruption and price-gouging in the space program, governmental agencies and military, we could easily eradicate homelessness. It all comes down to priorities. Because our government and its institutions still operate for the most part out of a third-dimensional, materialistic, negative-ego-based consciousness, we do not have proper spiritual values and spiritual vision. God living in human bodies is starving, homeless and hungry all over the United States and the world; however, apparently we have greater priorities than to take care of God. The spiritual leaders among all lightworkers must step forward to do their part to eradicate homelessness.

It is odd how people seem to feel compassion during Christmas and Thanksgiving and when it is cold outside, but at other times of the year the homeless are put back out in the street again. Taking responsibility for this problem might take the form of doing volunteer work, giving homeless people money, opening a shelter or helping to make political change in city, state or federal government. It might involve writing letters to influential people or political leaders. We all must do our puzzle piece, for no one individual can do all things.

Listen to the guidance of the soul, monad and mighty I Am Presence as we go through these professions and social issues and tune in to the ones you are supposed to move into and assume the rod of leadership.

Unemployment

What is it that causes so much unemployment? It is the negative ego running the climate of our economic affairs rather than the soul and mighty I Am Presence. When the negative ego is in control there is an economic climate of fear, pessimism, criticism, insecurity and self-doubt. Companies contract because of this fear and lay off workers.

If the soul, Holy Spirit and mighty I Am Presence were infused into the economic populace, fear would be eradicated. Instead of poverty consciousness, prosperity consciousness would reign. People would be empowered and filled with faith. Instead of contracting in fear, people would be expanding their business out of love and a desire to serve. People would realize that money must be kept in circulation, for to have all, one must give all. When we stop giving and serving, we begin losing what we have. We live in our society in an astral climate of fear, for this is the essence of negative ego.

From the perspective of the mighty I Am Presence, all that exists is perfection and there is wealth and opportunity for everyone. All else is illusion. This remains true for every person even though he/she might live in a society filled with a climate of fear. A lot of what goes on in politics is not what is actually happening economically, but people's perception of what is going on. Society at large is currently holding a mediocre to negative collective perception of the economic status of our country, and that belief is fueling unemployment. I think you can see that if our society were operating out of a fifth-dimensional consciousness, things would expand and flow again and there would be plenty of jobs for everyone. The fifth dimension is ascended-mastery consciousness.

The spiritual leadership of this world in all rays needs to fight this climate of fear, pessimism, criticism, doubt and insecurity and retain I Am consciousness to help uplift humanity instead of catching the psychological disease of humanity and being brought down with it.

Community

In our society because of the third-dimensional, materialistic, personality-level influence along with the negative ego, there is a great stress of importance on either independence or codependence. The average person might say, "What is wrong with independence?" At a certain level of development, independence is something everyone must develop. There is a stage of development that moves beyond codependency and independence, however, and this is *interdependence*. This is self-actualized people learning to depend on each other. This might also be called group consciousness. This is the goal of fifth-dimensional consciousness and beyond.

When one is in group consciousness, one retains his/her individual identity, but also maintains a conscious group identity. This identity includes certainly one's immediate personal family, one's extended family, one's community, one's race, culture or ethnic background, one's religion, all races, all religions, one's state, one's country, all countries, all humanity, then all of God's kingdoms on Earth, the solar system, the galaxy, the universe, all universes. Once one is in this group consciousness, he/she realizes that she and these aspects of self are all of God, or in other words, she is a cosmic citizen. One can maintain all of these connections including a sense of individual identity and group identity simultaneously.

In our society the heroes in movies portray strength through independence, not interdependence. The big male heroes like Sylvester Stallone, Mel Gibson and Arnold Schwarzenegger are the macho, independent violent types. Likable, but I wouldn't say spiritually or fifth-dimensionally focused.

This concept of interdependence and group consciousness is one of the least understood spiritual principles on this planet. Every soul on the planet searches and craves this sense of community and spiritual family. I know that I had searched for it in an outer sense during my entire spiritual path and could never find it. The different spiritual groups I got involved with were too narrow in their focus.

I loved Paramahansa Yogananda, but the group was too narrow and I had already become way too universalistic and eclectic. Sai Baba was the love of my life, but there was clearly an Eastern focus on this path. I loved Astara, but this didn't quite make it either. Finally I got involved with Djwhal Khul's inner-plane ashram, which was my true spiritual home, one I was meant to work from. It was out of this base of operation that I created with my wife an eclectic and universal ashram. It later expanded to a three-tiered ashram of Lord Maitreya, who runs all seven ashrams of the seven rays and then to Melchizedek, who runs all ashrams in the entire universe.

All spiritual teachers, spiritual paths, mystery schools, religions and spiritual teachings were welcome in our home and all were acknowledged, loved, respected and revered. Truly, all paths lead to the same place.

This theme expanded into the manifestation of the large-scale Wesak celebrations, which were really an expansion of this idea for the spiritual leadership group. All spiritual paths, all ashrams, all mystery schools and all spiritual teachings came together under the umbrella of Djwhal Khul, Lord Maitreya, Lord Buddha, Melchizedek and God.

The auditorium for 1200 people became God's ashram, or Melchizedek's ashram, under whose umbrella all comfortably fall. All are respected, all are loved and all are welcomed, including all masters from the inner and outer planes. What emerged was and is truly a coming together of spiritual family in the larger sense. The first Wesak festival at Mount Shasta in 1995 was absolutely extraordinary because of this tremendous sense of group consciousness and unity that was created within such a large gathering of people.

The level of God infusion and the number of inner-plane masters present was mind-boggling. Djwhal Khul said that in all his years of service work he had never seen so many diverse planetary and cosmic masters focused on one event. The combination of this universal and eclectic approach and the ability of the group to move out of the negative-ego and personality level to embrace group consciousness was extraordinary and magical.

The potentiality of the group became exponential. I think just about everyone was blown away by the collective experience. I personally had never experienced anything like that before, and I don't think anyone else had either. The key was the group consciousness and interdependence of everyone there.

Most people can relate to this in their marriages or families, where this sense of group identity and individual identity is often achieved. This must be expanded from this minute focus to a planetary and cosmic point of view, where all people are revered as one reveres one's earthly family. Once this expansion is complete, you will actually develop a group body and live within an individual and group body simultaneously. It is when you move into this state of consciousness that the negative ego can truly be released and the mighty I Am Presence can fully merge and take full authority over the four-body system.

One might look at this personality-level actualization as seeking independence; soul-level self-actualization is the movement toward interdependence; and monadic-level self-actualization and full group-body consciousness on all levels as planetary and cosmic citizenship.

It is for this reason that I invite every person reading this book to come to the Wesak celebrations held each year at the full moon of Taurus, usually falling in May, to experience this coming together of an eclectic, universalistic spiritual family in total unconditional love and acceptance. It is a wonderful thing to honor, love and respect all people, all spiritual teachers, all spiritual paths, all mystery schools and all spiritual teachings and to see them as *one*.

As we move toward the year 2000 and 2012, we plan to do these events for as many as 5000 people or more if we can. Melchizedek spoke to us about this event as the gathering of the spiritual leadership from around the globe and as the gathering of his initiates.

There is a lack of interdependence and growth consciousness in many places in our society. First off, people do not have a real sense of community, both in a spiritual sense and in an earthly sense. Most people do not really know their neighbors. Everyone lives in his/her own little box and keeps to him/herself. This is especially true in big cities. People are not usually friendly to the people they pass on the street. These are not strangers; they are brothers and sisters in a larger family.

People do not carpool. Every person has his/her own car and each person drives around in his own little isolated box called an automobile. Isolation gets so bad in some cities like New York that people can be beaten or mugged on the street in front of other people, and they will walk by as if nothing is happening. This is how numb we have become. Rural cities are better; however, none come even close to the full scope of the interdependence and group consciousness I speak of here.

The spiritual leaders of today and tomorrow must embrace and teach interdependence and group consciousness in all professions and all social activities. If there were true group consciousness, the Republicans and Democrats would not be bickering and gridlocked like spoiled children. A greater vision and identity would be maintained. If part of your identity was truly in a larger body other than your own personal one, how could you not want to help your brothers and sisters? How could you possibly think of hurting another? The answer is, you couldn't.

The true meaning of the law of karma, or cause and effect, would be understood. What you do to another is truly what you do to yourself, for all others are in truth your *self*. There is only one Self, and we all share that one identity regardless of the form or path we take to realize this.

Hunger

People are hungry in this world because of one reason and one reason alone: greed and selfishness. The motto of the negative ego is "I am out for myself. It is a dog-eat-dog world, and I will numb myself to the pain and suffering of others." This philosophy might increase your earthly bank account and belongings for a time. However, it also decreases your spiritual bank account, which will ultimately impoverish you on all levels—if not in this life, then on the inner plane and in your next life.

The figure is something like one percent of the population controls 75 percent of the world's resources. Then we take more and more services from the poor and give tax breaks to the rich. The only way people can achieve full ascension and get to heaven is by helping their less fortunate brothers and sisters. People are starving all over the world because people are not spiritually attuned and soul-infused. The negative ego cares only about self or family, not recognizing that one's true identity is not the personality or the physical body, but the eternal self that lives within the core of every person's being.

This eternal self lives within all things, not just in the limited fence of a physical body. This is the illusion of third-dimensional and negative-ego thinking and ultimately the cause of all suffering. To achieve ascension, every person must become aware of this first and then demonstrate his/her understanding of it in her daily life to graduate from this spiritual school. It is a travesty that people should go hungry and be malnourished.

The negative ego prompts the leaders of the countries of the world to spend money on wrong priorities. People cannot focus on things such as self-actualization if their survival needs are not cared for. Imagine what your life would be like if you were born into one of the Third World countries or an Arab nation or even the Soviet Union.

Abortion

I have asked the ascended masters Djwhal Khul, Lord Maitreya and Melchizedek many times about the issue of abortion, and they have very clearly stated that the position of the planetary and cosmic hierarchies is pro-choice. Abortions are not meant to be a form of birth control, however; it is up to the free will of the women and no karma is incurred.

This is because the incoming soul and the physical body are separate. You are not killing a soul, just a vehicle. The soul does not come into the body until just before birth or just after birth. Oftentimes when a woman has an abortion, the same soul will incarnate the next time she becomes pregnant, so in truth she is having the same baby. Fundamentalist Christians see the physical body and soul being the same thing, which is illusion.

Euthanasia

I asked Djwhal Khul about the masters' views on euthanasia, or mercy killing. He told me the Spiritual Hierarchy completely supports such a process. There is no karma incurred in this process. It is obviously important to consider such an endeavor only when doing this is in harmony with the dictates of the soul and not out of misguided thinking of the negative ego. However, as long as the negative ego is involved, this issue is one that the spiritual leadership of this world needs to raise consciousness about.

Again, here we have misguided Fundamentalist Christians and misguided doctors trying to save life at all costs, not recognizing the immortality of all people and the fact that death is illusion. The physical vehicle dies, but we are not physical vehicles.

It is interesting that third-dimensional people have no problem putting animals to sleep (to aid their transition), but to put humans to sleep (help with their transition) is considered a mortal sin. This seems quite hypocritical. Contrary to most people's beliefs, euthanasia *is* practiced by doctors all the time, not just talked about. Pulling the plug on life-support systems is euthanasia. Giving people enormous amounts of morphine or painkillers is really disguised euthanasia.

Many of the beliefs that are held in this world are extremely outdated and behind the times. Many political and social issues I discuss in this book might make some feel impotent to effect change. One way all can help is just by raising consciousness among lightworkers. Over time the hundredth-monkey effect will begin to take place. Others with specific ray configurations and missions will be directly guided to go into these professions and take on these issues head-on. Your soul and monad will tell you which issues comprise your mantle of responsibility, so to speak. The world is changing more than we think.

I find it very interesting that Bill Clinton and Al Gore are my age, were raised with rock music and experienced the '60s as teenagers. We are now seeing a whole new generation of leaders who cannot help but be different because of the radically different cultures in which they grew up. Very evolved souls are now incarnating. All of them are above third-initiation level. Those beneath this level will be incarnating on two other planets, which Sanat Kumara is now overseeing. From a spiritual point of view, this planet is the most evolved planet in our solar system except for Venus.

It is important to understand, however, that humanity's spiritual evolution is actually much higher than its psychological evolution. This is also true of most lightworkers. This speaks to the issue that one can ascend and still be run by the negative ego to a certain extent. Ascension and initiations have more to do with light-quotient levels than with psychological development.

The Space Program

I asked the masters about their views on the space program. The guidance I received is that they support the space program as an expansion of consciousness and a movement into our solar, galactic and universal heritage. From the perspective of the soul, however, the problem with the space program lies in the degree of corruption, lying, deceit and misappropriation of funds within the system.

An example of this is the Star Wars project. Look at how much money was spent on this boondoggle of a project, which was never developed and was finally scrapped. It should never have been focused on in the first place. If all that money were spent to help the homeless or feed the hungry, look at the difference it would have made in people's lives.

The space program wastes too much time on meaningless experiments. If we are going to have a space program, it needs to be balanced in relationship to the concerns of the people on Earth. I recently saw a newsmagazine show on television that featured a story on the enormous financial corruption in NASA—how money was being spent and the amount of money different firms were charging for their services. This is what happens when you have large collections of greedy people involved in such a project. The masters support the idea of a space program; however, it would have to be completely revamped, streamlined and prioritized from the perspective of the soul as to where taxpayers' money is best spent.

The Death Penalty

I asked Djwhal Khul about the Spiritual Hierarchy's position on the death penalty. He told me that they were against it, and the reasons were rather interesting. First off is the concept of the sentence coming out of punishment consciousness instead of rehabilitation consciousness. The death penalty is done out of people's anger. By doing this we are taking the lesson away from the person's soul or higher self. Remember that one of the Ten Commandments says, "Thou shalt not kill."

If you really think about it, to be in prison one's whole life is much worse than to be killed physically. I personally would much rather be killed than remain in prison. In prison, the soul would be forced to think about his/her crime and there might be the possibility of learning some lessons in the process, although the karma would have to be balanced in a future lifetime.

This issue is such a loaded one that I got a double confirmation from Archangel Michael. He emphatically stated that the Spiritual Hierarchy was indeed against the death penalty. He said that violence should not beget violence. The death penalty was and is an act of retribution and the true path of God is one of forgiveness. This does not mean that the person should not serve a prison term, for indeed this is obviously needed. However, the death penalty really stems from the negative ego's desire for revenge.

Archangel Michael told me I was courageous to attempt to speak of such loaded subjects. I replied that it was much needed, for there is much confusion on these issues among lightworkers. Archangel Michael also said that the death penalty would eventually be banned or outlawed for these reasons.

War

This is an interesting spiritual and philosophical issue. In the ultimate reality, war is a manifestation of negative ego; I think everyone would agree with this. From the perspective of the ascended masters, however, in the process of a planet's move from third- to a fully realized fifth-dimensional planet, wars do take place. They are sometimes supported by the Spiritual Hierarchy as vehicles of transition for achieving the ultimate goal of a peaceful and loving society.

The classic example of this is Adolph Hitler and World War II. Hitler was a high-ranking official of the Dark Brotherhood, which is an inner-plane hierarchy of sons and daughters of God who are steeped in delusion. The Dark Brotherhood was attempting to take over this planet, using Hitler as a vehicle. The Dark Brotherhood in essence serves the negative ego instead of God.

On the third and fourth dimensions of reality there is a constant battle going on between the forces of light and the forces of darkness, or the antichrist. This might also be called the forces of glamour, maya and illusion. Nazi Germany and Hitler had to be stopped, as did Japan, and the ascended masters supported the Allies in going to war.

I am one of the biggest admirers in the world of Mahatma Gandhi; however, if everyone had adopted his attitude, Germany would have won the war, not the Allies. When six million Jews and tens of millions of other people are being slaughtered in a mass genocide, it is the spiritual responsibility of the free nations of the world to stop this. Otherwise this would be a sin of omission, not commission. As Krishna said in the *Bhagavad-Gita* to Arjuna, "Fight for me and you will incur no sin." Failing to go to war to stop the Dark Brotherhood would have meant not completing God's divine plan on the Earth plane.

It is for this reason that in this transitional phase of Earth's evolution there might be what are called egotistical wars and spiritual wars. The same could be applied to killing. When the white man killed buffalo, they killed it for sport, leaving the buffalo lying dead on the ground for no reason. This was wrong and sin, or karma, was incurred. When an American Indian killed an animal, he/she saw the animal as a younger brother and prayed for it and thanked it for its service of providing food.

One cannot say that killing is always wrong even in our present day and age. Some animals volunteer to serve in this capacity. Transitional spiritual wars are sometimes needed to stop different antichrist figures from taking over this planet.

The recent war in Bosnia is another example. The Serbs and Serb leader were basically functioning as another Hitler, performing mass genocide of the Bosnian people. It is a documented fact that the Bosnian women were being gathered together and raped over and over again like the Japanese did in World War II. Should humanity stand around and allow this to continue? Should humanity have stood by and let Hitler and Nazi Germany kill six million Jews? I don't think so, and the ascended masters don't think so either.

So this issue of war and "thou shalt not kill" must be thought out a little more carefully. Another example is Saddam Hussein and his takeover of Kuwait. This man is another antichrist of the likes of Hitler who is destroying his country and the good people of Iraq with his Dark Brotherhood actions. The height of paradox was seeing him praying to Allah on television during the Gulf War. The danger here, regardless whether one is a Republican or a Democrat, was the possibility of his moving beyond Kuwait, which he most definitely had plans to do.

What this means is that for the time being it is still important for countries to have military forces, guns and police. It would be completely unrealistic to think that they could or should be let go of now.

The spiritual path is a process, not an instantaneous achievement. In the ultimate reality when all humanity has completed its seven levels of initiation, fully realized its ascension and become like Arcturus, then war, the military, police and guns will be completely removed, no longer needed. However, as long as we live in a world of third and fourth dimension, they serve an important function, acting as a stopgap until we reach this ultimate goal. These spiritual transitional wars force the world community to function like the United Nations police force or the NATO police force. If needed, such wars must be fought not out of hate, but out of love, recognizing that the people you are fighting are sons and daughters of God who are confused souls and who have been taken over by the negative ego.

This is the concept of the spiritual-warrior archetype. Now, unfortunately, the military leaders do not embrace love in their hearts when they go to war because they do not see the bigger picture: that they are being used by the Spiritual Hierarchy and by the soul and monad for the proper outpicturing of the divine plan on Earth.

The people who have been guided to work in the military should feel proud. Many, contrary to popular belief, incur very good karma for selflessly giving their lives to help their country and fellow comrades. They often learn self-discipline and self-mastery in a way that no other path could have given them.

I bring this up because the common spiritual belief among lightworkers is that the military is all bad, but this is not true. It serves a very important function in our society, as do the police and sheriff's departments, the CIA and the FBI. The problem comes from the corruption of the negative ego, which does not see its purpose as the soul sees its purpose.

This philosophical argument about war and killing can be taken one step further by taking it to a more personal level. If someone broke into your house and wanted to rob, kill and rape your wife and kids, or in the case of a woman, to rape you, would you send him unconditional love and let it happen, or would you see it as your spiritual responsibility to stop him from hurting you and your children?

From the perspective of the ascended masters, you incur no karma by protecting yourself and even killing the intruder if there was no other way to stop him. I bring up these types of issues in this book, for many light-workers are confused on some of these points. This is why I asked the masters their opinions on the political, social and philosophical issues of our time. This present discussion brings us to the issue of gun control.

Gun Control

As discussed in the previous section concerning war and the philo-sophical issue of violence, guns still have their place in our society. As we all know, owning a gun is a right bestowed upon Americans by the Bill of Rights in the U.S. Constitution. We can clearly see that for the time being until our ultimate spiritual goals are achieved, the police and military are going to need to have guns.

The next question is, how about the general public? From the perspec-tive of the ascended masters, Djwhal Khul told me they support the right to bear arms. I think we all can agree that our government, police depart-ments, CIA and FBI are not always trustworthy. This is because of the negative ego that controls a great many of our political and law-enforce-ment officials. Given this fact, people bearing arms is kind of a political equalizer and prevents all the power getting into the government's hands.

From the perspective of the physical body, we also live in a very dis-turbed and dangerous world. There is an enormous amount of crime, rape, robbery and the likes, especially in the big cities. We cannot always de-pend on the police department to protect us. People have a right to protect themselves. It is like learning the martial arts.

Learning martial arts is a wonderful thing; however, if guided by the soul, the ultimate ideal is never to use it. Just as one needs to develop psy-chic self-defense on mental and emotional levels (see "Psychic Self-Defense" in *Soul Psychology*), one must also develop physical defense to protect his/her physical life.

Now, I will be frank with you here. I personally have never owned a gun and never will. I am choosing to rely completely on God, the masters and my own good karma and positive thinking to protect me. Even though this is the case, I still recognize people's right to protect themselves if they need to. The masters support this position also.

The danger arises when people own guns who are emotionally imbal-anced, not connected to their higher self and soul and are run by the nega-tive ego. In fits of emotional passion, they might use them. These people are not necessarily criminals—most of the time they are not. These are crimes of passion, so to speak.

The key philosophical question here is how to balance the right to bear arms, yet keep guns out of the hands of emotionally imbalanced and deranged people and criminals. In my opinion, people should not be able to buy a gun off the street without out some kind of delay and check of police and psychiatric records. This seems simple common sense.

The gun lobbies, of course, are never willing to see the whole picture or budge in the slightest. Politicians are more concerned with getting reelected than in looking at the good of all concerned.

Many people might be surprised that the ascended masters support the right to bear arms in this temporary phase of the ultimate goal of God realization.

After writing this section I wanted to be 100 percent sure that I was not coloring this with my own personal views on the issue, so I asked Melchizedek about this issue for a second channeled confirmation. What he said surprised me.

He said that guns in and of themselves are neutral. Guns are not in and of themselves either of the negative ego or spiritual. It is the person who uses them that makes them so. The original idea for guns came from the inner plane as a divine idea for helping in the process of hunting for food. It was certainly a better idea than bows and arrows. But humans misused the idea when they started using guns to kill each other.

It is true that one does not need guns on the inner plane because one does not need a police force or an army or food. As a divine idea in the transition between third- and fifth-dimensional society, it had divine potentiality. As with everything in our society, however, the negative ego has misused it. I found it very interesting that Melchizedek spoke of it this way, but it did make sense.

The true essence of this additional point is that guns were originally a divine idea, not a negative-ego idea. He did confirm, however, that there were no guns in the higher dimensions of reality. He also confirmed to me again that the Spiritual Hierarchy did indeed support the right to bear arms.

Sometimes on some of the more controversial issues I like to double-check my channeling to make sure that I am receiving 100 percent-accurate information. As I am writing this book I am very excited to be getting the Spiritual Hierarchy's view on all these political and social issues. I am actually learning a lot myself, as I am comprehensively speaking with them about each one of these issues.

Most lightworkers and most spiritual books I have seen or read have not comprehensively explored this area with the masters in this way. It is actually quite an exciting project for me, one that came about quite spontaneously in the flow of my automatic typewriting of this book.

From the Hierarchy's perspective, the right to bear arms is an eternal right. The real truth of the matter, however, is that the more evolved we become, the less we want to rely on physical armament and the more we rely on God. At one point in our evolutionary process we might feel compelled to pick up a gun for protection, but at a later stage the protection we call on might be from Lord Michael, Lord Maitreya or Sai Baba.

As we continue to move to ever higher levels on our path of initiation and ascension, the way we use certain inalienable rights automatically changes. For example, we have the right to free speech. A person who is not spiritually oriented might choose to exercise that right in cussing, gossiping or writing tabloid articles. A more evolved soul would use that right to speak freely about the spiritual path and encourage his/her brothers and sisters in their own evolutionary process. The same basic right pertains to both freedom of speech and bearing arms. The use of that right, however, dramatically changes as one proceeds along the path of initiation.

In discussing gun control thus far, it is important that you are aware that this issue was being addressed from a third-dimensional perspective. All that I have written has specifically addressed this issue from the point where humanity is currently operating. In other words, the particular lens through which this situation was looked at and spoken about is the limited lens of the current status of our civilization.

After writing about it from this perspective, the masters requested that I broaden the lens and address this issue from the point of view of the fifth dimension, or spiritual kingdom. The advantage of doing this would be to encourage the reader to help move your consciousness to that higher vantage point. It became evident to me that when discussing various world problems, the masters like to analyze them both from the state of consciousness that the world is currently functioning at and from the higher spiritual spheres where they see the greater potential. Their goal is to make the lightworker aware of all these various levels so that he/she can see the world as it is and yet help manifest the vision of what the world will one day be. From the Hierarchy's point of view, they see us moving into a fifth-dimensional frequency in which the problem of gun control—and all weapons, for that matter—will not even be an issue. For those of us who hold this frequency within ourselves, the call goes forth to help bring this into manifestation now.

This does not mean that we should hide our heads in the sand and ignore the third- and fourth-dimensional world that swirls around us with all of its violence. What it does mean is that each of us should live our lives to the highest and most spiritually attuned frequencies we can reach. As greater and greater numbers of us learn how to stay fully centered in the love and light of God, the world around us will begin to reflect that light and love back to us.

As more and more of us feel that we are able to do this without owning and therefore potentially using a gun, the quicker this will manifest as a reality. We will have the one-hundredth-monkey effect as guns become less and less an option. This, of course, must be done in one's own time as each follows the dictates of his/her own inner guidance.

The Hierarchy wishes us all to be aware that we each have the power to help turn our planet into one of peace rather than aggression. The quickest way out of our present violence is through changing the reality of our personal world. What is requested from each of us is that we put as much peace into the planet as possible in order to more quickly establish love, light and peace as a living reality upon this Earth.

Nuclear Bombs and Nuclear Energy

The masters are totally against both. Testing nuclear bombs creates massive holes in the aura of the Earth. They cause earthquakes in different parts of the globe. They are weapons of mass destruction and should be completely abolished. Nuclear energy should also be abolished.

First, humankind does not have the needed knowledge and understanding of what it is working with. This can clearly be seen in the Chernobyl disaster and all the other reactor accidents.

Second, we have absolutely no way of dealing with nuclear waste. Nuclear radiation is the single most toxic substance that exists on this planet for humankind and for the Earth herself. Third, what happens if there is a massive earthquake at a reactor site? We even have reactor sites in California over the San Andreas fault! It doesn't take a brain scientist to figure out that this is insane.

Fourth and most important, there are other ways to create energy that do not destroy a substance. Nikola Tesla proved that his energy rods could be placed on every home and attract free energy. The greedy energy companies and oil companies stopped this because they would go out of business. Many such technologies are known by these companies and kept under wraps. Patents are bought up; people are killed. The secret government and greedy power elite that run this world are doing everything in their power not to let this happen.

The spiritual leadership of this world needs to step forward, raise mass consciousness and stop using all forms of energy that pollute our environment—nuclear energy being the worst. There will obviously be a transitional period before these new-age methods are allowed to come out en masse.

Extraterrestrials

The biggest cover-up of all time is the fact that extraterrestrials are visiting our planet en masse and have been doing so for a long time (see *Hidden Mysteries*). How we have allowed our government to get away with this deceit and corruption is beyond me. It is time for the spiritual leadership of this planet to demand honesty and accountability on this issue.

The full story of how the American government has shared bases with extraterrestrials and has stored hundreds of bodies of many different species will have an enormous impact on the collective consciousness of humanity. There is still a large number of people who do not believe this. This issue alone shows how untrustworthy our government really is.

When the extent of extraterrestrial life in our solar system, galaxy and universe becomes completely known by the people of this world, it will open people's eyes to spiritual realities like nothing they have ever experienced before. This realization will leave people thinking, If this is true, then almost anything is possible.

Opening this lid will catalyze the way for more open and direct communication with extraterrestrials, which will radically change our society more than any other factor. They have so much knowledge and information to give us that it will make our planet's knowledge look like that of a nursery school. This more open and direct contact will lead the way to our planet's becoming a part of the solar council and galactic council of planets. The restricted lens we have been operating out of will open up, and we will see ourselves as solar, galactic and universal citizens, not just an isolated, alienated planet.

The way we currently look at our planet in relationship to the universe is the height of egotism. The spiritual leadership of this world must step forward and raise consciousness about this issue. In every form of media possible there must be a demand from the lightworkers on this planet and the new group of world-servers to the governments of the world to stop hiding this information.

The people of Earth must also be made aware that we are under attack by a small group of negative extraterrestrials, who are the ones doing all the abducting and alien implantation. The world must see this war in perspective, as the people's minds are under attack, which is the level at which the war is operating. In addition, humanity must be advised of the enormous help that is available to us from the positive extraterrestrials such as the Arcturians, Ashtar Command and Pleiadians, to name a few. The spiritual leadership of this planet must embrace this understanding and see it as an integral part of the whole spiritual picture.

Foreign Aid

There are certain political leaders going around saying that we should stop all foreign aid and take care of our own countries. This is also the height of egotism. For are we not our brother's keeper? Of course, foreign aid can go too far and must be thoughtfully balanced with the United States or any other country's home concerns.

This whole issue usually has to do with the illusions of the negative ego. Think about the nations of the world. Are there any actual lines that separate countries? The whole idea of nations is a man-made idea. Man through his greed and egotism has divided up the world into large plots of land that different governments own. This, of course, changes as power-hungry governments gobble up different countries or, on the other side of the coin, people in these countries seek independence and form smaller new countries. It is all arbitrary, relative and, from the ultimate point of view, illusion.

For planetary and cosmic citizens to care about only one small plot or one egotistical group of people is absurd. Even the ideas of "belonging" to a country and patriotism are really egotistical. Why should one root for one country over another when all are God? There is nothing wrong with having pride in one's country as long as the negative ego does not intrude, making one superior and another inferior, which most countries do. Every nation thinks theirs is the best. The spiritual leadership of this world must get out of thinking about countries, religious preference, race, culture, gender, creed and color and see the unity and oneness.

Most people see life through an extremely small lens. Melchizedek said that most people see life through the lens of a fly instead of through the lens of a God-realized ascended master. The purpose of this book is to look at the subject of leadership and the political, social and philosophical issues of our time from a much larger lens than partisan politics and the above-mentioned lens of nation, religion, race, creed, color, culture, gender, social status, economic status and so forth.

What we are developing here slowly but surely is the ability to look through the lens of the Holy Spirit and the mighty I Am Presence, which transcends duality and the negative ego's separative vision.

The United Nations

The concept of having a United Nations is a very good one and definitely inspired by spirit. The problem is that the United Nations has had no real power and has been rather ineffective in its functioning. For many years it was in a state of gridlock because of the Cold War. This has begun to change because of the fall of Communism in the Soviet Union and East

Germany. People must remember, however, that Russia is a heartbeat away from moving back to its reactionary ways. In more recent times in the Iraq situation and slightly in Bosnia, we have seen some leadership asserted by the United Nations. In the future it will be stronger because the United Nations will ultimately be connected to the Federation of Planets in our solar system and galaxy.

Earth has not yet evolved to the point of being a consciously working member. *Star Trek's* Federation might serve as more of a prototype than we realize. It will eventually be run by high-level initiates and ascended beings and function like an externalized Shamballa. We will always have different countries; however, group consciousness and/or global consciousness will be much more a part of humanity's thinking process. Third-dimensional thinking and negative ego have kept the United Nations from fulfilling its full potential.

Immigration

It is absolutely tragic how immigrants are treated in this country, especially with this recent wave of conservative rhetoric. All people are God whether they have U.S. citizenship or not. Sure immigration laws and proper border control are necessary. However, even the labeling of immigrants as "aliens" is wrong. *No one* is an alien; everyone is our brother and sister in Christ.

Environment and the World's Economy

Another social comment I would like to make here is that taking care of our environment can actually aid the world's economy and not automatically harm it, as the Republican Party seems to assume. Environmental protection can create an enormous number of jobs. Politicians need to change their mindset on this issue.

Plastic Surgery

A client recently asked me about plastic surgery and whether it was spiritually okay to do such a thing. When I tuned in to the masters, the answer I immediately got was that in some cases it would be acceptable and appropriate. The problem is whether a person's self-esteem and self-worth are tied too closely to the physical vehicle and appearance.

You have all heard stories where some people get carried away and have hundreds of operations to look like a movie star. This would be doing it for negative-ego reasons, not soul reasons. People have plastic surgery often for the wrong reasons, and this needs to be looked at very closely. There are many exceptions, however, so there is no hard-and-fast rule.

One must also realize that plastic surgery has a traumatic effect on the physical vehicle and etheric body. Etheric-healing teams need to be called in to make these repairs. The anesthesia and painkillers taken after surgery poison the liver and suppress the immune system. There is a long healing process that people must go through. If people were truly aligned with their soul and monad and were clear of negative-ego control, it would not be used very much; however, the ascended masters do not have a rigid stance against it. The same would apply on a much simpler level to makeup.

Isolationism vs. Internationalism

I asked Djwhal Khul about the Spiritual Hierarchy's position on this most important political and philosophical issue. Isolationism is the political philosophy that America, for example, should be concerned only with her own problems and not be spending money or sending troops to help the world in any way, shape or form. According to this ideology, every country should take care of itself. I am using the example of America, but this philosophy applies to any nation in the world.

Internationalism is the opposite political philosophy. It states that we have a responsibility to be our brother's keeper and be a leader in service to the world. The Spiritual Hierarchy's view on this is quite obvious. The path of isolationism is a path of selfishness and egotism on a national scale. Every country on Earth has a global responsibility. Being our brother's keeper applies to nations as well.

Djwhal Khul said that this political philosophy of internationalism must be tempered with wisdom. The United States cannot be the policeman for the world. Each country must pick its battles and find a selfish/selfless balance. Vietnam, for example, was a mistake. On the other hand, the Spiritual Hierarchy supports troop deployment in Bosnia. It is important to see that the Hierarchy has firm positions on such issues and that they are not so ethereal that they are separated from the political issues of our planet.

The answer to this political issue is easy to understand if you apply isolationism versus internationalism to yourself as a person. Is it appropriate to be an isolationist in the way you live your life? The answer is no. We each have a responsibility to serve our brothers and sisters at the highest level we possibly can.

This is the destiny of all soul-merged and ascended countries. Each country is governed by a personality ray and soul ray. The spiritual ideal is for each country to move into leadership and manifest the higher expression of its soul, and eventually monadic, ray. Leadership and service are forever the touchstones.

Surrogate Mothers

The next philosophical issue I would like to discuss has to do with women who become surrogate mothers for women who are unable to have children. I asked Djwhal Khul about this and he said that the Spiritual Hierarchy is totally in support of this when done appropriately. This is a great act of kindness and love that can be a beneficial exchange for all concerned.

The Fundamentalist Right

It is very interesting to me that the right-wing Fundamentalists, claiming to be the political party of God, take virtually the opposite view that the Spiritual Hierarchy and ascended masters do, who truly represent God on this planet. It is amazing to me how a political party based on a belief in God and Jesus Christ can be so run by the Dark Brotherhood. The cause of this is negative ego. The relationship to its own members and to God and Jesus has been so incredibly contaminated by negative ego that the Fundamentalists have actually become a major vehicle for the dark forces rather than the forces of light. This is quite a paradox in reality.

Ecological Concerns

This is a most pressing concern for the spiritual leadership of all professions around the world. This stems from the third-dimensional negative-ego consciousness that sees the Earth as being separate from self, nonliving and an object to be plundered and destroyed for one's own self-centered, greedy needs. In our current society, making money always comes before any ecological concerns.

Humankind has literally raped the Earth. We have polluted the water, the air, the rivers, the lakes, the oceans and the soil. We have damaged the lungs of the planet by cutting down the trees in the rainforest. We have damaged the ozone layer and created a hole as wide as a continent. The burning of fossil fuels has created a greenhouse effect. Our farms have poisoned the earth and water tables with pesticides. We cover the surface with cement so Earth cannot breathe. Our cities are filled with noise pollution. Our homes and cities are filled with electromagnetic pollution from power lines and electrical appliances.

We blast our food with microwaves, which puts holes in the aura of the food and is most definitely not a new-age form of cooking. We have greedily raped the Earth of her natural resources to satisfy technology and commerce. We don't thank the Earth or look at her as our mother. We don't look at her as a living being in a state of evolution and initiation just as we are.

It is amazing that with one massive catastrophe she hasn't rid herself of the parasite called humanity. We have alienated Pan, the devic kingdom and nature kingdoms, who have left our farms because we don't recognize them, instead using chemical farming. For the first time in the history of our planet we have acid rain, in which no living plant or human can thrive.

Is it any wonder we have so many natural disasters? It is humankind's abuse that creates much of this. We have thrown off the ecological balance of this planet. Animal species are dying. Cutting down too many trees around the world is depleting the oxygen of the planet. We have poisoned the Earth with nuclear waste. We litter our streets, throwing trash on the ground, occupied only with ourselves.

We keep taking and don't give back. Is it any wonder that so many people are physically ill and have deficient immune systems? What we do to the Earth we also do to our own physical bodies, for these cannot be separated. This is the path of the negative-ego, third-dimensional, materialistic mind, which does all these things and still doesn't care. The fifth-dimensional society works in harmony with the Earth and gives back to her.

Economic success and ecological sanctity can work hand in hand. Al Gore wrote a wonderful book about this. This is just another example of what happens when we don't see life from the eyes of the soul, spirit and Christ vision. The Earth Mother is suffering as an abused wife or mother would, yet she still forgives and supports us.

For every tree cut down, at least one tree should be planted. Paul Solomon, the great universal-mind channel, was asked in trance what was the single most important thing a person on this planet could do to serve the divine plan. The Source said if every person on this planet simply planted one tree, that would be the best suggestion It could give.

In the future everyone will recycle and every day will be Earth day. We will work in partnership with her, Pan and the nature kingdom of elementals and devas. The burning of all fossil fuels must stop and we must find new forms of energy from universal and extraterrestrial sources. Trees and plants must also be looked at as our younger brothers and sisters and as living spiritual beings.

We must get rid of these crazy aerosol spray cans. Fluorocarbons are destroying the ozone layer. We must have a 180-degree shift in our priorities on a global level. This is beginning to happen, but we need to go much further much faster. Our lives and the lives of our children are literally at stake. This is one of the most pressing problems of our time.

The lightworkers and humanity at large must persuade our government officials to change their priorities. If companies cannot do their business in a pollution-free manner, they should be shut down by the government until they do. The Environmental Protection Agency should do what it was created to do and become one of the most important and backed agencies on our planet.

The FDA needs to get on the stick and employ people who know what they are doing and who will stop the irradiation of our foods, pesticides on our produce and parasites in our drinking water. The FDA actually condones the things that are killing us, telling us they are safe. Lightworkers and high-level initiates must infiltrate all these organizations and gain positions of power. There must be a new political movement called the Green Light party, "green" for protecting the Earth and "light" for spiritual priorities for all facets of Earth institutions and life.

One very interesting area of environmental awareness and activity that I recently became aware of is the advances being made in the cultivation of organic cotton. Using no pesticides or chemicals whatsoever, extremely soft cotton is growing in greater and greater abundance.

Relying on the natural tendencies inherent in nature herself, certain insects are being brought into these cotton fields. These insects feed on the worm pests that normally invade the cotton plant. Rather than using the toxic chemicals that most do, select groups of motivated individuals have discovered a way to let nature take care of the problem. They are working daily to get more of a handle on this natural process and have even succeeded in growing cotton in an ever-expanding variety of colors. This is but one example of what can be done in this area when our minds are focused in this direction.

Extraterrestrials will help us in the future to clean up our environment with such things as smog-sucking machines. They will also show us how to tap into universal energy so we can get off fuels, coal and electrical power lines. We will use free energy from the universe, as Tesla spoke of and actually invented. Animals, trees, plants and even the mineral kingdom will be protected in the future.

Anything the spiritual leadership can do to raise the consciousness in these areas and many more I have not mentioned must be done as a top priority before we do too much more damage. Better ways need to be developed to deal with our landfills, which also poison our soil, air and water. We need to cut down on the amount of waste and garbage we create and recognize there is not an endless supply of resources.

Ecology will be revered in the future as an important science and as important a part of schooling as reading, writing, arithmetic and spiritual studies. The Earth Mother has been good to us, and it is now time that we return the favor. This can happen only by waking up the soul and monadic consciousness within humanity and the leaders of this world.

It is not only the waking up but also the willingness to take action personally, spiritually, politically and socially on an ongoing basis. The American Indians may be our best teachers.

NAFTA

The North American Free Trade Agreement (NAFTA) was being voted on when President Clinton first came into office. I asked Djwhal Khul about the Spiritual Hierarchy's views on this and he said that they did not have views on it and that it was up to the free choice of humanity. I wish to say here that many times when I ask such questions I am told this. They take stands on about half of the issues, which is a fact that I thought lightworkers would find interesting. One does not often think of going to vote and asking the ascended masters what to vote on.

I suggest that in the next election you take Lord Buddha and Lord Maitreya into the voting booth with you. When asked if you are a Democrat, Republican or Independent say, "None of the above. I am a mixture of all of them," or "I belong to the Ascended Masters party."

I am joking here; however, there is a seed of truth and a real point I am making. Ascended masters and the Spiritual Hierarchy are not Democrat or Republican or Independent, for they are beyond duality. They take each issue as it comes and see what is good for the whole. When I asked Djwhal Khul about individual candidates in city and state elections whom I had never heard of, he would tell me who had the most light in his/her aura. This is another interesting way to vote and another factor to consider.

In terms of NAFTA, the Spiritual Hierarchy supported this treaty because of its focus on greater group exchange and communication.

Voting

This is another issue that the Spiritual Hierarchy has very strong views on. Many lightworkers are too heavenly and ephemeral, and need to get more grounded and manifest their spirituality on this Earth plane in the real world. True ascension is not going up but is rather a descension of the soul and monad to create heaven on Earth. Voting is a spiritual responsibility of every lightworker. To not vote is a sin of omission.

The masters this morning told me that part of the purpose of this book and all my books is to create impeccability. This means to have integrity, consistency and responsibility at all levels of one's being at the highest level of perfection one can attain, while still allowing for mistakes as part of the learning process. It is the civic and spiritual responsibility of every lightworker to vote, say the ascended masters.

Lightworkers are often so busy in the heavenly and etheric realms that they are of no service to the real world. This must change. Many lightworkers dislike politics because of how argumentative and corrupt it has become, and this is understandable. I have a love/hate relationship with it myself.

How is this world going to change unless the lightworkers en masse vote in other lightworkers? Do not be lazy in this regard. I have been guilty of this myself in the past. The past is all forgiven. Just begin from this day forward. Become familiar with the candidates and issues and vote.

Please remember that the first-ray department is totally focused on politics as its main focus in God's divine plan. All need to focus on politics, not just the first-ray people. When lightworkers become disgusted by politics and do not enter politics and refuse to vote, they surrender the real world to the Dark Brotherhood. The Dark Brotherhood is delighted when you are lazy and reject politics. It is counting on this.

The problem with this world is that we have systematically separated the soul from every aspect of life including politics, when instead it should be integrated with the real world. The spiritual path is not living in a cave; it is living in the marketplace. Anybody can be spiritually isolated from the real world. The real test of the ascended master and bodhisattva is be involved with every aspect of Earth life and retain this consciousness. This includes romantic relationships, parenting and service work of all kinds and politics. In the future there will actually be a spiritual or light party being run by people with the highest integrity.

I just received a phone call today from a man who wanted to speak with me about a woman who was running for president who was overlighted by the ascended masters. As I already mentioned, Clinton was a third-degree initiate when he came into office and has achieved near completion of his fifth at the time of writing this. This is also true for Al Gore. It is beginning to happen, and that is why it is time as never before that lightworkers move back into the political arena in whatever capacity they can. This might involve raising consciousness or doing volunteer work or just speaking out on the issues.

As you can see from this book, the ascended masters and Spiritual Hierarchy have very strong views on a great many political and social issues of our time. We are meant to be their hands, arms, legs, feet, eyes, mouths and ears to manifest change in this world. They are enormously appreciative that we are still in physical bodies, for it is very difficult for them to make the changes they desire without physical bodies. We are their instruments and channels.

This concept of an Ascended Master Party might be just the concept you now need to get involved in politics. One of the men I respect most and one of the great masters who has lived on this planet is Mahatma Gandhi. Where would India be now politically if it were not for this great soul? In

Mahatma Gandhi is God made manifest in the political arena. It is now time for us all to integrate the Gandhi archetype and demonstrate this in our daily lives. Martin Luther King was another fine example of this political consciousness.

The whole push now of the Spiritual Hierarchy is to have millions of people ascend and remain on Earth. This is a whole new dispensation and understanding. In the past, ascended masters died or transcended after taking this initiation. Why do you think Sanat Kumara, Lord Buddha and Lord Maitreya, our spiritual planetary leaders, took this new course of action? It was so that lightworkers of a very high level could make changes in the real world. These ascended beings and high-level initiates are meant to take over all the different agencies and professions I have spoken of in this book. This is the divine plan.

In the not-too-distant future we will have an ascended master as president. We will have ascended-master senators and congressmen. There will also be ascended-master lawyers, doctors, United Nations officials, psychologists, scientists, artists, ministers, rabbis, religious leaders, business people and financiers. This plan is in its beginning stage of manifestation. The real world is always the last thing to change.

The job of the spiritual leadership of this planet is to ground spirituality. For too long spirituality has been made manifest on the spiritual, mental, astral and etheric planes, but not into our physical bodies, the Earth and the real world. As the sixth ray is now being phased out on a planetary level and the seventh ray is now coming in, this is about to change. The seventh ray is the grounding of spiritual energy.

The clarion call now goes forth to the spiritual leaders around the world of every ray and every mission to help in this noble work. I know it is difficult. We are the lightbearers for the new age, the pioneers. In truth, our job is the most difficult of all. We will take much abuse from the third-dimensional world for our efforts just as Christ did.

We are now being supported by a wave of energy the likes of which this world has never known. We are living in extraordinary times of

- mass ascension
- the externalization of the Spiritual Hierarchy
- the inbreath and outbreath of Brahma
- the beginning of the Aquarian Age
- the beginning of the end of communism on this planet
- the incarnation of universal and galactic avatars on this planet, Lord Sai Baba and Lord Maitreya
- the activation of the Order of Melchizedek
- the end of the Mayan calendar

- the end of the Pyramid prophecy
- the end times of which the Bible has spoken
- the end of a number of solar, galactic, universal and cosmic cycles
- extraterrestrial activity the likes of which the world has never known
- the activation of the archangelic and angelic kingdoms
- the movement of the Earth herself into the fifth dimension
- an increase in the number of lightworkers in the world
- the flourishing of the ascension movement in a way and manner the world has never known
- the coming together of the United Nations in a new way
- Buddha taking over the position of Planetary Logos
- the externalization of the inner-plane ashrams
- the Earth becoming a sacred planet esoterically
- an influx of light to this planet such as the world has never known
- an influx of spiritual knowledge, information and spiritual books, the likes of which this world has never known
- the existence of Babaji, the yogi Christ, still manifest on this planet
- the externalization of at least fifty senior members of the Spiritual Hierarchy to join Lord Maitreya in his work on Earth
- an aspect of Kuthumi living on this planet, with the pseudonym John of Penial
- millions of lightworkers who will be ascending and remaining on Earth
- a focus on this planet by solar, galactic and universal energies the likes of which this world has never known.

If this doesn't inspire you, then check your heart monitor! Jesus had a tough go of it because he didn't have the support that we have now. Two thousand years later Lord Maitreya and Sai Baba have come again to lead their army of lightworkers into spiritual battle to transform this world into a fifth-dimensional planet.

Can you possibly think of a more noble mission and spiritual battle to participate in? The eye of the cosmos is literally upon us. Being on this planet at this time, working as you are, is the spiritual résumé of all spiritual résumés. Take up your rod of power and join in this great work of grounding spirituality into the real world. It is the work of which legends are made. More progress will be made in the next forty years—1988 to the year 2028—than in the past 3.1 billion years of evolution on this planet. In truth, if you have the eyes to see and the ears to hear, you should be honored to be here.

How can we lose this with his holiness Lord Sai Baba and Lord Maitreya leading the way and sacrificing themselves to come to Earth on a mission of mercy? Christ has returned again after two thousand years, not through a channel, but in person. We all stand on hallowed ground. Take up your rod of power and join his army of light and love to completely turn this third-dimensional world into a heaven on Earth. As Krishna (Lord Maitreya) said to Arjuna (the Buddha) in the *Bhagavad-Gita*, "Get up and give up your unmanliness. Get up and fight! This self-pity and self-indulgence is unbecoming of the great soul you are."

We can see the signs of this coming victory beginning to happen. In this moment they are now calling you forth as they have never called you before to help in the great cause of making the divine plan manifest on this earthly plane and in this real world.

Leadership, they have just told me, is empowerment. So take up the rod of Buddha and the rod of Christ and electrify this world with your love, devotion, perseverance, steadfastness, single focused service and real-world groundedness until final victory is achieved. We are each cells and puzzle pieces in God's body. If each person simply does his/her part, heaven on Earth will be achieved and God will be made manifest.

IQ Tests

This is another third-dimensional imbalanced system our society relies on. The problem stems from the fact that unconscious third-dimensional people create them. They will be abolished in their present form. They are not balanced in their approach, for if they were balanced they should also test emotional quotient, spiritual quotient, physical quotient, right-brain quotient, past-life quotient and even social-behavior quotient.

What if you do have a high mental IQ, but are emotionally damaged and socially inept? I remember a dream I had not too long ago where I was given a test for my aptitude to achieve liberation. I had this dream prior to taking my ascension. The tests we presently take don't mean too much because the people who create them see through the lens of a fly and are not balanced or evolved themselves, except maybe in their mental body.

A true IQ test would test all the factors and include an astrological reading, ray reading, numerological reading and higher-self channeling. An IQ test focuses on the concrete mind. But what about aptitude in the higher mind and abstract mind? What about aptitude as a mystic, channel, psychic, clairvoyant and our right-brain abilities?

This discussion also applies to the scholastic-aptitude tests given in high school to go to college. These tests are written by upper-middle-class, self-righteous, white, unconscious racists. They actually believe that these tests are fair to African Americans or other minority groups. Do these kind of tests really determine who should go to college? The only realistic IQ test and scholastic aptitude tests would have to be written by the higher selves and mighty I Am Presence through an ascended master. Humanity has too many lenses it sees through that are prejudiced and imbalanced.

AIDS Awareness

AIDS, as we all know, is a modern-day plague. It was created by the United States Government war department and was given systematically to fringe groups, from the war department's perspective, to see what its effects were. These people, being run by the Dark Brotherhood, have created this epidemic. All this business about AIDS being created by a monkey in Africa is absurd. HIV and AIDS are not a death sentence. Some people's natural immune system has the ability to fight it off. There are cures that are being facilitated by the use of herbs, homeopathic remedies and an overall bioenergetic and holistic approach.

It is awful how people who have AIDS are treated in this society. This prejudice is because of fear and, of course, negative ego. The nature of the negative ego is to be concerned with self and not have compassion for others. This fear makes these individuals who are run by negative ego act in very cruel ways. AIDS is not a homosexual disease but a human disease. No one is immune to it and it crosses all boundaries of race, creed, color and sexual preference. Those who have HIV or AIDS must use it as the tremendous catalyst for spiritual transformation that it is. People must learn to release their fear and prejudice in this regard and know that it is only transmittable through blood or sexual exchange.

One of the disturbing aspects of the AIDS movement on the reverse side of the coin is how radical some of the gay activists become in their pursuit of raising consciousness about AIDS. This is hurting the cause rather than helping it. It is like pro-lifers who attack people or kill doctors and think that in God's eyes they are being righteous. Nothing could be further from the truth.

The masters have told me that there will ultimately be a cure for AIDS in the form of some kind of future vaccine. As I mentioned earlier, a lot of the drug treatments that the traditional medical practices are using are actually making HIV and AIDS patients sicker. A lot also depends on belief. If you believe you are going die, the battle is already half lost.

Recreational Drugs

Here I am speaking of marijuana, psychedelics, mushrooms, ecstasy, cocaine, heroin and all the rest. The ascended masters are most definitely against taking drugs and are very emphatic about it. One does not find enlightenment, ascension and God realization through a pill. There is no judgment upon any people who have used them in the past. In this current new generation there are very few who haven't, including myself. They might have actually served a certain purpose of opening some spiritual channels.

Using recreational drugs is the child-level phase of the spiritual path. It is not for the true advanced initiates. If you want mind-altering experiences, then learn to meditate, and the experiences you will have will be a million times more profound than anything you can experience with drugs. Drugs catalyze an experience; however, there is always the downside when it is over, and you will need the external pill to create it again. It clouds the aura and poisons the liver and kidneys. Meditation will clear the aura and strengthen the liver and kidneys and make you healthier, not weaker. In the very beginning of one's spiritual path they might have a place for some, but not for serious initiates on the path.

The Tobacco Industry

I am very glad to see that the tobacco industry is finally getting busted for its past abuses. It doesn't take a brain scientist to figure out that cigarettes are cancer producing, that nicotine is addictive and that the tobacco industry has been manipulating nicotine levels to purposely cause drug dependency. Cigarettes are drugs.

Cremation vs. Burials

Djwhal Khul has stated most emphatically that burials are in truth a third-dimensional practice, and as humanity moves into the fifth dimension they will eventually be outlawed. This is because most people have all kinds of viruses, bacteria, infections, cancers and numerous other health problems when they die. When you bury someone, you are in a sense poisoning the Earth Mother, energetically and physically. The masters are more and more encouraging (not demanding) people to consider cremation. All disease factors are burned to ash. It is like the sacred ash of *vibhuti*. It is ecologically, environmentally and spiritually a better practice as well as being less expensive.

It is recommended by the ascended masters that the physical vehicle be preserved for three days prior to cremation so the soul can complete its three-day bardo experience (see "Death, Dying, and the Science of the Bardo" and "Between Lifetimes" in *The Complete Ascension Manual*). Since we are in a transition to a fully realized fifth-dimensional humanity, burials will be around for some time. The spiritual leadership of this world can begin to prepare humanity for this transformation.

Halloween

As the process of writing this book continued, I got more and more into this process of asking the masters about every possible aspect of Earth society. One day I asked Melchizedek, the Universal Logos, about the holiday of Halloween. As a little kid it used to be my favorite holiday of the whole year because I loved to get all the candy. As an adult, however, it came to be my least favorite. It seemed to indulge the dark side of life and I would see the news reports where every Halloween there would be hundreds of fires all over the country. On a whim I asked Melchizedek his thoughts on this. The force of his answer surprised me.

He said that Halloween was indeed a dark holiday, one that seemed to give children and adults permission to indulge in the dark side of life. He said this was a holiday that was not supported by the Spiritual Hierarchy and that in the future it would be abolished. He went on to say that even the appeal for children of receiving lots of candy is part of this lower-self indulgence.

When I was in school, I always noticed that shortly after Halloween everyone and their mother would start getting sick. I am convinced it was because of the overindulgence in sugar and the repercussions of this on a mass scale. Bacteria, viruses and disease grow when sugar is present. I found Melchizedek's views to be quite interesting.

Taxes

Right after I asked Melchizedek about Halloween I asked him about the Spiritual Hierarchy's view on taxes. I began by sharing my personal opinion that in an ideal society set up on real spiritual values, the poor and even middle class should not pay taxes and only the rich should pay. Melchizedek agreed with this, but then said something I had never considered before. He said in the golden age of the planet all taxes will be abolished. I was shocked.

He went on to say that in the future taxes will not be needed because people will be so spiritual and service-oriented that they will want to give money to help their brothers and sisters in need. Taxes are really only needed in a selfish, third-dimensional, ego-based society. Did not Christ say we are our brother's keeper? Imagine if we lived in a society of ascended beings and high-level initiates. The sprit of giving would be so great and contagious that I am sure there would be more money than could be possibly generated now by taxes. This will be something to look forward to.

Patriotism

There is nothing wrong with feeling good about one's country as long as it is not colored by egotism, which it usually is. Just as individuals can compete, so can countries. To identify oneself as American, Russian, Chinese and so forth, is illusion. It would be more truthful to call yourself an Earthian. Even this in the ultimate sense of truth is illusion, for in reality we are all cosmic citizens. Such limited boundaries and fences are unbecoming of the great souls we all are. In past lives we have lived in all countries, all places, been all religions, all sexual preferences and all genders. In this vein we see how absurd it is to identify with just one and think that it is the best.

The history books of most countries, including the United States, are filled with patriotism, nationalism and propaganda. Be proud of your country; however, retain your cosmic citizenship and do not let the negative ego tinge the pride you have for your country, race, religion or creed.

Feminism

Feminism was a natural and important backlash to the macho and patriarchal society in which we live. It was needed to counterbalance how totally overmasculine and yang our world has become. You might see feminism as a needed pendulum swing. The problem is when the women and people involved in such movements do not see this from the higher perspective. To be overidentified with the women's or men's movement is to be caught in duality.

In the ultimate sense we all are androgynous. We must let go of all lenses and identify with all facets of the prism, so to speak. The same is true when people overidentify with being gay, bisexual or heterosexual. This is such a small facet of our total being and identity. People stuck in third-dimensional consciousness make this facet or sliver the crux of their whole identity, which is absurd. This is why Melchizedek has often told us that much of humanity sees life through the lens of a fly. Get beyond such petty differences as male or female, gay or straight. I am not saying they are not important aspects to integrate, explore and embrace in a given phase of life, but the idea is to move on to greater and more important issues such as merging with your soul, monad and the ascended masters.

Animal, Human and Godly Identification

There are three phases of evolution with which every person can consciously and unconsciously choose to identify. These are as an animal, human or God (planetary, then cosmic, with various substages in between). Even though every person is born as a human, he/she does not live that way. A great many people live like animals. We have all heard the term "dog-eat-dog world." This manifests when people are run by their lower self. When a person is run by his/her lower self, he has animal consciousness.

In reality many animals are more evolved in their consciousness than some humans are. As people evolve, they embrace human values. This is the phase of development of personality-level self-actualization. As evolution continues, they hopefully then embrace the soul and/or higher self or oversoul, which is the next phase of development and soul actualization. The next step is monadic or spirit actualization, then comes group-soul actualization, group-monadic actualization, solar actualization, galactic actualization, universal actualization, multiuniversal actualization and God or cosmic actualization. These might be considered the phases of self-actualization and evolution.

Often I hear people say such things as "I am only human." It must be understood that this statement is in truth illusion. You are not human; you are God. The word *human* is broken down into "hu" and "man." The word *hu* means "God." Both the science of Eckankar and the former Tibetan Foundation use the *hu* mantra as one of the main mantras for realizing God. So the actual word *human* means "God-man." The key question here is what you identify with. Do you identify yourself as a physical body or as the Christ visiting and temporarily living in a physical body? This is the difference between third- and fifth-dimensional consciousness. It is also the difference between truth and illusion.

The truth is that you are God living in this body. To move into the fifth kingdom from the fourth kingdom (human to spiritual kingdom), you must identify yourself with the identity above your level. You are not a human; you are God, and so is everyone else. This is one of the keys to enter the fifth kingdom. You must also completely transcend animal, carnal and lower-self consciousness. This is called ascended-master consciousness.

People often use this excuse of being human so as not to have to act like a god. There is nothing wrong with making mistakes, for even gods make mistakes. Do not, however, use being human as an excuse for indulging in negative emotions and lower-self consciousness. We have been built and created for much nobler things.

Technology

The ascended masters think that technology is wonderful and God-inspired. The problem is not technology, but rather letting technology be more important than humanity, spirituality and the Earth Mother. The problem with our society is that our material development has developed faster than our spiritual and psychological development. This is an unequal development of our four-body system (physical, emotional, mental, spiritual) on a planetary level. This leads to the exploitation of people, the environment, animals and plants. In essence, it is materialism and the drive for the almighty dollar.

Movies in our popular culture such as *Jurassic Park, Powder, Soylent Green* and others have played upon such a theme. Here again we see the split between the East and the West. In the East, spirit is developed and the material world extremely undeveloped. This is not good either. In the West it is exactly reversed: The material side of things is greatly developed and the spirit is not. There must be an integration or blending of the two.

Modern technology is wonderful, but we must make sure that spirit and the essence of things is valued as more important and that modern technology is used to support the true purpose of life, as God would have it be.

Pornography

Djwhal Khul told me that pornography is a manifestation of the lower self and is something that lightworkers should phase out of their reality. Pornography will not be part of our future fully realized, fifth-dimensional society. It is of the carnal influence. There is no judgment upon this, for all have been bombarded by such glamour growing up in this world. It is a natural progression to evolve beyond this, just as one evolves toward eating a better diet and viewing less violent movies and the like.

In the fifth dimension sexuality is used only as an expression of love and in a more tantric manner toward achieving union with God and union with your partner simultaneously. This again is the process of moving from animal to human to God consciousness. The raising of sexuality and kundalini is used to build *ojas* (brain illumination), and the sanctity and sacredness of this form of energy is honored.

Sexual Harassment

The process of sexual harassment is of course a byproduct of men, for the most part, looking at women as sexual objects instead of divine spiritual beings. Eastern religion teaches every person to see every woman as the embodiment of the divine Mother. Instead of seeing life through the third eye, crown and heart, those who sexually harass are seeing life through the eyes of the second chakra, also known as the lower brain. This is the direct byproduct of seeing life from the third-dimensional perspective rather than the fifth-dimensional perspective. Said another way, it is seeing life from the negative ego's eyes rather than the eyes of the soul and the Christ consciousness.

It is interesting that for the first time this is beginning to come out and women are beginning to stand up for themselves and not tolerate this. This is a very pleasing step from the perspective of the ascended masters. Although it was going on in the past, most women just endured it.

It is essential now for women to come into their full power. It is absurd that they do not get equal pay and equal leadership positions in all phases of government and industry. We still clearly live in a patriarchal society, and this must change. I always enjoyed the fact that one of Jesus' teachers was Judy, according to the Edgar Cayce readings. It is also very interesting that in most spiritual groups and at spiritual events anywhere in the country the majority of the people are women. Its significance needs no explanation.

If women were more in power we would have a much more loving, spiritually guided world. It is time for women to step forward and claim their full power and not be intimidated by the patriarchal system we all live in. The preservation of our globe and the planetary-ascension movement depends on it.

Sports

According to the masters, as we move toward a fifth-dimensional society some of the more violent and even barbaric sports will be phased out. A couple of examples would be boxing, wrestling (the Hulk Hogan type practiced on television) and the violence and condoned fighting allowed in hockey. Only a consciousness steeped in negative ego and third-dimensional thinking can enjoy this kind of violence.

Sports will always be a part of human life, and the ascended masters recognize sports as a true art form. Great athletes like basketball's Michael Jordan, baseball's Barry Bonds or football's Joe Montana are amazing to watch. It is important for those who play sports at a semiprofessional or professional level to serve as role models for the young people of this world. This role modeling is not just at the physical level of the game but in all areas of life. Sports figures can have an enormous impact if they can play sports from a soul perspective rather than the negative-ego perspective.

This concept might come as an interesting insight to some, but it applies to every person in this world, for we all play sports at some time in our lives. When the negative ego is involved in sports, the person playing gets angry and curses frequently. He/she gets in fights and has no sense of sportsmanship. All he cares about is winning no matter what. This might be called egotistical competition.

There is, however, a form of what might be called spiritual competition. This would be the attitude of doing one's best, competing with oneself. An example might be trying to jog a little faster around the track than you did the previous day. When interacting with others, this spiritual competition is being sportsmanlike, complimenting your opponent on a good shot, helping him/her up if he falls down, laughing, joking and being friendly with your opponent even though you are also trying as hard as you can to win. When the game is over, you would shake hands with your opponent, congratulating him/her on a game well played whether you won or lost. Spiritual competition is not getting so caught up in winning and losing that you lose your Christ consciousness.

A lot of lightworkers think that competition is always bad. It is only bad if there is no Christ consciousness connected with it. Competing can be fun if no sense of separation is created in the process. People who are run by the negative ego lose track of this attunement. Competition and cooperation can merge together into sportsmanship. The spiritual leadership of this world needs to teach sportsmanship by always speaking of one's opponent in the highest terms.

This applies to politics, business and all phases of human life. Imagine a society where politicians and businesspeople put love, respect and generosity above winning elections and making money. The problem with this world is that too many people have too many false gods and idol worship such as winning, power, fame, greed, lust and material desire. We all must let go of these false gods and put love first. Then we will be rich in spirit, which will also lead to being rich in a material sense. For has not the Bible said, "Seek ye the kingdom of God and all things shall be added unto thee"?

One aspect of sports that the Spiritual Hierarchy really likes is the energy created at the various sporting events. Djwhal Khul told me the masters and angels gather at these major professional sports events and collect the energy that is created from the excitement and enthusiasm and then use it for spiritual purposes.

Sport Hunting

Killing animals for fun will most definitely be completely outlawed in the future. It is one thing if someone uses the game for food, but to kill animals just for sport is completely barbaric. It is up to the spiritual leadership of this world to raise the consciousness of this planet that animals are our younger brothers and sisters for whom we are responsible just as the ascended masters are responsible for humanity.

Animals have within them the potentiality to move into the human kingdom in some cases. In killing animals for fun, it is not too different from killing a child. It is barbaric and must be stopped. This applies as well to the wearing of animal furs. These animals are inhumanely caught in traps and tortured. Great species of animals are becoming extinct because of the greed of humanity. Those who feel guided to do so must take up this banner and not stop until this genocide of the animal kingdom stops.

Animals are a thousand times more intelligent than people realize.

I would like to share two very sweet animal stories. When my former wife and I were first married, she brought with her two cats who were around seventeen years old, one named Patches and the other Rags. I had never had cats before. Early on in our relationship my wife went away for the weekend and I was in charge of the cats. As my full pet-loving tendencies had not yet become fully realized (as they did later), I ended up going to the Whole Life Expo that weekend and did not see the cats much except to feed them, give them water and clean the kitty box. When my wife (who was extremely bonded to cats) came home and asked me how it went taking care of them, I said, "Oh, fine. It went great."

She then asked, "Did you give them lots of love?" I said, "Oh yes, lots of love."

My former wife, being very clairaudient, immediately heard Patches say, *No, he didn't. He was barely around the whole weekend!*

She proceeded to tell me what Patches had said telepathically to her and, boy, was I busted! I was busted by a seventeen-year-old smart-alecky cat. I learned my lesson. I came to love these cats very much. Rags literally sat on my desk and helped me write my first five books. She had me wrapped around her paw.

The cats ran the household, not us. Every time we would have a group meeting in our home, Patches would take one of the chairs or sit on someone's lap as an equal group member. This cat's light-quotient factor must have been off the scale.

One incident that shows how spiritual cats and animals really are happened after Rags passed away after her twentieth birthday. She had been hanging around our home in her spirit body as she went through her kitty bardo. My former wife came out from a session and saw Patches sitting out in the patio looking up toward the Sun. She spontaneously asked, "What are you doing, Patches?" As she looked closer she could see Rags in her spirit body sitting next to Patches. Patches responded to her question by telling her that they were praying together. Isn't that the most adorable story you have ever heard?

All animals have this intelligence and telepathic ability; it is just that humans are generally too dense to hear their communication. Animals can speak in words, have opinions, have all kinds of emotions and have very specific types of spiritual missions to complete just as we do.

One time my former wife and I and Patches and Rags were all watching television and Patches said, *O.J. Simpson is not guilty.* This came right after we had watched a news report on the trial. We were floored. I don't know if Patches was right, however, but the fact she had an opinion on this knocked my socks off.

This is why the cruelty that is going on with animals around the world is so awful. Let all the lightworkers on the planet join together to honor and cherish our younger brothers and sisters.

Earthly Law vs. Spiritual Law

In the continuing discussion here of the social, political and philosophical issues of our time from the ascended masters' perspective, we next come to the issue of earthly law versus spiritual law. From the perspective of God and the soul, spiritual law stands above earthly law. Now, it so happens that in most cases they are compatible and in harmony. However, this is not always the case.

An example of these laws being harmonious might be laws against stealing or murder. This is obvious. An example, however, where they might not be in harmony would be a person who was asked to go to war as a soldier by his/her government and whose conscience told him that for him personally, killing another human being was an impossibility. What is the person to do in this case, follow earthly law or the guidance of his soul?

God's law comes first. Another example might be euthanasia, which is against the law. However, the guidance to perform euthanasia might be one's inner-soul guidance. One more classic example was when Rosa Parks was told to move to the back of the bus and obey the law in Alabama at that time, but she wouldn't do it, and thus became the mother of the civil rights movement. Another example would be a woman who might be guided by her soul to have an abortion although her state might have laws against it.

This does not apply to our country alone. Look at the law that Mahatma Gandhi had to fight in India. He followed a higher law, which eventually changed the earthly law. Earthly laws are not always in harmony with God's laws, and this must be clearly understood. I am not encouraging breaking earthly laws, but making an important philosophical, spiritual and social point.

Open Marriages

I asked Melchizedek one day about the concept of an open marriage to understand the Spiritual Hierarchy's views on such a thing. An open marriage, of course, is an agreement between two people who are in a romantic relationship to have sexual relations with other people while still being married and having sex with each other. When I asked about this I was actually unsure myself about what the masters would say. Melchizedek was quite firm and adamant about this.

Open marriages, he said, were out of harmony with universal law and were not supported by the Spiritual Hierarchy and ascended masters. I asked Melchizedek if this was also the case when the two people had made a personal agreement in this regard. He said that it did not matter, as it is still not spiritually right. Melchizedek said that it created a great amount of negative-ego problems regardless how people tried to rationalize it.

This brings up the philosophical issue of a person's personal laws or value system often being out of harmony with universal law.

Affairs

The next issue that stemmed from the last one is their views on extra-marital affairs. They said that affairs were most definitely wrong from the perspective of the soul and monad. The whole idea of having an affair is that it is done in a deceitful way and behind the back of one of the marriage partners. This is not honest. If it were honest, the person would ask the permission of all parties concerned.

Anything that hurts another is spiritually wrong. Anything dishonest is wrong. Anything that breaks a commitment of marriage between two people without the consent of the other party is spiritually wrong. In saying this, for those who have had affairs, I don't mean this to be judgmental, for everything in God's universe is always forgiven.

It must be understood that karma is created when one embarks on such a path. The whole purpose of life is to balance one's karma, not create more. People often get into this through mental and spiritual weakness, being overcome by the astral and desire body. The key word here is having *integrity* and being a master of one's energy, as well as having right human relationships.

Mixed-Race Marriages

This, of course, is totally accepted and honored by the ascended masters. The isolation and separatism between religions and races is a byproduct of the negative ego, not the spirit. All people are God and the eternal self is simply clothed in the human body. This human body changes colors, gender and religion each lifetime. Only someone who is completely run by the negative ego and who thinks he/she *is* a physical body rather than a soul living in a physical body could be against such a thing.

The bottom line is *love*, not the color of one's skin or the religion you happened to be born into. There is nothing wrong with honoring, respecting and enjoying one's race and religion; however, do not use this to create separation among people. Unity in diversity is achieved simultaneously. If you have a preference about this personally, there is nothing wrong with this; however, do not project your preference onto other people as if it is God's law. This is a byproduct of the ignorance and prejudice of the negative ego.

The Political Independents

This is something that the ascended masters greatly support. The Republican and Democratic parties keep people stuck in duality. Registering as an independent leaves open the possibility of transcending duality and politics as usual, which usually means gridlock. A third party, regardless whether you like its candidate, leaves room for more dialogue, making all candidates more accountable and less rigid. I encourage lightworkers to support such a widening of options.

Child Abusers

This next section is just a social commentary I would like to make. Child abuse or child molestation is a terrible thing. However, one of the things I have observed in our society is that when these people who have committed such a crime get out of jail, they are treated worse than mass murderers. No community will let them live there and their pictures are plastered all over the community in which they are trying to live.

People who commit murder and get out of jail are not treated this way. I am not condoning the crime; however, if they pay their dues in prison, they should be forgiven at some point and allowed to try and redeem their life. This was brought home to me recently with the movie *Powder*, which was an absolutely brilliant ascension-focused movie. If you have not seen it, do rent it on video.

The man who directed it has spent time in jail for such a crime. When the movie came out, even though he had paid his dues in jail, there was a big uproar that no one should go to see the movie. It is a brilliant masterpiece and the man has obviously moved on to a new-age spiritual path in order to create such a movie. This continual witch hunt must stop; it is not right. People who continue such behavior are egotistical, self-righteous, judgmental and unforgiving. As Christ said, "Let him that hath no sin cast the first stone."

Advanced Ascended-Master Abilities

A great many lightworkers in the ascension movement are very interested in developing what I have termed their advanced ascended-master abilities such as dematerialization, teleportation, materializing things and the like. The realization of these abilities is a natural byproduct of complete realization of the ascension process. However, it comes only in the very advanced stages of activating and actualizing the twelfth dimension of existence, not just the fifth dimension as many have believed. Melchizedek, Lord Maitreya and Djwhal Khul have asked us not to focus on this too much.

The masters' guidance has been to focus all energies into world service and leadership. Their guidance on this issue is that all the focusing and practice on this will not get you there any sooner. The powers that can eventually come from ascension are not as important as love, service, leadership and egolessness. Focus on these things, which are the true basis of the spiritual path. Live a life totally dedicated to these principles and in time the advanced ascension abilities will come.

They are not what should be focused upon now, for they can be a distraction and even dangerous for some. We have seen in India where some masters have been more interested in the *siddhas*, or powers, than in love and service.

Most lightworkers do not have enough control over their emotional body, desire body, subconscious mind, inner child and negative ego to be allowed to have these powers anyway. Most lightworkers are more advanced spiritually than they are psychologically. Until their mental, emotional, etheric and physical bodies catch up with their spiritual bodies, it would be a disaster to have such abilities.

This is why the masters governing this planet have pushed the maturing of these abilities back to the attainment of the twelfth-dimensional level. This allows for the maturing time that disciples and initiates need. Masters in previous times had more time because things moved much slower in past centuries than they do now. Take the time to mature properly on all levels and remain focused completely on love, service, leadership and egolessness. Then you will be moving like an arrow to the ultimate attainments of these abilities because you will be mature enough to use them wisely.

The Government and Militia Groups

In the times we live in our government has about as much credibility as a used-car salesman. Most people are very cynical about government and politics. Congress' popularity is at an all-time low. The sad thing is that people have a right to be disgusted with our government. The United States system of government might be one of the best systems in the world; however, it has been extremely contaminated by the negative ego.

First of all, the American people are disgusted with the gridlock and the partisan politicians, the childish bickering between parties and the inability to cooperate for the good of the country. They see the corruption, selfishness and egotism of most politicians. People have lived through Watergate and the corruption in that administration and the Vietnam War and the terrible decisions that were made then.

Most people also realize that John Kennedy was assassinated by a conspiracy in which many government officials were involved. Everyone knows there was a massive cover-up. Most people are also aware of the secret government and how the wealthiest power elite in this world is controlling our economy and world. Then add to this the massive amount of fraud, waste and corruption that goes on throughout all our governmental agencies. This is not all the politicians' fault, but it is an overriding example of the contamination of the negative ego throughout our society and government.

On top of this we then have the worst cover-up of all, which is the extraterrestrial activity I wrote about extensively in *Hidden Mysteries.* The government has actually had living extraterrestrial guests and hundreds of crashed flying saucers and hundreds of dead bodies of aliens from all different kinds of civilizations, yet everything is kept hidden from the public.

Then we have senators and congressmen who serve in this capacity for twenty to thirty years and who form a good-old-boys club, which prevents any true change from taking place. People are sick of all the arguing and negative campaigning. True loving statesmanship has been lost. Politicians would actually sell their soul to the devil to get elected, and often do.

The press and the two political parties add to this negative perception of government by mercilessly attacking any politician with any substance who enters the race, to feed their own egos. Most politicians are not very spiritually or psychologically developed and are not in office to serve the people and the nation. Even if they were, the system and the good-old-boy society won't let them.

Our government is also a racist institution. We have never had a black or a minority person, including a woman, as president. This might also be a product of the patriarchal, white-racist society we live in. People don't like to hear this, but it is true. It might not be as racist as it was during slavery or earlier in this century, but it is still racist in more subclinical and often unconscious ways.

Adding to this state of affairs, people see the corruption in the police department and the abuse of power in the CIA and FBI, which most people are a little wary of. When all of this is put together, there is a negative stigma, a gray cloud, which again is a byproduct of the contamination of the negative ego over a government and political system that has enormous potential and that the ascended masters actually helped to create.

People are also now becoming disgusted with the jury system due to the Rodney King, Menendez brothers and O.J. Simpson debacles. People see the corruption in welfare, the trillion-dollar national debt and the misuse of our tax dollars in infinite numbers of ways, all of which reflect on the government. Then the media adds to this negative perception by using what they call journalism to dig up dirt and skeletons on any and all political figures.

Hence the American people are pessimistic and dissatisfied. That is why an independent or third party or the idea of candidates such as Ross Perot or Colin Powell and others like them strikes a chord. The American people are disgusted with the status quo, and a great many do not trust the government.

The corruption and often blatant dishonesty of our government along with the secret government that is operating behind the scenes has led to the development of these militant groups. This, I believe, is the natural pendulum swing to the other extreme. It was inevitable that they would develop given the misuse of power of many facets of our government.

These militia groups are also quite paranoid and create conspiracy theories that, though often not true, are based on a grain of truth. People do not realize that slowly but surely we are losing a lot of our basic constitutional rights. Even though I do not personally relate to or support these militia groups, I can see from a larger perspective why they have developed.

The key question here is, what can we do to change this whole situation? I personally don't trust our government. I don't trust the police. I don't trust the judicial system and I don't trust the CIA or FBI. There is too much abuse of power going on and too many people in control who are third-dimensional and run by the negative ego.

The only way we will change this is for lightworkers to get involved in every aspect of Earth life. This might not be a pleasant view of things, but this is our mission. If we abrogate responsibility, then we deserve what we get. If we avoid responsibility, we are saying, let the people who are controlled by their negative ego run things. The purpose of life and the divine plan is not to ascend and leave, but to bring heaven to Earth.

The cause of all the problems I have mentioned here comes from one source, and that is negative-ego thinking and lack of Christ/Buddha thinking. The more people are educated to become right with self, right with God and then to develop right human relationships, the more this world is going to change. This is happening. Communism would not have fallen in the Soviet Union and Germany if this were not the case. If everyone in the world would just do his/her little puzzle piece perfectly, the world would change with infinite speed.

What we need is spiritual people in politics as lawyers, businesspeople, ambassadors, policemen, heads of the CIA and FBI, senators, congressmen, presidents, bankers, journalists and news reporters. People need to get involved, write letters and make a fuss when things are not right.

This is what Marilyn Ferguson referred to in *The Aquarian Conspiracy: Personal and Social Transformation in the 1980s:* people from all walks of life banding together in a spiritual conspiracy to change the world. I will admit we have a very tough nut to crack, especially when dealing with traditional institutions. The proper attitude to take is that every little bit helps. The hundredth-monkey effect will take place at some point. There is also a new generation taking over the old positions that will help greatly. The public has got to stop being passive and instead write letters, make phone calls, send e-mail and complain. The public needs to take back control and not sit back passively while it is being victimized. This is all our spiritual responsibility.

There are sins of omission and commission. Not to act is a sin of omission. We have all volunteered and contracted on the inner plane to incarnate at this time to make these changes. Look at the effect that one little spiritual man wearing a loincloth had in India. Do any of us have any less potential? If each person just took responsibility in his/her chosen profession to make this change, a revolution in our society would instantly take place. It has begun to happen, but your input is needed now more than ever. This is where the group consciousness is needed. None of us can do this alone, but together as a group we can make the inroads and changes that are needed.

The biggest problem in the past is that spiritual people have detached from Earth life and have chosen not to be involved. This might have been okay in the past, but it is not anymore. We have entered a new age. With the end of the sixth ray and the beginning of the seventh-ray influence on a planetary level, it is time to ground spirituality into the Earth, which has not previously been the case. In the past masters left after ascension; now 98 percent of them will remain on Earth to serve.

The push now is not to go up but to come down and bring heaven to Earth. It is time to put on your mental, emotional and spiritual armor and get involved. Jesus lived in the marketplace, not in a cave or in a bedroom.

As Sai Baba says, "Hands that help are holier than lips that pray." Even better is helping *and* praying. We each do not have to take on the weight of this whole problem ourselves. All we have to do is our puzzle piece, whatever that might be. We need to recognize that we are each part of a massive group body that is doing this work. Ask yourself, can God, the ascended masters and the sons and daughters of God be stopped? What are we fighting? In truth what we are fighting is negative ego, or really just glamour, maya and illusion. Can God and the God force lose against illusion?

This world is going to change and it has already begun. It is just a matter of time. Our job as lightworkers is to shorten the need for time. Remember that we are not alone. We share this burden with our brothers and sisters in our group body as part of an Aquarian Age conspiracy of a most positive nature.

We have the ascended masters helping us. We have the angels helping us. We have a vast array of positive extraterrestrial groups helping us. We have the externalization of the Spiritual Hierarchy led by his holiness Lord Sai Baba and Lord Maitreya helping us. We have cosmic energies and cosmic intelligences such as the Mahatma, Melchizedek and the archangels helping us. In truth, the spotlight of our entire galaxy and even universe is now on the Earth to make this quantum leap in consciousness.

Starseeds, star children and advanced initiates are now incarnating to help in this great work. Those of lower than a third-degree initiation will not be allowed to incarnate on this planet anymore. Sai Baba has agreed to incarnate for a third time in an avatar incarnation to help in this great work. Over fifty senior members of the Spiritual Hierarchy on the inner plane who have long since achieved their ascension and liberation are incarnating at this time to help in the great work.

We are now living at a time of the inbreath and outbreath of Brahma. We are ending the 2000-year cycle of the Piscean Age and entering the Aquarian Age. We are living in a time of mass ascension from 1995 to the year 2000. We are living at a time of the ending of the Mayan calendar in 2012. We are living in the end time that the Bible spoke of and are at the dawning of a golden age.

Vywamus has said that the anchoring of the Mahatma energy is the single biggest event that has ever occurred in the history of planet Earth. The Order of Melchizedek has now been officially reactivated and reinstituted. The ascension movement has begun to take hold and is gaining full force. Very soon the lid will be blown on the extraterrestrial movement, which will have a radical impact on the consciousness of humanity.

More change will occur from 1988 to the year 2028 than in the previous 3.1 billion years. The Earth has recently taken her sixth initiation and moved into the beginning stages of her ascension. Humanity is beginning ascension en masse now. Communism, a godless philosophy created by the negative ego, has fallen in the Soviet Union and Germany. The Berlin Wall has fallen. There is a renewed interest in religion and spirituality as never before in the history of the Earth.

My friends and brothers and sisters, if there was ever a time to focus on your own ascension and service to humanity, the time is now. We are all involved with a great wave of energy and consciousness shift that is radically altering our individual and collective landscape. The time to take action and get involved is *now*.

Death

The masters told me that in the future funerals as we now practice them will be abolished. They will be looked at more as celebrations of the eternal existence of the human spirit. People's feelings of missing their loved ones will of course be honored; however, there will be much more focus on the fact that the person is not really dead. In reality, he/she has just shifted dimensions and is still as alive as always. The soul has been freed from the confines of the limited physical body and is now living in one of the higher heavens. In India, death is seen as a happy occurrence not a sad one, for everyone there believes in reincarnation.

As more and more people take their higher initiations, the veil between the inner and outer worlds will grow increasingly thinner. Those who have passed on will be easily able to contact those who remain on Earth and vice versa. The utter despair of loss will be obliterated, as those left behind will know for a fact that those who have passed on are indeed alive and well. The loss of a loved one will be seen as temporary. Death will be seen as the transition it really is and life will be known as eternal.

The Superheroes of Our Children and Adults

Another change that will take place in the future is a shift in the protagonists and superbeings for both children and adults in our society. For children, their superbeings fight for good, but they are all incredibly violent. Be it the Power Rangers, Superman, Spiderman, the Ninjas, they are always fighting and beating up people. What kind of message does this teach our children? The cartoons are some of the most violent of all. Adults are not much better. Our idols are Clint Eastwood, Arnold Schwarzenegger, Sylvester Stallone and a number of others. What kind of society do we live in?

In a fifth-dimensional society the superheroes for both children and adults would be more like Sai Baba, the Buddha, Jesus, Lord Maitreya, Saint Germain, El Morya, Kuthumi, the Virgin Mary, Isis, Quan Yin and new ones that could be created by living out the Christ/Buddha archetype. Can you imagine kids getting up on Saturday morning and watching these types of superbeings? Instead of using guns and beating up people, they would have ascended-master abilities and solve all problems with love and forgiveness. Can you imagine what a teaching aid this would be for providing children with proper morals and values? Video games and schoolbooks would be created using the ascended masters. It would be universal, so no one religion would be emphasized.

This applies to adults also. I remember that old television show called *Kung Fu* where the peaceful priest would travel the world solving problems in a peaceful, loving and spiritual manner. That was a very popular show. People loved the movies *Gandhi* and *Little Buddha*. Those in the media and movie industry must begin to make more movies with a spiritual focus that feeds our soul and spirit, not just our personality level. This is the key.

The beings who are now held in high esteem in our society have not yet entered the soul level. This must change. Those of you who are the writers, producers and directors and have power in media must help make this change. The world is hungry for soul and spiritual beings.

Our Credit-Card Society

There is nothing inherently wrong with credit cards. The key issue here is that they are meant to be used only for an emergency. The problem is that a great many people including our government use them as a lifestyle. Djwhal Khul was very adamant in speaking about this. Living on credit is being out of balance with the laws of karma. There is an enormous seduction in using credit cards, for there is a false feeling created of having money when in fact you do not. Credit-card companies play upon this seduction and illusion, and before you know it you are deep in debt and you do not know what happened.

The United States government is the worst perpetrator of this false psychology. Our government is approximately one trillion dollars in debt. How can you run a government that is constantly losing money? It does not take a brain scientist to figure out that this is insane.

The use of debit cards, even in the form of an ATM debit to your bank account, is a frightening reality. With the zip of your card through a slot you can instantly spend hundreds of dollars without even being aware of that fact. No money is exchanged, no familiar checks are written, yet in an instant your bank account is immediately depleted. This is instantaneous rather than a debt that must be paid over a given time period, as is the case with credit cards. The masters tell me that this is getting into dangerous waters and that we all should be very careful not to fall prey to the potential danger of all debit cards.

This is another example of how the negative ego has contaminated the psychology of our governmental officials. Being too wrapped up in consumerism is part of being run by the emotional and desire body. It must be stopped and turned in the opposite direction, or the interest alone is going to bankrupt us.

Term Limits

I personally feel that term limits for politicians is a healthy thing. It would get rid of the good-old boys and constantly bring in fresh blood and new energy. In addition, I believe that it would help eliminate some of the gridlock. This influx of new opinions would raise the level of consciousness of the members of Congress, for some of them seem to be locked into social and political views of the Middle Ages. It would force people who really want to serve to enter office, rather than the ones who are simply there for a fat paycheck. It would get rid of the deadwood. Presidents have term limits, so why not Congress? Congress has not passed it because the power elite and the old guard do not want to lose their manipulative control. This is my personal opinion on this one.

Evolution vs. Creationism

This has been one of the great philosophical arguments of all time. I asked the ascended masters about this and they said that in this argument both sides are right. There is an actual point of creation by God and the God force. There is also a most definite evolutionary process also taking place within our consciousness and physical vehicles. One example of this is the changing of lightworkers' DNA from two strands to twelve.

The masters have said that our blood might eventually become golden in the distant future. There have been certain genetic transformations introduced by various extraterrestrial groups. All aspects of our being and four-body system are in a constant state of evolution. It is not true that humans came from monkeys, however. Apart from this debate, creationism and evolution work perfectly together.

Science and Religion

In the past there has been a schism between science and religion. This was mostly caused by ignorant scientists who do not believe in God or spirit realities simply because they cannot see them with their five physical senses. What scientists of this third-dimensional, concrete-mind type do not realize is that we have many more than five senses. We have astral senses, lower-mental senses, higher-mental senses, buddhic senses, atmic senses, monadic senses and logic senses. Some of these senses are intuition, spiritual discernment, clairvoyance, clairaudience, clairsentience, psychometry, imagination, telepathy, comprehension, healing, idealism, divine vision, all knowledge, realization, beatitude, active service, response to group vibration. All these are actual senses we all have.

In reality, science and religion go hand in hand. Part of my work as an author and spiritual teacher has been to explain the scientific and mechanical laws that govern the planetary and cosmic-ascension process in an easy-to-understand manner. The spiritual path is actually scientific and logical, being based on exacting spiritual law. The problem with traditional scientists is that they have limited themselves to using about one-tenth of all the senses that are available to them. Was it not Einstein who said we use only seven or eight percent of our brain? As one opens to the soul, the monad and/or mighty I Am Presence and God consciousness, this begins to change.

This illusionary separation between science and religion was created by ignorant scientists and materialistic third-dimensional people, but it is not recognized by the ascended masters. In truth, science and religion work perfectly together. The science of the future will be and is currently the science of God on all dimensions of reality, not just the material plane, which is merely a small fragment of the total spectrum of vibration and light frequency.

The Christian Right

It is quite a paradox that a political party that is supposed to represent God, religion and the teachings of Jesus should be diametrically opposed to the ideals for which it stands. To begin with, the Christian Right is against pro-choice, which is antithetical to the ascended-master views. Members of the Christian Right are blatantly anti-homosexual, which is against the ascended masters' views. They are extremely judgmental and self-righteous in their approach, which is totally contradictory to what Jesus actually taught. This gets into the contamination of the Christian religion by the negative ego.

The ascended masters do not support the views of the Christian Right even though the masters follow the guidance of the Christ and the Buddha. The Christian Right is ultraconservative and the ascended masters do not follow an approach that could be labeled conservative, liberal or moderate. They take each issue as it comes and make the appropriate decision as God would have it.

Some decisions might be considered Republican, some Democrat, some Independent and others none of the above. All is one in their eyes. They do not fit into labels. The ascended masters would support prayer in schools, not in a Christian context but in a universal context.

A problem with the Christian Right is that anybody who does not believe what its members believe is considered of the devil, or Satan. According to the Christian Right, the entire New Age movement and even the ascended masters are a product of Satan. The truth is that this is a projection; it is actually the Christian Right that is to a great degree overshadowed by the Dark Brotherhood. The contamination of the negative ego is enormous.

This brings to mind the Pope as another interesting topic. I happen to like the Pope and feel he is doing a lot of good work. I really like the way he is traveling around and seems to be much more open to a universal approach, at least in his honoring the leaders and the validity of other religions.

One of the amazing beliefs in the Catholic Church, however, is that they believe the Pope is incapable of making a mistake. From a philosophical approach and without trying to be judgmental, some Catholic views on a wide variety of subjects are completely out of harmony with the ascended masters and even the master Jesus. At least the current Pope seems a little more open and universal than some of his predecessors.

He is a good and loving man, even if a great deal of the doctrine he speaks of is archaic. I recently saw a poll taken of Catholics in the United States in terms of their practices and views, and I was amazed by the high percentage of people who did their own thing, not following the dictates of the Pope on many issues such as birth control, abortion and so on. Even though they did their own thing, they still considered themselves Catholics.

Sex in the Media

As we all know, sex pervades every aspect of our media and advertising. It pervades commercials, magazines, billboards, television, movies and now even the Web and sex phone lines. Why is it so pervasive? The reason is because it gets people's attention. Advertisers aren't stupid; they go with what works. The next question is, why does it work? Because our society is extremely materialistic and obsessed with appearances, glamour and sexual energy itself. As humanity evolves and moves into a fifth- and sixth-dimensional society and spirituality becomes the all-consuming focus for humanity, this will change. It will change because humanity won't be interested in it. It won't get their attention in the same way.

It is like violent movies. If people didn't go see them and money couldn't be made, then people would have to stop making them. People in this world are way too preoccupied with physical looks and see life way too much through the physical eyes and ego's eyes. When humans learn to see life through their spiritual or Christ eyes, they will focus more on seeing their brothers and sisters as gods and goddesses, as incarnate Christs and Buddhas.

People will see God first because that is what they are interested in. They will be more interested in seeing life through the third eye than through the second chakra. Each chakra is like a lens or spectacles. Humanity will eventually transcend interest in the lower self and be interested in only the higher self. Everything that happens in the world is a product of mass consciousness.

Magazines like *The National Enquirer, The Star* and shows like *Hard Copy* and others like it thrive because people read and watch them. It is very important that people be strong in their values and not support with your attention those things you don't believe in. This applies to where you put your attention every moment of your life, as well as not buying magazines, watching junk TV or going to movies that you don't believe in.

The most dangerous thing we can do in this world is flow along on automatic pilot and let society spoon-feed us with its mental and emotional garbage. Unfortunately, this is what a great many people do. They watch or partake because it is there in front of them. They eat junk food because it is in the house or in the neighborhood. They watch garbage TV because there is nothing else to do. They go to violent movies because that is what they always did in the past. They read the magazines because they are right in front of them as they pay for their groceries.

Your attention is the single most important piece of your consciousness. Where you put your attention is where you live. When you walk or drive down the street you can place your attention on the billboards the advertisers want you to look at, or you can place your attention where the Holy Spirit wants it to be. You can be extremely discerning about what television and movies you see, or you can just flow along with the gang. You can place your attention on judging a person's body as he/she walks down the street, or you can place your attention on the Christ identity that she truly is.

The powers that be in our third-dimensional world are betting that you will be lazy and like a sheep, flow along with the rest of humanity. God, the ascended masters and the Holy Spirit are betting that your desire for God and God realization will inspire you to keep a disciplined mind and a pure heart and keep your attention on your own mighty I Am Presence. When enough people take this stance and set this example, it will inspire others to do the same. And soon the hundredth-monkey effect will take place and the collective consciousness will no longer support these practices.

Necessity is the mother of invention, so the advertisers will then have to come up with fifth-dimensional advertising, and the media will have to come up with fifth-dimensional television shows and movies. Sex and how people look will not be that interesting. People will be more concerned with inner beauty rather than outer beauty.

There are no neutral thoughts. Djwhal Khul says, "Learn to keep your mind steady in the light." The problem is that most people are not strong enough within themselves to defray the effect of the environmental influences. Most people are weak-minded. This is what has to change. It is the job of the spiritual leadership of this planet to set and teach this example.

Everyone wants to do this, for everyone is a soul and son or daughter of God. Many people have just forgotten and need inspiration. Each person is a great soul who has waiting deep within him/herself the opportunity to live and to demonstrate this nobility of spirit. Change of society begins first with change of self. Get your house in order first and attain self-mastery over your attention and focus. Then you may help and demonstrate a better example for others.

This pattern I have mentioned in this section will continue only as long as the collective consciousness feeds it. Let us all commit to stop feeding this negativity with our attention from now on. This is a large part of developing ascended-master status. It is not just passing initiations, which have more to do with light-quotient level; it is also, more important, living and demonstrating the consciousness and psychology of an ascended master. Hold to your values and ideals as a drowning man wants air. As Jesus said, "Be ye faithful unto death and I will give thee a crown of life."

This means right now in this moment that you must choose whom you shall serve. Do you want the lower self or higher self? Do you want God or the ego? Don't choose a life serving both God and Mammon. Do not remain in the twilight zone. Do not sit on the fence. Do you want truth or illusion? Commit yourself 100 percent to maintaining a spiritual consciousness at all times no matter what the spiritual test or temptation. This is the consciousness of the fully realized ascended master you are destined to be and the consciousness of the spiritual leadership you are now meant to realize.

Cults

The first key question here is what exactly is a cult. Cults are headed by sons and daughters of God who lead spiritual communities and who as leaders have been severely contaminated by negative ego and improper integration of the mental and emotional body. It must be understood here that every spiritual teacher on this planet, bar none, has some negative ego. The closest examples of perfection would be Sai Baba and the Lord Maitreya.

Cult leaders have a massive amount of negative ego and misunderstanding, which moves it into the realm of a cult. Not every spiritual group or organization is a cult. Cult leaders usually put themselves above their students and in truth are not interested in empowering them. The real interest is a conscious or unconscious ego trip. The leaders of cults are usually very charismatic. Charisma is a positive quality to have, but it can be used by either the negative ego or the soul and spirit.

Cult leaders are also usually self-righteous. They are prone to fits of anger. They are not into universalism and usually try to convince their followers that their teachings are the best and highest, or the only true teachings on the planet. These are all signs to watch out for. Another sign is that many cult leaders portray themselves as being special and better than other prophets or leaders. There is also usually the need to separate the followers from the rest of the world. They are also into getting the followers belongings and material possessions.

The forms that cults take are varied and multifaceted. A lot of times their teachings are based on the end times, Armageddon, and catastrophes, which play upon the fears of the followers. Cult members tend to be very impressionable and undiscerning.

In some cases the cult leaders have sex with many of the followers. Another sign of a cult is the unneeded accumulation of material possessions by the cult leaders, like owning fifty Rolls-Royce cars in one case that I know of. There is often a psychology represented of them vs. us, that "soon the Great War will come against the Satan-worshipers." They are most often based on communes or spiritual communities because they can have more control in live-in communities.

Some cult leaders have formed death pacts with their followers, such as the case with Jim Jones and David Koresh of the Branch Davidians. These followers often see themselves in a megalomania sense of being the Christ, not realizing that *all* are the Christ.

There is also a bizarre psychology that I see in lightworkers who automatically give their power to channels. Be aware that so-called channels run some of the worst cults around. They might even channel the ascended masters (which makes this even more seductive), but the truth is, the channelings are filled with negative-ego contamination. Without trying to be judgmental here, it is my opinion that Elizabeth Clare Prophet and her organization belong in this category. I usually do not like to name names; however, in extreme cases I consider it part of my responsibility. This is not to say that she does not do some good work. However, I would personally guide lightworkers away from this organization.

Also, in my opinion one of the worst cults out there is Scientology. It is a spiritless cult that preys on the vulnerable. The leaders of Scientology have developed a psychological system that has a sliver of truth in it, which allows them to get in the door. Once they get in, they become incredibly proselytizing and won't take no for an answer. The leaders have been charged with much fraudulent, even criminal activity. Stay away from this organization at all costs. I have some friends who had been immersed in it for a long time, and some of the deeper-level teaching the leaders disseminate is some of the most bizarre stuff I have ever come across. To the public, it is a godless psychological system.

In other cults there is an enormous amount of fraudulent information. People get sucked in because it is often based on a grain of truth. Younger souls are drawn to this information but are not discerning enough yet to see the enormous negative-ego distortion. The amazing thing is that the people running these cults cannot see what they are doing.

The key principle here is that these are often sincere spiritual people who are quite unclear psychologically. Just because someone is spiritually developed doesn't mean he/she is psychologically developed. This is one of the biggest lessons lightworkers need to understand. The leader might be excellent at bringing in high transmissions of spiritual energy, but this does not mean that his philosophy is developed at all.

Also, people channeling the ascended masters sometimes channel their negative ego or astral entities parading as ascended masters. Realize that astral entities are capable of lying and misrepresenting themselves.

Many spiritual teachers on this planet are what is called twilight masters, which means the negative ego controls them. They are half in the light and half overshadowed by the Dark Brotherhood. The Dark Brotherhood is an organization of misguided souls on the inner plane who have actually set up a hierarchy to serve the dark side of life. Whenever a person is run by the negative ego, there is a definite danger that the Dark Brotherhood will begin hooking onto his/her energy field. Lightworkers need to be aware of this potential within themselves and within the leaders they follow.

Another aspect of cultism is New Age groups that hook into an old thought form that is no longer active. For example, early in this century this planet and humanity was headed for major catastrophes regarding earth changes. Many of the great prophets and seers spoke of this, and at the time they gave these predications they were accurate. Lightworkers must remember, however, that the purpose of prophecy is to *give humanity an opportunity to change the future* by exercising its free choice. The reality is that this is exactly what *has* happened! Most of the earth-change prophecies and predictions of an axis shift and mass evacuation by the Ashtar Command and the Galactic Brotherhoods are now completely outdated. This information was once true, but is not now. Groups have formed with leaders who still believe this old information. This is because they read it in books and think it still holds true. This is the problem when you do not directly receive updated communication with the masters.

Groups then form because of the fear that is created by such prophecies. Cult leaders then step in to fill this void, which in truth is a massive power trip. Some even claim to channel and create illusionary maps that have no basis in reality. There is the claim that these maps come from the ascended masters. There is no judgment intended here, but these maps are a product of channeling a combination of a false thought form that has been created by masses of people who have read this outdated material. In some cases astral entities give this information. In other cases it is the negative ego contaminating the channel because of the need for power.

If any channel tells you that his/her channel is not colored to a certain extent by his personality, run for the hills. There is not a channel on the planet whose information is not colored to some degree by personality. Some are clearer than others, but the nature of channeling by definition comes through a person's information banks and filters. If a person has done a lot of reading about earth changes and this has had an emotional impact on him/her, channeling false information through that lens is not that far a step. Lightworkers need to be much more discerning in regard to channeling. The best place to get your information is through your own channel.

Wherever there is too much pushing to get you into the fold or too much control and/or manipulation, get out. There might be ten percent you can use from a given spiritual leader. Gain the pearls you need, then get out of the program. Ideally, it is better to find a spiritual teacher who is well developed spiritually, mentally, emotionally, etherically, physically and psychologically with his/her head screwed on straight and who strives for egolessness. A spiritual leader and teacher who is well-developed and well-integrated on all these levels is hard to find. Always remember that your true spiritual teacher is God, the Holy Spirit, your own monad and mighty I Am Presence. You can also always rely on the ascended masters on the inner plane through your own channel.

This new age is no longer the age of the guru. The true spiritual teacher and guru will teach this. Those of the highest quality who held this position in the past and still have followers today always guide their students to find the God within themselves. A wonderful example of this is Paramahansa Yogananda and the lineage of Self-Realization Fellowship masters. Their only aim in life is to see you empowered and as an equal. Gurus were a great part of the Piscean Age. The energies of the Aquarian Age, however, are much more focused in individual alignment with the higher self, monad and God. The ascended masters on the inner plane do not portray themselves as gurus. Djwhal Khul has told me quite specifically that he does not want to be looked at in this fashion. Sai Baba, who is the cosmic Christ and the highest spiritual being who has ever walked this planet in a physical body, has as his main message that he is God, but so are you. If you are looking for a spiritual teacher on Earth, he would be the ultimate choice. Study his books and teachings.

Cultivate the Christ quality of spiritual discernment and discrimination if you are new to this work. I have attempted to make the ascended masters' teachings as clear, simple and easy to understand as possible. I have also attempted to synthesize the best of all schools of thought as well as channeling in the future dispensation of ascended-master teachings.

The Flat Tax

One of the candidates running in the presidential election in 1996 was Steve Forbes. His whole candidacy was based on this main issue of setting up a flat tax for all people in the United States. When I first heard about this I thought it was a crazy idea, but the more I heard about it, the more intrigued I became.

I asked the ascended master Djwhal Khul about the Hierarchy's views on this issue and he surprisingly told me they were all for it. It is an issue they had been supporting quite fervently for a long time. The concept is that every person in the United States would pay a flat tax of 17 percent, or in some other versions of this plan it has been 13 percent. There would be no deductions. This would prevent all the big corporations and fat cats from not paying taxes. According to how I understood it, people making under $35,000 would not pay any taxes at all.

The problem in our society is that the rich don't really pay taxes. There are so many tax loopholes that their high-priced lawyers and accountants can help them pay nothing or at least a fraction of what they should. In this flat-tax system this would all be avoided. The rich would have to pay more than the middle class because they would have to pay 17 percent of what they *truly* earn. Everyone would be the same and it would create more equality and less separation. Doing taxes would also be a million times easier, for no one would have to worry about all those complicated tax forms.

This was an idea I rejected when I first heard it; however, after conversing with the masters I see it has great merit. There are many other candidates who are now coming around to this idea. Djwhal Khul wanted me to add that the Hierarchy's flat tax is different from the earthly models because there are no deductions in their model. Djwhal was very adamant that I make that point clear.

Three Strikes and You're Out

I asked Melchizedek about this controversial law of three strikes and you're out. This is the law mandating that if a person commits three crimes, he/she automatically spends his entire life in jail no matter what. The ascended masters believe in the law of forgiveness, not the law of punishment. There is nothing wrong with having tougher penalties for violent crimes. However, three strikes and you're out is a very punishing, not rehabilitating, attitude and policy.

One example I heard was of a young man who had been convicted of two crimes and then stole a piece of pizza from a young boy. According to the law of three strikes and you're out, he had to spend the rest of his life in prison for stealing one piece of pizza. The purpose of life is to learn from one's mistakes. Did not Jesus say forgive forty-seven times seven? He also said, "He that has no sin cast the first stone."

Campaign-Finance Reform

One other political issue of our time that is incredibly corrupt is the whole issue of campaign-finance reform. It was really after the Watergate affair and the enormous amount of illegal money that was being laundered into President Nixon's campaign war chest that the first step in this direction came about. A law was passed that a contributor could give a maximum of $1000 no matter what. This was an attempt to stop what can most aptly be called legalized bribery. The only problem is that there are so many loopholes in the campaign-reform laws that this reform is almost meaningless.

First, contributors can give as much as they want to the Republican or Democratic parties, but not to a single candidate. Second, a candidate can set up a nonprofit organization that serves as an educational vehicle and a contributor can give as much money as he/she wants to this representative organization. The representative organization can then produce TV ads and commercials, which are in truth almost the same as if the candidate did it him/herself. It is a joke.

Third, candidates are allowed to receive up to $5000 from what is called PAC (political-action committee) money, which is another loophole. On top of this they are allowed to receive what is called soft money, which is separate from the $1000 limit established by the above-mentioned law. They are also allowed to borrow as much money as they want to spend on their campaign, which is yet another loophole. Finally, they are also allowed to receive what might be called independent money and assistance.

In this example an independent contributor, instead of giving money directly, will pay to produce commercials and written material on the candidate's behalf. In essence, it is almost exactly the same thing as giving it to them, except that someone else's name is on the checks.

Do you really think our government officials don't know these things? Of course they do. They do not have the integrity, courage or desire to change the system. They also run into the gridlock caused by the negative egos of our political leaders who care more about themselves and their party than true collective change.

Legalized Drugs

The political discussion of whether to legalize drugs is another interesting philosophical discussion, which I posed to Djwhal Khul. He said quite adamantly that the ascended masters were against legalizing drugs. He said that in his opinion it would just make drug use much worse rather than correct the problem, as some would say. This had always been my thought on the subject; however, it was nice to get confirmation on this.

Using Marijuana for Medical Purposes

I asked for the Hierarchy's opinion on legalizing marijuana for medical purposes and the answer I received was a definite yes. They said that despite the fact that this might encourage a greater temptation to use the drug for recreational purposes, as it would be more readily available, the benefits outweigh the potential problems. There would have to be strict supervision in order to contain the use of marijuana within the medical domain. However, this is already done with a vast array of narcotics.

One of the reasons for legalizing marijuana for medical purposes is because of its effectiveness in reducing some of the worst effects of chemotherapy. As so many people are currently undergoing this ominous treatment for cancer, why not relieve them from as much suffering and as soon as possible? I have also been told that there are many beneficial uses for marijuana not within public awareness at this time. Just because certain aspects of nature have been misused does not mean that we should deny their positive uses. This seems to be the case with medicine and marijuana, and something tells me that this is not an isolated occurrence.

Assignments

It is very important for spiritual leaders and lightworkers to understand that your mighty I Am Presence, the Spiritual Hierarchy and the ascended masters will give you assignments to fulfill. In my profession, for example, the masters would give me both intuitively and directly certain assignments they wanted me to complete such as teaching classes, public speaking, writing articles, counseling and putting on the Wesak festival.

As I fulfilled these different assignments, my progress and success would be charted by the masters and greater assignments and job responsibilities would be given. It is very important to be in touch with the assignment and mission you have been given and to fulfill that properly. When you are ready, ask and pray for your next spiritual assignment.

Flexibility

Another very important lesson in learning proper leadership is to learn to be flexible. Leadership is often a juggling act between having a right relationship with self and the group body and staying clear from negative-ego control issues. Advice given by the masters in one situation might not apply in another.

Circus Animals

This practice of using animals in the circus is another barbaric practice and is most definitely cruelty to animals. The problem is that we do not look at animals as our younger brothers and sisters and as God beings just as we are. Just because they do not have the same level of intellect we have does not mean we can treat them like slaves. Is that how the ascended masters treat us? Then why would we allow animals to be treated in this manner?

Frog Dissection in Public Schools

This is another incredibly barbaric practice. The kids in school hate it, and it is not as if they are studying to become medical doctors. It is a needless cruelty.

Lobster Rights

Another issue that most people have not really thought about is lobster rights and the barbaric practice of throwing a live lobster into boiling hot water. Lobsters are God too, and how would you like to be thrown into boiling hot water? It is a barbaric practice and should be stopped. If a person has to eat a lobster, then it should at least be done in a humane way.

Electroshock Therapy

I happened to be watching *Donahue* and the topic was electric-shock therapy. I am here to tell you that this practice is barbaric, to say the least. They actually fry the person's nervous and electrical system and call this therapy. The inner-plane ascended masters can easily do this without damaging the physical or etheric body. Depression comes from faulty thinking, and as usual, our barbaric medical profession is dealing with symptoms rather than causes.

The Minimum Wage

The ascended masters totally support an increase in the minimum wage, for who can truly live on five dollars an hour in this society? There is already too much discrepancy between the rich and the poor, so the masters are for any change that can be made to remedy this disparity.

Gays in the Military

As long as homosexuals or heterosexuals do not force their sexual preference on another person, what is the problem? There is the belief here that gays are going to do this, and I ask, why don't they think this of heterosexuals? It is ludicrous, that is why. The newest policy is, don't ask, don't tell. This is an improvement over what existed previously but does not go all the way.

Politics and Perception

One of the interesting insights about politics is that what is "true and just" does not really hold much water. What I mean by this is that in the political arena and media, it is not what is true that counts but the *perception* of truth. For example, in the Whitewater hearings involving Bill and Hillary Clinton, whether there is fault is not the point from the Republican point of view. If they can create the perception of fault, this is all they care about. The Democrats, of course, do the same thing to the Republicans. This is the basis of all campaign advertising.

This goes beyond just politics, of course. Whether Michael Jackson was guilty or innocent of molesting a child is not the point. His reputation was already destroyed. The way America's judicial system is supposed to work is that when someone makes a charge, we are not innocent until proven guilty. Instead, in our society we are tried by the media and proven guilty until found innocent. By the time the media is done with you, even if you are innocent, after two years of being dragged through the mud and conflicted by judgmental reports, your reputation is destroyed and the gullible public does not believe the verdict of innocence anyway.

This understanding that perception is everything and truth means nothing is the basis of politics in our society. Even if, for example, Bill Clinton was doing a great job, if the Republicans could create a perception he wasn't, then he would not be reelected. Facts mean nothing; perception is everything. Even if the economic numbers show that the economy is doing well, if the public has a perception of gloom, doom and fear, it doesn't matter what the numbers or facts tell you.

This understanding about perception being everything in politics is the key insight as to how Republicans and Democrats destroy one another. They do not hold truth and integrity above all else; they hold winning and power above all else. You can see how dirty politicians who serve their negative egos and the Dark Brotherhood can literally plant lies and destroy other politicians even though none of it might be true.

The American people and people around the world need to be much more spiritually discerning about what they hear in the media and much slower to make judgments. Just because it is in the newspaper or magazine or on television does not make it true. The media can create just about any story to get ratings and make money. We all must hold to the truth that other people are indeed innocent until proven guilty. We must be much more discerning about what the media says and what politicians say to us. If they are run by their negative ego, they will literally say anything to win and get elected.

Divorce

The ascended masters' and the soul's views on divorce are quite different from that of the Catholic Church, which says stay together at all costs. From the perspective of the soul, divorce is often a very positive thing. As a psychologist I often intervened, not to bring people back together but to help them to separate. What is spiritually wrong is to stay with another person for ego reasons that are not in harmony with the dictates of the soul.

There are sins of omission and commission.

I use the word "sin" here as nothing more than a mistake. One should most definitely work on one's marriage and exhaust all possibilities of communication before taking this step. When the time is right, however, no karma is created by making this move. In actuality, staying in a bad marriage longer than one is supposed to often creates the spiritual karma. This brings to mind women who are being beaten by their husbands and yet keep coming back for more.

Child and Spousal Abuse

This is a most serious issue. It usually stems first from an individual who was abused him/herself in his upbringing and who has not learned to become right with self and right with God before moving into marriage and having his own children. The person in truth has an abusive relationship with self. The real reason for this is our educational system, where students are instructed to study and memorize useless facts. Instead, from the very youngest age a curriculum should consist of classes that teach how to be right with self and right with God, the world's religions, how to clear the negative ego, how to learn inner parenting, the dynamics of romantic relationships, how to become self-actualized, how to achieve the seven levels of initiation, the laws of karma, how to parent, how to control the astral and desire bodies, how to stay in harmony with your own soul and tools for practical living.

Can you imagine how interesting school would be for children if this was taught along with reading, writing and arithmetic? Our school system is a joke. It is soulless and teaches no morals, values, psychology or spirituality. The soul and spirit have been systematically extracted from earthly life and the real world.

Traditional religion fills us with even more faulty thinking. Most psychologists and counselors have not even merged with their own souls and are working from personality levels at best. Is it any wonder that there are so many screwed up people and that child abuse, spousal abuse and divorces are rampant in our society? In the future, people will not get married until they are first right with self and right with God. Abuse stems from the person involved not having learned how to control his/her own negative ego. Often alcohol is involved, but not necessarily. People who are abusive are often not even aware that they are doing anything wrong; that is how unconscious they are.

If every person on this planet was inundated with practical training in school from the ages of three or four until eighteen, this would make an enormous difference. What is more important—memorizing useless, meaningless facts, or learning how to live properly and be prepared for real life?

When problems arise in the future, courts will recommend not only counseling but also spiritual schools that people will have to attend for long periods of time. Most counseling is not effective because most counselors don't have the first clue about what the negative ego really is and do not understand psychology from the soul's perspective.

If you are living in an abusive situation, set your boundaries and don't let it happen. You deserve better. Many women who accept this often have extremely low self-esteem. Hence there is a codependency in operation.

Children need to be protected by adults, so if you ever see abuse happening, call the appropriate authorities. Ideally, parents should set the proper example; however, this is not always the case, so that is why our educational system is the key. Most children are in school six hours a day for thirteen years, if not longer. Do you see how much could be accomplished during this time if this time were used wisely?

I have seen children who have come out of the schools that Sai Baba has set up in India. They learn the teachings of Sai Baba along with their regular earthly studies. These kids are like supermen and superwomen. In our society we wait until we are adults and completely screwed up and going through a dark night of the soul before we begin. Can you imagine starting at three years old or even earlier?

Future schools will become temples of God in a universalistic and eclectic sense, with no one fundamentalist theory shoved down the students' throats. The separation of church and state was set up to protect children from the extreme right-wing Christian ideology, but this detachment has gone too far and instead the baby has been thrown out with the bath water. Or more aptly stated, school officials have thrown the soul out with the bath water!

Crime

Crime develops in the same way that child abuse or spousal abuse does: lack of spiritual and psychological education by parents, extended family, school and society. It is bizarre to watch how politicians in our culture deal with the issue of crime. Their answer is to hire more police officers. There is nothing wrong with hiring more police officers, but as is usual with our third-dimensional leaders, they are dealing with the symptom rather than the cause, just as Western medicine and traditional psychology do.

To think you are going to solve the issue of crime by hiring more police officers is absurd and almost beyond belief. The fact is, as we have seen from the O.J. Simpson trial, many police officers are themselves criminals. The cause of crime is lack of spiritual and psychological training and education in school and at home. We compound this by then sending criminals to an absolutely barbaric prison system, where there continues to be no spiritual or psychological training. To make matters worse, because the prisons are so crowded, they let the criminals serve only a quarter of their sentence because they have no money and room to keep them in prison. Is this a vicious cycle, or what?

Until our educational and prison systems are shifted from negative-ego to soul-inspired systems, you can hire all the police officers in the world and it is not going to make the slightest bit of difference. On top of this you have traditional religion, which is supposed to supply some moral training but is also completely bankrupt and corrupted by the negative ego. Then add to this the psychologists and counselors who are for the most part operating out of a personality-level understanding (and not very effectively) and have not integrated the soul themselves. So how are they supposed to help these types of people both psychologically and spiritually?

I am not saying they are of no value, but they are operating out of a very limited capacity, as are the ministers, rabbis and priests in traditional religion. This is the job of the spiritual leadership in this world to help completely revamp this whole system and bring back the living soul into all facets of our society in the third-dimensional world.

Gangs

Gangs are an interesting phenomenon in our modern society. There have always been gangs, but nothing like what we are experiencing at the end of this century. The reason for gangs is multifaceted. They often form in the ghettos and among minority groups. This is quite understandable. These youths are uneducated and often come from broken homes and families. They do not do well in school, which lowers their self-esteem. Their families are poor and often live in a type of ghetto in the poorer section of our major cities. As minorities, they live in a racist society where the white people do not even realize how racist and privileged they are. They live in a consumer-oriented culture that is soulless and where materialism and negative-ego values pervade every aspect of society.

They get no spiritual or psychological training in school, and traditional religion is bankrupt. Their fathers are often out of the house and the mothers cannot control them as they move into adolescence. They live in a ghetto environment of violence and crime that is much different from the environments in which most of us were raised. They have no real opportunity to go to college because of lack of education and money. This relegates them to minimum-wage jobs that can support no one.

If by chance they stick it out in school, they then have to take the scholastic-aptitude tests, which are one of the most racist aspects of our society. These tests were created by white, well-educated, self-righteous, third-dimensional, negative-ego based people who are actually so ignorant that they think these tests are fair.

One more obstacle for these young black children is the violence they see on television, which proves to be true moral training, as they in turn act out that same violence in the streets. In truth, these souls never really had a chance.

Anyone who believes that the American dream is equally available to all should have his/her head examined. These kids had few chances, if any, from day one. Their karma of being born into such a situation prohibited much else. I am not saying it is impossible to get out of a poor environment, but the obstacles are enormous.

Added to this is the enormous peer pressure to join gangs. If they don't, their lives are often on the line. The Dark Brotherhood on the inner plane is having a field day in this environment. In addition, the drugs and alcohol in school (prevalent even in the upper-middle-class white schools) has its debilitating effect.

Then these kids see Rodney King being beaten for forty minutes by twenty-five police officers on video tape and the police officers are set free by our wonderful judicial system—which then causes riots and destroys their city (Los Angeles in this case). They clearly see from this example and thousands of others that justice is not colorblind.

I just saw a report on television that blacks in our society get much stiffer penalties than whites, proving racism. Minority youth are constantly being harassed by the racist police officers in every city in the United States. This is an absolute fact and was proven in the Rodney King case, the O.J. Simpson trial and the tapes of Mark Fuhrman in that trial.

Even minority judges, lawyers, business people and millionaires can be harassed and humiliated by the police. We still live in a completely racist society, and anyone who disagrees needs to wake up and smell the coffee.

Gang members often get in trouble and go to juvenile hall or prison for a little while, which environment makes things even worse and where gangs are even more prevalent. Gangs are almost a survival mechanism. They provide a community of friends, support and protection. The problem is that once they get in one it is very hard to get out. I know that a lot of these kids want to get out. They know they can't or they will face gang retribution. It is a very tragic situation and a vicious cycle. The concept of having a community of friends is obviously a soul-guided principle. The problem here is that the gangs in these cases have been taken over by the negative ego and Dark Brotherhood.

What could be a good thing or have positive potential becomes more like a Mafia crime syndicate, completely controlled by the negative ego.

Drive-by shootings, drug trafficking and criminal activity of all sorts are the mainstay of these gangs. They actually spread to different cities and become like a network crime syndicate. Once this path is followed, it is very hard to get off. The temptation for easy money, drugs and other lower-self values is too great.

These young men and women, not having spiritual training, are extremely angry with everyone and everything. They could not possibly understand the law of karma and that on a soul level they have chosen to come into this situation as part of a spiritual learning experience. Society, being totally bankrupt in regard to these issues, provides no real alternative for them. This is the problem.

These are sons and daughters of God who are essentially good kids, but who see no way out of their predicament. Imagine being born in Iran or Iraq, and you would see the enormous impact one's environment has on one's life. I am sure that most people reading this book had an incredibly good karma to be born into your situations. I am not saying there were no problems, but they were probably nothing like being born into poverty in the ghetto.

Much compassion and tough love is needed. When our society transforms more from a third-dimensional to a fifth-dimensional society and from a negative-ego-based to a soul-based society, there will be many more opportunities for these youths. The spiritual leadership of this world needs to address this issue and programs must be established for rehabilitation and training to help them reacclimate and become healthy, functioning citizens. I don't claim to have all the answers here. I am simply putting out the clarion call to those with expertise in these areas to step forward and to begin making inroads.

The world changes brick by brick. If each person will just take responsibility for laying the bricks as your soul and mighty I Am Presence guides you, the world will change faster than we all think.

Veterans

As I mentioned previously, I feel that one of the most disgusting aspects of our society is how veterans are treated. These are young men and women who give their lives in service to our country. The military could obviously care less about them, for in their eyes they are all pawns in their third-dimensional militaristic and egotistical warring consciousness. MIAs were left in Vietnam to rot in the prison camps; they were given up on and forgotten about for political reasons. They were and still are treated terribly at home.

Prior to going to Kuwait to serve in the Gulf War, American soldiers were filled with vaccines out of fear of germ warfare. All these shots are absolutely poisonous to the human body. Of course, this is contrary to what the military doctors tell the soldiers. Tens of thousands of soldiers are now deathly ill from this—and of course the military takes no responsibility for helping these young men and women whose lives they have destroyed. This negligence also applies to those who have been injured in war.

From a spiritual frame of reference we should be proud of the men and women who have served in the military to protect our freedom. The problem is that they are quickly forgotten after these wars. Many also suffered severe psychological trauma from the killing they experienced firsthand and are not properly helped upon returning home.

The consciousness of the military is to bring them in, use them and then spit them out. This is terrible and must change. They give up their normal lives to serve their country and should be helped to find jobs and reintegrate into society when they return home after serving their country.

These issues were even more pronounced in the Vietnam War, which was such an unpopular and useless war. This war was fought mostly by young men who did not have the money to get out of it by going to college or getting married. During this particular war Agent Orange was used supposedly to destroy crops. What the government knew but did not tell the young men and women in the middle of that war was that it also destroyed lives. By simply providing gas masks, countless lives could have been saved. Soon after the war many of these young men immediately got cancer and died. Now, almost a quarter of a century later, men in their forties who were in areas where Agent Orange was used are also ill and dying of cancer. Clinton has recently acknowledged some of this publicly. One wonders why this was not prevented in the first place, when the horrific results were foreseen at the outset. Could it have possibly been the few dollars saved on gas masks?

To add salt to this already festering wound, the blame for this war is put on the men and women who served, rather than on the corrupt government that got us into it in the first place. The veterans who served were just following the orders of corrupt leaders driven by the dark forces. The veterans were mistreated, blamed, dishonored and not helped as they should have been.

Prostitution

It is tragic in our society that women, men and even children have to sell their bodies to make money. The institution of prostitution might be the oldest profession. It is often practiced in an informal sense and under a different guise. For example, a woman might sleep with a director to get a movie part. This is not formal prostitution, but it meets the requirements in a larger context. People prostitute themselves all the time to get what they want or need. So this must be looked at in a larger context, as our society is incredibly oversexed.

Sexuality is the second most powerful force after the force of personal power focused upon the spiritual path. Our materialistic third-dimensional society is absolutely obsessed with it. If someone has an attractive physical body, then he/she can be an instant supermodel even if there is nothing upstairs. Our entire society uses sexuality in advertising, television, movies and so forth.

I asked the ascended master Djwhal Khul about pornography and he said that this was of the lower or carnal self. I spent a great deal of time discussing the spiritual aspects of sexuality in *Soul Psychology,* so I am not going to repeat myself here. Suffice it to say that in the future humanity will have a much greater understanding of sexuality. Humans will understand more clearly the karmic bonds that are created when you share fluids with another. Once they understand more about these energy cords that are set up they will be far less likely to want sex with just anyone. Sexuality is meant to be an expression of love, not treating another person as carelessly as a piece of beef.

People will learn the importance of raising this energy and not debilitating the body by overindulgence. Sexuality in the future will become more a sacred act. People in the future will have more control over their desire body, astral body, emotional body and lower self. They will not put as much importance on appearances and instead will focus on the energies of the emotions, mind and spirit. In our current times, AIDS has actually put a damper on the free-sex movement.

It is interesting how our society works. Prostitutes are picked up, booked and imprisoned; however, usually their male clients aren't—another example of our patriarchal negative-ego based system. Prostitution will be around for a long time because of the incredible power of sexual energy, even among the most advanced lightworkers.

The most important lesson here is that we as lightworkers do not prostitute ourselves in any area of our lives to get something the negative ego or desire body wants. I am not speaking here of just sexuality but all areas and facets of our lives. The ascended masters obviously don't support prostitution; however, they are very philosophical, nonjudgmental and understanding, having lived in physical bodies themselves and knowing the difficulties of earthly life. Many people in this world are living in survival mode. In the future when our society becomes more spiritualized, a lot of these survival needs will be better taken care of on a collective basis, which will allow people to move from survival to a path of self-actualization and service.

The O.J. Simpson Trial and Verdict

Just as I was writing this section the O.J. Simpson verdict was coming in. The group consciousness of the United States was incredibly charged on this issue, certainly more than any trial in the history of the United States. Everyone I spoke with had a strong opinion and feeling. I spoke with a friend the night before the verdict and she had a strong feeling of gloom and doom, which I believed was her sensing the hammer about to fall, not just on O.J. Simpson, but also on the group consciousness that was overidentified with this process.

Sixty-five percent of the blacks polled said he was innocent and 75 percent of whites thought he was guilty. This is quite a statement about our society. I decided to ask Melchizedek about his views on this, since I was writing this book. I had refrained purposely from speaking about the trial with him in the past because I thought it would be too frivolous and maybe indulging in glamour on my part.

I did not feel this way now, for this had turned into a real lesson for all of humanity, and there was the potential for riots in Los Angeles and other places. My psychic feeling was that there would not be physical riots, but psychic riots, especially among the black community at large.

This, however, was now much bigger than the tragedy of O.J. Simpson, Nicole Brown Simpson, Ron Goldman and the children and families. It had become a group-consciousness lesson as well.

This issue of group consciousness was one of the reasons a great many people had been rooting, so to speak, for O.J Simpson. The individual evidence was obviously quite extensive against him and most people realized this. On a group-consciousness level, however, people were viewing this as O.J. Simpson, the hero and idol, and O.J. Simpson as a black man. Some people did not want to see their hero tainted and others were looking at it from the perspective that he deserved to get off because of how racist our society is toward blacks.

Finding him innocent would balance a little bit of the karmic slate of all the mistreatment and injustice to blacks. This might sound strange to look at it this way; however, this was one of the themes operating on a group-consciousness level. The following is what Melchizedek had to say: "Part of the lesson here is for people to look more to themselves and not put others on a high pedestal. It is only the negative ego that has created this situation, not only the negative ego of O.J. Simpson, but also the negative ego of Nicole Brown, who had a certain codependent relationship with him."

Melchizedek went on to say, "It is also the negative ego of the public that puts one in such a position to take such a large fall." He said this was part of the shakedown and cleansing process on a group-consciousness level. He said part of the lesson here was pinpointing the danger of fame. Here was a man who was in the limelight literally all the time, and everything he did had an effect on the group consciousness.

Melchizedek said this was why those who are now moving into leadership need to be in a place of total clarity and impeccability on all levels, even more than the average lightworker. This is because you are in the spotlight much more. Everything you do will be examined with a fine-toothed comb and will have a great effect on the group consciousness.

Melchizedek said a corollary lesson here for those who move into leadership and fame is to learn how to step into the limelight and back out of it, becoming neutral or even go backstage when needed. Many who move into spiritual leadership, after getting a taste of fame and the spotlight, do not have the ability to step out once they get that fix, so to speak. This is the negative ego feeding on the drug of fame and power.

Every lightworker, Melchizedek said, must be able to be a wallflower and be supportive of other leaders when need be. This is an extremely important point about leadership that Melchizedek had also spoken to us about on other occasions. He said that when one does not have this ability and balance, it creates an O.J. Simpson. Here is a man who gained the whole world but lost his own soul. This is very big lesson for humanity, and it really struck a chord throughout the world. The tragic fall of O.J. Simpson crossed many boundaries. Look at the youngsters and adults who idolized this man as one of the greatest college and professional football heroes of our time. Then there was his career in movies, on Monday-night football and in commercials with Hertz Rent-A-Car. O.J. Simpson was the epitome of fame, glamour and stardom.

Melchizedek made another interesting point of how O.J. Simpson also crossed the barriers of color. The black community obviously idolized him, but so did the white community on a group-consciousness level. He was a man all could relate to. He had made something of himself. It is for these reasons that the group consciousness reacted so strongly. This is an issue that the spiritual leadership and lightworkers must consider more in their daily processing of reality—how things affect individuals and how they affect the group consciousness. This is part of the lesson of developing full ascended-master consciousness.

We each have an individual body and a group-consciousness body. It is usually only at the beginning and realization of one's ascension that people begin to become aware of this. It is like looking at all of humanity as one being and seeing how it is reacting. The masters do a great deal of work on the inner plane administering to this larger group body by sending energy, light and rays of energy to balance the group-consciousness imbalance.

Melchizedek said that the masters on the inner plane were very interested to see how the group consciousness reacts to this verdict. I am actually writing this section the morning the verdict is about to be given. I pretty much know what is going to happen on a personal level, but I do not know exactly what the group consciousness is going to do with this lesson. My intuition is that there will be psychic riots and depression among the black community; however, I do not think it will become physical. Melchizedek said to me, "Joshua, not everyone is as objective, detached, calm and rational as you are." And I realize that that is the case for the most part.

I grew up in Los Angeles and used to go to the USC Trojans football games when O.J. Simpson was in college. He was the greatest running back that college football had ever known. There was also a part of me that was looking at this whole thing from a group-consciousness lens, recognizing the enormous racism and prejudice toward blacks in our society. I was looking at this whole process almost as if I had a black body. How could one *not* root for the blacks in the face of the incredible racism of the Los Angeles Police Department as demonstrated by Mark Fuhrman?

I asked Melchizedek if this trial made racism even worse. He said no, it did not make it worse or better. It was just bringing to light what has always been there. He said that we have made little progress in our society on the issue of racism. He was very emphatic on this point.

The feeling of doom that my friend felt was what Melchizedek described as the psychic group-consciousness or collective-consciousness feeling of being shaken to its core, in terms of what it has held dear. Melchizedek said, "Instead of looking within and to the Source, it has looked to a god of clay."

Melchizedek said that this lesson should be listened to very carefully. He said that just as individuals must be cleared on the path of ascension, countries must be cleared also. This lesson is bringing up for collective clearing a great many lessons. For all must realize that the United States (every country on the globe, for that matter) and the planet herself are in their own initiation and ascension process. In a larger context this lesson is good, for it is bringing to the surface what has been buried.

Melchizedek went on to say, "Only when humanity begins looking within and not without can the true work begin here. People will no longer be satisfied with their paper heroes." He said that many people will never give this power to one person again because of this lesson. Melchizedek continued, saying that if there were one word to describe the Spiritual Hierarchy's frame of mind in watching this lesson unfold, it would be "thoughtful." He said that they did not know exactly how humanity would respond, for humanity has free choice. This whole lesson and what was about to come about was a spiritual test, and the ascended masters were watching the outcome unfold as carefully as we were.

In concluding this section I have to admit that I find it fascinating to look at these earthly group-consciousness lessons from the perspective of cosmic and planetary ascended masters. It really makes me think about the future when we will have an Ascended Master political party that transcends the duality of Democrat and Republican and will look at earthly lessons from a more transcendent point of view. This might be the true future Independence Party. I believe the movement that has been started at the end of this century to push for an Independence Party is a beginning step toward a more transcendent political and social viewpoint.

Won't politics and the great social issues of our time look different and be more exciting? We will be working to elect ascended masters as president and senators and representatives. We are not that far away from the time when this can become a realistic potential.

When the verdict came in this morning that he was found not guilty, I was really shocked. No one knows for sure his guilt or innocence. I was under the opinion that he was guilty; however, I obviously did not know for sure. The not-guilty verdict was obviously very popular among the black community and for a lot of other people. I asked Melchizedek about this phenomenon of people cheering as the verdict came in. Melchizedek said it was just demonstrating how much the astral plane was involved in this whole procedure.

What Melchizedek said was that this decision had created an enormous rift in the astral plane of the whole planet and most specifically over the United States. Given that over 75 percent of white America thought he was guilty, this verdict created a stunning wake-up call to people all over the world. One of the prime lessons a great many people are learning is how incredibly unjust our "justice" system is.

The black community already knew this. Rodney King and the Menendez brothers trials were subtler wake-up calls. The O.J. Simpson trial was a nuclear explosion heard around the world. The black community to a large extent, but not completely, is celebrating, and the white community to a large extent, but not completely, is in stunned disbelief. On a large group-consciousness level this can be viewed through one lens as karmic justice. Melchizedek told me that there is an enormous amount going on here beneath the service that we do not as yet fully understand. One thing I will say is that it has been one of the most interesting group-consciousness lessons of our time.

As I reflected on this situation for the rest of the day and watched the news programs, a number of lessons that humanity was being forced to examine came to me, no matter which side a person had taken. They include the following:

1. Our justice system is really extremely *unjust*. Any American propaganda on this issue among blacks and whites is now completely bankrupt.
2. Racism is incredibly prevalent in our society on all sides of the spectrum—much worse than most people realized.
3. A person with money, fame and power who can afford to hire top-notch lawyers can get away with anything.
4. People with no money, fame or power are going to face the opposite side of this spectrum.
5. The black community was looking at this trial, not on an individual basis, but as a group-consciousness referendum on all past injustices inflicted upon them in the United States. In this sense this trial was a balancing of karma on the group-consciousness race level. This might be the only redeeming factor of the whole process; however, it sets a dangerous precedent for people to look at all future similar events in this vein.
6. Lawyers can go too far as advocates for their clients. As the saying in the Bible goes, "For what is a man profited if he gain the whole world and lose his own soul?"
7. The astral nature of humanity got overinvolved in this case. Seeing people cheering as if this were a football game after the verdict seemed inappropriate to me. That two people were murdered seemed to get lost.
8. It is a sad commentary on our media, which focused an obsessive amount of time and energy on this trial when there were so many other worldwide events of far greater importance (the war in Bosnia and the peace settlement between the Arabs and Israelis).
9. The defendant has an advantage, which in the bigger picture might be a good thing. It is probably better to lean toward letting a guilty person go free than putting an innocent person in prison.

In conclusion, what is most stunning to me is how many people in the United States were looking at this through a group-consciousness and race/class-struggle lens rather than just as O.J. Simpson's personal guilt or innocence. Melchizedek said that we have made little progress on the issue of racism and class struggle in our society—far less than the average man/woman thinks. The positive side is that this has all been brought to the surface of humanity for cleansing, where before it was buried and unconscious.

O.J. Simpson's conviction in the civil trial had a kind of balancing effect. Unfortunately, because it was a white jury there is still the projection that this is a race issue rather than an evidence issue. If the jury would have been comprised of more African Americans, this automatic assumption might have been transcended had the result been the same.

The only other social commentary I would make is that it is quite bizarre to me that a person can be found completely innocent in a criminal trial and then be tried for the same crime in a civil case. I say this, not speaking specifically about O.J. Simpson, but about the judicial concept. In judicial language I think this is called double jeopardy. This means that you cannot be tried for the same crime twice, regardless whether the person is found guilty or innocent.

Chain Letters

One day in the recent past I received a chain letter in the mail and decided to ask the masters their opinion of chain letters. What they told me was interesting, and it clarified something I had been feeling but had been unable to theoretically frame in my mind. They said that they are against most chain letters because of the veiled threat inherent in most of them. By this I mean the warnings or stories of people having extremely negative things happen to them if they did not continue the chain. It is the negative ego that uses fear to make people send money and participate in the program. On very rare occasions you will see a chain letter that does not involve money and has a more christed approach. The guidance was clearly not to be involved with any chain letters that contain any type of threat, which I personally felt was good advice.

Pyramid Moneymaking Schemes

What I mean by pyramid moneymaking schemes has nothing to do with multilevel marketing and/or network marketing, which are perfectly fine. Pyramid moneymaking schemes circulate around the United States even though they are not really legal in a third-dimensional government sense. Some of these pyramid programs seem to be spiritually based but in truth are not. The masters told me that the problem lies in the fact that when the pyramid program runs out, which it must do eventually, there will always be losers at the bottom of the pyramid who not only did not make money, but lost their investment. This goes against spiritual law, which is always based on a win-win concept. The pyramid moneymaking scheme cannot be win-win if there are losers at the end. Be aware of the fox in sheep's clothing.

Governmental Cover-up of ETs' Existence

The biggest governmental cover-up in the history of Earth would most definitely have to be how the United States government and many other governments around the globe hide the existence of UFOs and extraterrestrials. It is not the purpose of this book to explore this in any great depth since I have already done this in *Hidden Mysteries;* however, it is sufficient to say that this cover-up is indeed happening. The United States government has met with extraterrestrials face to face and has over a hundred dead bodies of extraterrestrials of varying races. This is fact, not fiction.

The government's attitude—or maybe I should say secret government—is that it would create mass panic. But given that recent polls have shown that as many as 60 percent of the people in the United States believe in the existence of alien life, as Bill Clinton likes to say, "This dog just won't hunt." People of the United States have a right to know, and in my personal opinion, it is time to let this information out.

The fact is that 95 percent of the extraterrestrials contacting our planet are of a positive nature, so there is nothing to fear. The release of this information would also have a very spiritualizing effect upon all the inhabitants of planet Earth and would break down some of the egotism that pervades this planet. It would also leave the door open for the positive extraterrestrials to have more overt contact and to teach us about their advanced spiritual and material civilizations.

The United States government shares underground bases with an alien race known as the Grays and also has in its possession at least twelve crashed crafts from extraterrestrial races. There might have been a time in the past for some short-lived secrecy on this subject; however, it is the opinion of this humble author and of the ascended masters I work with that this time is long gone.

J.F.K. Assassination and Other Cover-ups

I do not believe that it is any big revelation to my readers to make them aware that the John F. Kennedy assassination was a conspiracy and not the act of a lone gunman as the Warren Commission claimed it was. I have checked this out with the ascended masters and they confirmed this fact. As to whether it was the CIA, Cubans, Mafioso or some other group, the ascended masters would not say; however, they definitely confirmed the conspiracy theory.

One has to ask him/herself, why does the government lie to us so blatantly and purposely on such issues as this and ETs/UFOs? In my mind this is a statement of tremendous negative-ego corruption at the highest levels of government let alone the assassination itself. The officials in government are playing God, and the last time I read the Constitution, this is a government by the people and for the people. If the government has so blatantly lied about UFOs and the J.F.K. assassination, you can only imagine all the other things they lie to us about. This deceit often does not necessarily come from the President or even Congress, but more from the CIA, officials at the Pentagon, Majestic-12, the FBI and secret branches of the government that operate like rogue elephants, secret even from the President himself.

The current AIDS epidemic has been another cover-up, as AIDS was created by the United States government and military as a germ-warfare experiment that went awry (see *Hidden Mysteries* for more details). In a new-age form of government controlled by the ascended masters, this obviously would not be allowed and would not be the way a christed government would be conducted.

The Destruction of All Nuclear Weapons

The Hierarchy would love to see the destruction of all nuclear weapons. These weapons pose a great threat not only to individuals and humanity, but also to the very core structure of Earth. In the event that nuclear weapons were ever used to any degree of the capacity now available, it would cause the complete destruction of every kingdom evolving upon this planet. Many of the spiritually evolved extraterrestrials have backup plans for Earth's evolution in the event that this ever came to pass. These plans involve the immediate evacuation of masses of humanity and certain animals onto their spacecraft.

This, however, would not prevent the enormously traumatic effect that such mass destruction would have upon all the souls involved. Nor would it save the Earth herself. This would be a cosmic tragedy of such monumental proportions that words could not describe it. It is obvious, therefore, that every effort be made so that this does not come to pass.

The unfortunate truth is, however, that the Hierarchy would not recommend a mass destruction of all nuclear weapons. This is because it is not within humanity's nature to carry it to its conclusion, and it would only result in more havoc and problems of the gravest kind. What would happen in the event of forced nuclear eradication is that there would be underground nuclear centers set up with only the appearance of nuclear disarmament. Those countries that were most cooperative would unfortunately be at the mercy of other nations that were less cooperative. The Third World nations would seek to take complete advantage of these situations, creating an even greater threat than that which currently exists.

For this reason the Hierarchy as well as the extraterrestrials mentioned above keep close watch over humanity's actions in this area. They are there in the event of an absolute emergency. Primarily they are there to guide humanity into the fifth, or spiritual, kingdom, in which case the dismantling of all nuclear weapons could become a fact. This, my beloved readers, is the ultimate goal.

The true potential for the mass destruction of all nuclear weaponry lies within the domain of lightworkers everywhere. The more infused each of us becomes with the Christ/Buddha energy, the more able we are to anchor it as a reality upon the physical world. In the ultimate attainment of our true spiritual natures lies the elimination of all nuclear weapons. We therefore need to work as the masters do for the upliftment of humanity and for the manifestation of the kingdom of God. Then and only then will we joyfully be able to dismantle finally nuclear and all other weaponry and remove these instruments of destruction from the face of the Earth.

China: Most Favored-Nation Status

I asked the Hierarchy what its point of view was regarding giving China the most-favored nation (MFN) status in the United States trade agreement. This particular issue seemed to be overflowing with pros and cons. From one extremely important point of view, giving them this status seemed very wrong, based on some of their barbaric and horrific practices of human rights abuse. When looked at from this perspective it seems absolutely wrong to be sanctioning a nation that conducts itself in such a severely totalitarian manner.

On the other hand, there is truth in the statement that the only way you can change something is from within. If we wish to help enlighten the government of China to any degree whatsoever, the stronger a bond between our government and theirs, the more possible this becomes.

What is interesting is that the Hierarchy supports both of these points of view. They tell me that there is great validity in not supporting a nation that is acting so out of sync with spiritual principles. They go on to say, however, that the more involved we become with China, the greater the potential to influence her for the better. They tell me that the timing of this could have been a bit better, but that in weighing both options we made the right choice in giving the MFN status.

By giving China our friendship and support we have brought her closer to America and the basic value systems by which our government functions. This provides an opportunity for change within her system. If we kept China alienated, there would be no possibility whatsoever to influence her.

The Hierarchy does tell me to bear in mind that this is a monumental task and one that will not take place over night. Every government is allowed to govern as it sees fit, and there is nothing that America can overtly do to interfere with China's governing processes. It is hoped, however, that by giving China the MFN status and maintaining friendly relations, some of America's better precepts will take hold within the hearts and minds of China's governing forces.

The Hierarchy is most emphatic that the barbaric, brutal and inhumane practices conducted within China must stop. The ascended masters do not wish us to misinterpret their support of giving China the MFN status to mean that they condone what is going on there. Their primary reason for supporting the MFN status is that they hope that in time, the darkness of what China is doing will be revealed in the light of America's more humanitarian conduct and thus change will be brought about.

Cloning/Genetic Engineering

The masters tell me that humanity must be very careful in developing the cloning process, as there is much potential danger in it. There is also much potential good; for example, the cloning of limbs to replace those that are severely diseased or lost in accidents. In regard to cloning, the balance is a very delicate one, as humanity has freedom of choice whether to use it for good or for ill.

Just as certain negative extraterrestrials use cloning to create drones to carry out specific functions, it is also possible that humans could use clones to create their own drones of sorts. One of the most negative uses of cloning would be to do this for the purpose of manufacturing soulless killers programmed to fight and destroy. These clones could be used either in the warring of nations or in the private wars within nations. In either case, the prospect is quite a frightening one and definitely not aligned with the Hierarchy's intent.

Cloning for the purposes of healing is another matter entirely. Just imagine the horrific suffering that would cease if people who had lost their arms, legs or even other parts of the body were able to have a replica cloned for them. Certain extraterrestrials are already doing this procedure.

The Hierarchy has indicated to me that the secret government has already made major advances in this area that would stun anyone who knew. They would not tell me precisely what these advances are, but they did indicate that there are dark forces behind a lot of what is currently going on. They tell me that this is an area of science that most of humanity relegates to the realm of science fiction, and that doing so is a big mistake. When the time comes that cloning is made a public issue, we should all pay very close attention to what is and is not being said.

Cloning is a wonderful tool for healing as well as one of the most vile tools for manipulation and control. As long as the government is functioning via the third dimension and the negative ego is the controlling factor of nations, we must be very careful about what we consent to.

As soon as the reality of cloning is brought forth into public awareness, the call will be sounded for initiates everywhere to become involved in this science in order to help it maintain its integrity. The potential dangers are quite severe.

If this little section has piqued the interest of those of you who feel drawn to this area, then it will have served its purpose. This emerging science is in definite need of the Hierarchy's guidance through the disciples, initiates and embodied masters who are working within the world. If this resonates at all within you, stay open to the fact that this science might manifest as a reality that needs your input sooner than you think. Many of you might have seen the movie *Multiplicity* with Michael Keaton. This demonstrates that this seeming science fiction concept has in truth now entered mainstream consciousness.

CIA: Drug Sales to Finance Nicaraguan Rebels

I asked the masters whether or not the CIA did indeed sell drugs in Watts in order to finance Nicaraguan rebels, and their answer was a simple and direct yes. They said that this was most important to bring to public attention, as this was not an isolated incident by any means.

Both the FBI and the CIA are supposed to function within very strict and rigid purviews, but these are generally ignored. The fact that this one situation was brought to light on the television news shows and in hearings in Watts is at least a beginning in mass awareness of activities that go on behind the scenes. This is equally true for both the public government agencies and the secret government.

These institutions were set up to protect us. They should be run honestly, aboveboard and with integrity. This is certainly not the case, as the above example demonstrates. The masters tell me that there are a legion of things we do not know about the government, FBI and CIA. Their guidance on most of the matters that I present to them remains consistent. Pay attention to what can be known. Work daily on maintaining an ever greater connection to your own God-self and take action in the social areas to which you feel most drawn. Maintain Christ/Buddha consciousness at all times and follow the advice of beloved Jesus to be "wise as the serpent and gentle as the dove."

Social Commentary on the Word "Christmas"

Everyone pronounces the word "Christmas," *Chris-mas*. I got to thinking one day that it should truly be pronounced *Christ-mass*. In my humble opinion humanity has somehow misinterpreted the proper pronunciation of this word and in a sense, its true meaning. Isn't this exactly what the masses of humanity have done in regard to the holiday itself in making it more about presents and material concerns than about giving and truly being of the Christ consciousness? The pronunciation of the word is the perfect symbol for the misinterpretation of the true meaning of Christmas itself.

Wearing Furs

As so much discussion has been focused upon the issue of wearing animal furs, I decided to ask the Hierarchy for its point of view. The masters told me that at an earlier time when humanity was functioning at a more primitive level and with less access to various cottons, clothes and shopping malls, the using of animal skins for warmth and clothing was quite appropriate. Now, however, humanity equates the owning and wearing of animal fur as a symbol of wealth and status. The Hierarchy obviously does not approve of this. It should be noted and never forgotten that despite the fact that we are living at the end of the twentieth century, we must honor those existing cultures that still live at the above-mentioned primitive level. Bear in mind that this section deals with the large number of cultures living in the modern world; however, we must keep in mind that this planet is evolving at various levels of development.

The ways in which animals are trapped and then slaughtered for these purposes are quite barbaric. Both the killing of the animal and the status of owning furs in today's modern world bears no resemblance to the way, for example, the Native American would use animal skins. In these instances, the animal that was killed was blessed. The skins were then worn to provide necessary clothing. The meat of the animal was consumed with a spirit of thanksgiving. All was done in unison and harmony with the Earth.

In our modern world we have ample means to clothe ourselves without using animal fur. Our status should not ever be measured by material things, but by our inner progress upon the path of God realization. We must learn to look upon the animals that we share this Earth with as our younger brothers. Adorning our bodies with their fur is not the way to do this!

One thing must be made clear, however, and that is that we must not participate in some of the cruel tactics used against those who own and wear furs. We can actively seek to educate them into a greater understanding, but we must definitely not seek to intimidate them by pouring red paint on them or by using any other form of coercion. In this case two wrongs simply don't make a right, as the saying goes.

The planet is moving toward greater and greater awareness and the love and respect of the animal kingdom is part of this awareness. It is up to each of us to live to our highest standards and to educate by example. As the hearts of humans open ever wider, so will their actions be ever more reflective of hearts that hold all of creation within their keeping.

Nuclear-Waste Disposal

When we look at the disposing of nuclear waste, we must realize that we are dealing with the proper containment of one of the deadliest elements of all times. The fact that groups of individuals have been willing to look the other way for a price and dispose of this radioactive metallic chemical in a cavalier manner bespeaks of a consciousness that has utterly separated itself from the Earth on which we live.

The first and ultimate rule that must be adhered to when dealing with disposal of plutonium and other nuclear byproducts is caution of the highest order. We are discussing the fate of the living, breathing, sentient Earth here as well as that of humanity and all life that dwells hereon. As we are dealing with elements that in their pure form came from within the Earth, they should ideally be returned back to the Earth. It must be remembered, however, that even when placed within the depths of the Earth, there are those who dwell within the hollow Earth to be considered. Therefore, the ideal would be to consult with high-quality psychics and spiritual telepaths to learn the best places to bury this waste product.

The dire problem of how best to do this arises because humankind has tampered with the natural flow of the elements and created such hazardous and toxic waste that there is no easy and simple solution. The best and highest standards must be adhered to in the continued development of more secure containers within which to place this waste. What can be recycled should be recycled within the nuclear plants now in existence. This would also require the utmost care.

The ideal is for those in the proper fields to work equally if not harder on developing alternative sources of power—for example, Nikola Tesla's discoveries and solar power. The goal is to work in harmony with our planet rather than disharmony. Only by a full understanding and use of alternative sources of power will the problem of toxic waste be eliminated. Until that day is reached, however, the strictest rules, laws and precautions must be taken so that this most deadly waste will remain forever hermetically sealed and placed as far out of harm's way as is humanly possible.

The National Debt

The national debt of the United States, as of the Clinton administration, is $5 trillion. We, the taxpayers of America, are paying off this debt. To whom are we paying it?

The central banking system of the United States is not governed or operated by the federal government. The Federal Reserve System is owned and operated by thirteen banking families. The idea for the current Federal Reserve System was created and brought to fruition at a secret meeting in Jekyll Island off the coast of Georgia in 1910. The seven financiers who attended this meeting were representatives of the Rockefellers, J.P. Morgan and the Rothchilds and Warburgs of Europe. The name of Baron Nathan Meyer Rothchild is almost synonymous with the Bank of England. The

Federal Reserve Act of 1913 created the Federal Reserve System, which consists of the Board of Governors, twelve privately owned and operated Federal Reserve banks, the Federal Open Market Committee and the Federal Advisory Council. The United States is divided into twelve districts, which are controlled by the twelve Federal Reserve banks. All national banks are required to become members of the Federal Reserve System.

The Federal Reserve System has virtually locked the United States of America into perpetual debt. We, the taxpayers, are paying back the interest on the debt, which is in the hundreds of billions of dollars and growing every year. This interest on the national debt is consuming well over 50 percent of all the revenues collected from our income taxes without even touching the principal. The bottom line is that as long as the Federal Reserve System is owned, operated and controlled by private families, the national debt will never be paid off. The present system is similar to a cartel that is officially protected by the federal government.

Conclusion

As we are in the process of moving through the third and fourth dimensions and into the fifth, it is a most appropriate time to take an in-depth look at our world's institutions and earthly civilization. This time period also coincides with the movement out of the age of Pisces and into Aquarius. The sixth ray that has governed our planet for two thousand years is now being replaced by the seventh ray, and a whole new structure is being called into manifestation.

In order to help effect the changes that must take place as we move from one era into the next, it is essential to take an in-depth look at our planet as a whole. As we examine the existing institutions as well as some of the vital issues of our time, we have the opportunity to see what is good about them as well as what is out of alignment and in need of healing. This has been the purpose of this chapter.

The ability to do the necessary work of healing and restructuring lies within the domain of lightworkers everywhere. If I were to quickly summarize the need of the hour, it is to bring light, love, integrity and the ability to perceive and act out of the Christ/Buddha mind. That is why it is up to all of us who abide in the light to bring forth that light into whatever area we are most drawn.

Each of us has our own unique ascension mission and divine puzzle piece. Some of us are physical/etheric healers and others are writers. Some are artists and some function within the business world. The work you are best suited for will most likely be within the specific arena that you are already functioning in.

Yet we must never forget that we are all a part of the world and are either a cause or an effect of the world's various modalities. For example, political decisions have an influence upon all of our lives. Although it is obviously not all of our callings to participate within the political arena itself, we are all capable of voting. Through our vote and through our prayers we can help to elect into public office those people who most resonate with hierarchical intent.

The main point is that it is time for lightworkers everywhere to begin anchoring that light into the Earth and within the institutions and civilizations of the Earth. The frequencies of the spiritual realms are not meant to remain isolated in those realms. The time for these frequencies to be fully anchored and activated upon the physical is now. This is something that we must do, my beloved readers, as it requires the actions of those of us who have contacted and activated this light and love within ourselves to bring it forth into manifestation within the world.

This chapter and indeed this book have been written with this intent. As we become more and more aware of the status of the world's governmental institutions and civilizations, so we become equally aware of where we might bring our particular brand of service to them.

These are most complex issues, yet the simple solution is to act out of your higher self and monad at all times. Beloved Saint Francis actually hit the nail on the head when he said, "Lord, make me an instrument of Thy peace." This is something that we are all being called to do in all walks of life.

The schism between the spiritual and the earthly must cease. In truth it is only an illusion, a product of faulty thinking. The statements "God is one" and "God is all and that I Am" are statements of fact. If God is everything and everyone, then does it not logically follow that it is God manifesting through all institutions and civilizations and every aspect of life? As this is so, is it not then up to those of us who are more awake to our own God-selves to help awaken the less evolved aspects of ourselves in order to bring about a world reflective of the highest potentiality?

The first step in this process is awareness. The second step is in the willingness of each of us to participate in the areas that we most resonate with. The third step will be when we all do this as a group body of lightworkers, each bringing our diverse gifts and insights into play. When this is done, Earth life will be functioning at a fifth-dimensional frequency and light will be infused into all facets of existence.

All problems that have been revealed within our institutions and civilizations have been brought to light only so that they can be healed all the more quickly. We cannot begin the healing process if we allow ourselves to remain unaware of the very problems that need healing. For example, if you have a toothache that is causing pain in one side of your face, then you go to the dentist so that you can identify which tooth is causing the problem and see what is wrong with that tooth. Only then is the dentist able to prescribe and implement the necessary treatment.

It is not news that much of our societal structure is hurting. The reason I write so specifically about various institutions is not unlike that of the dentist who seeks to isolate the problem so it can be treated properly. The major difference lies in the fact that the subjects addressed herein cover a large area and require the help of many hands. These hands, dear readers, belong to *all* lightworkers everywhere who have access to the benevolent healing energies of God and their own creative minds and likewise have the will to bring these energies forth into manifestation.

The power to change things and to establish the kingdom of God upon Earth is ours! There is an old adage that says, "God helps those who help themselves." As I conclude this chapter, the masters have asked me to rephrase this quote to say, "God helps those who help the *world*." All it takes to shift things are a lot of good people doing their own puzzle piece in the divine plan. In serving God we cannot help but serve self. In serving self, we cannot help but serve the world. In serving the world, we cannot help but serve God and self. It is all one circle, and we are each at the center of it with the ability to make monumental changes by simply doing our part. Let us each look fearlessly at the issues at hand and then do what is appropriate for us individually to help uplift the planet as a whole.

The last point I would like to make is that it is not God's or the inner-plane ascended masters' job to change the world. It is our job as the externalized masters, initiates, disciples and new group of world-servers to do this with God and the inner-plane masters' guidance. The masters are there to work with us as we call upon their love, energy, direction and higher vision, but the actual third-dimensional work and transformation is ours to do.

4

The Ascended Masters'
Perspective on Leadership

I dedicated one of my meditations to conversing with the ascended masters on the subject of leadership, and the following information is the product of this conversation. The masters began by saying that leadership is, in essence, *empowerment*. Melchizedek, Lord Maitreya and Djwhal Khul went on to say that it is the turning of your personal energy, talents and strengths over to hierarchical service and acting in accordance with the divine plan to establish a base within your own community or sector of the world or globe to distribute the energies of light.

They also said leadership is for the purpose of focusing universal values, laws and understanding and bringing each individual into his/her full empowerment as a world server and in service to the universe and God.

They continued by saying that leadership is the ability to bring in one's own lessons in a compassionate way to help others move forward. It is also the ability to connect with others and help them understand what they are really going through. Moreover, true leadership is having compassion from a dispassionate view and being able to stand in this place because you know that you have walked this road. True leadership is to remember that you have done this but not dwelling on any past experience. Just hold this energy and know that you can reach out to someone and understand. The key, they said, is having this understanding and compassion.

Melchizedek, Lord Maitreya and Djwhal Khul remarked on the importance of being an example as a world server and a spiritual self-leader, but not imposing your own personal model as the model for others to follow. Rather, they suggested, act as a model of possibility, allowing each person's style to come under the jurisdiction of his/her own being so that it is not a religion or guru that is espoused.

One example that the masters offered is vegetarianism, a lifestyle that people often turn into a religion. The ideal in leadership is where there are no personal morals imposed on other people. The masters went on to say that there is so much lost in leadership when the leader puts him/herself so far above the others that he loses the connection to the people he is leading. You cannot lead well if you do not understand who you are leading. The danger is that you separate to the point of losing this contact. This can happen not necessarily purposefully, but simply through the pressures of leadership.

They continued by saying that much of leadership is self-leadership. It is really about planting seeds and providing inspiration. The leader is still responsible for making certain decisions that affect the group; however, the ideal leader encourages everyone to come into their full power. The need here is to keep this connection and balance.

The Pressures of Leadership

The masters began this discussion by saying that as leaders we are constantly in a state of perfecting our own being. We have been given the spiritual job of externalizing the inner-plane Spiritual Hierarchy. In the past we thought that in this ascension process we were going to immediately disappear into the light or that the inner-plane ascended masters were going to materialize out of the etheric to solve Earth's problems. In the larger context the fact is that neither of these alternatives is going to happen immediately. The fact is that the transformation of this planet is up to normal, average people like me and all of you who are reading this book. We are the ones materializing the hierarchical plan on Earth. Therefore, we are in a constant state of perfection, improvement and change.

People who cannot work with the idea of guidance coming through their own intuition might accuse you of not liking them or not holding favor with them. People might want to hold you literally accountable and not allow for changes in inner guidance. They might feel that if you think they are not ready to do something, then you don't like them. In other words, they take things too personally. These are some of the pressures of leadership.

The masters went on to speak of the incredible need to remain unattached. There is also the issue of being able to see and sense certain things going on in the fields of one's fellow disciples and initiates that these people are not ready to discuss or handle. Therefore, there is the constant need to discern what can or can't be given at any one time and what needs to be put on hold. These are further pressures.

The masters continued their discussion by saying that there is undue adulation given to many leaders, which places a danger on the leader's ego if he/she is not clear on this lesson. The secondary lesson is that no one can live up to this sort of false expectation in the disciple's eyes, so a fall is inevitable.

A corollary of this, the masters said, is the one where the leader is expected to be perfect. This is of course an impossibility. The disciples project their spiritual fantasies of what they want a spiritual teacher and leader to be. It is essential for true spiritual leaders to break this illusion and admit their mistakes, which then allows the team members to make mistakes also. A true leader constantly gives power back to others and demonstrates that he/she is equal to them.

Often leaders try to make themselves special, which is a manifestation of the negative ego. All are special in God's eyes. Sai Baba allows his physical body to age and does normal human things around his ashram so people can relate to him. He does this as a service to humanity, for as a universal avatar he has the power to be completely unlike the masses of humanity if he wants to. This is the grace of Sai Baba.

Views on the Hierarchy

Djwhal Khul, Lord Maitreya and Melchizedek continued this discussion by again speaking of the need to blend the idea of having one leader who uses consensus to reach decisions. They went on to say that there is most definitely a hierarchy of leaders. The difference between the Spiritual Hierarchy and earthly hierarchies is that in the Spiritual Hierarchy even though there is a leader, all are seen as equals. Consensus is always achieved at the end even though there might be differences of opinion among the various masters in the beginning. Each person is seen as an extremely valued part.

The divine plan cannot work without each person fulfilling his/her puzzle piece and gift. Each person's place in this hierarchical puzzle is earned by her overall knowledge, good deeds, leadership abilities, light quotient, initiation level and special gifts. Each person is automatically placed by the powers that be in the exact perfect service place for his/her stage of evolution. No person can fill all blanks in the puzzle. God is infinite, and each soul has been built to fulfill certain functions in God's infinite divine plan. God pulls, in a sense, all the functions of the big plan through us, like pouring liquid through a sieve.

According to the masters, the key essential ideals are self-responsibility, self-accountability and integrity. No one master is the expert in all things. They said that when a question is asked of one master and another knows more about that subject, the more knowledgeable master is allowed to respond. This is another aspect of transcending negative ego.

One way of understanding this is through one's ray structure. Djwhal Khul, for example, is a second-ray monad and soul. If someone asks a first-ray question about politics or a fifth-ray question about science, Djwhal might ask El Morya or Hilarion for help in answering it.

God has built us to have gifts in certain areas through the ray structure. However, it far transcends even the ray structure. I, for example, was built to write, teach and counsel. This is because of my second-ray monad and second-ray soul and how I have been built. If you put me in front of an easel with paints and brush, I couldn't even create an image of a stick figure very well. I marvel at fourth-ray people who are gifted in the arts and those who are good at mechanical things, areas in which I am completely ignorant.

The curious thing is I am the ultimate spiritual and psychological mechanic, but my mechanical abilities do not extend to physical objects. I simply accept this about myself and focus my energies on the puzzle piece God has given me. For me, leading and running an inner-plane ashram is what God built me to do. This is where I am totally in my element.

Get in touch with what your ray structure is and meditate on how God built you and what you are supposed to do. Some are meant to be healers, channels, counselors, psychics, gardeners, comedians, politicians, lawyers, scientists, ministers, teachers, the list is endless. God needs agents and workers in all aspects of society, and one is no better than another.

The most important concept is, never try to live another person's puzzle piece. The fastest way to God realization and ascension realization is to live out perfectly your own puzzle piece even if your ego tells you it is not as glamorous as others. This stems from the ego's need to compare rather than be quiet and listen to the inner guidance of the still, small voice within, also known as the Holy Spirit.

One other very important understanding about the ascended masters is that they do not—I repeat, *do not*—have all knowledge. Do not project this upon them. When it comes to my personal life, at times I have received guidance that I didn't agree with. I have always been one to trust my own inner guidance more than an inner or externalized master. I listen to the advice, but then I make my own decisions. This, I feel, has been one of the real keys to my personal success. From a relatively young age I have not given my power to the masters, and I think it is why I feel a strong sense of equality with them now, as well as respect. It is also why they respect me and why I have been given leadership positions. I trust myself more than I trust any external being.

The masters are not insulted by this, for you must understand that such ones as Djwhal Khul, Jesus, Saint Germain, Kuthumi and El Morya are only one inch up a ten-inch ruler of their own cosmic evolution. We have projected upon them an all-knowingness that they really don't have. They are in truth much wiser than we are, but not omniscient as God is omniscient, omnipresent and omnipotent.

The key lesson is trust yourself. The masters have told me that they don't want to make a lot of these personal life decisions. These are meant to be made ourselves. I am extremely circumspect and discerning about what I do and don't ask the masters. I rarely ask them questions about my personal life. To be honest, a great deal of the time I really don't want their advice, and this is good. I like to ask them questions for my books and for help in certain areas and/or activations of all kinds. On rare occasions I will ask about a personal matter. Most of the time my own inner guidance from my mighty I Am Presence and/or the Holy Spirit automatically tells me everything I need to know. I also use my dreams in this manner.

There is almost a kind of etiquette in talking with the masters, taking advantage of their help but not overusing or abusing the privilege and/or wasting their time on trivia. I don't want to make people afraid to approach them, for they want to be approached. I am saying that one must stay balanced in relationship to them.

On the other side of the coin I have seen certain channels who have this wonderful ability to communicate but who never ask questions. They know how to channel but do not know how to ask questions, so the potential for the channel is greatly diminished. This can be helped by having friends who ask the questions, which will serve the group and humanity.

Every person on this planet has a job that they have contracted on the inner plane. Some serve in a clear leadership role; others will serve in subsidiary leadership roles. Some missions are to serve in a support role, although all are leaders and equals. Melchizedek said that often everyone wants to be the chief and no one wants to be the Indians. This is a manifestation of the ego and of not being in tune with what one's true mission is at any given moment. Even major leaders must learn to be neutral and take the backstage at times. If they can't do this, or won't, it means the negative ego has contaminated their leadership mission.

Every leader is also a supporter on a higher level. Everyone is really a leader and supporter simultaneously between dimensions and on Earth herself. The biggest lesson of this entire book is not letting the negative ego become connected to your leadership actualization.

Djwhal Khul emphasized quite emphatically that even though he is the figurehead of the synthesis ashram on the fifth-dimensional level, the senior initiates have equal knowledge. He said he has been given the leadership role in the ashram for karmic reasons. Djwhal said he is dependent upon the whole organization. Often, he said, when disciples ask for him on Earth prior to taking the fourth initiation, it is the group body of the ashram that responds, not necessarily him personally. In other words, a third-degree initiate might be communicating with a senior initiate of the second-ray ashram. This senior initiate might be just as wise as Djwhal Khul though not the leader of the ashram.

Remember, in the ashram there is no separation between the individual and group body. The group body is an extension of Djwhal Khul and he uses it as such. Even for higher initiates there might be an occasional time when he or other masters are called forth and they do not come for an appointment because some major crisis is going on in the world. When I realized this, it actually made this whole thing more believable. The other possibility is that he would send a high-level initiate in his place. What I have mentioned here does not apply only to Djwhal Khul but to all the masters.

A person at a lower level of initiation might call Saint Germain or Sananda, and in response a high-level initiate from these masters' ashrams might serve in this capacity. This is a part of the way the high-level initiate helps out. The leader individually does not have to do everything just because he/she is the leader. Djwhal Khul emphasized here that the initiates he sometimes sends in place of himself are just as qualified and they function as his voice—kind of like soul extensions function as the voice of the oversoul and as the oversouls function as the voice of the monad, or mighty I Am Presence.

Some members of the ashram might be more developed in some areas or have specialized gifts. Leadership itself is a specialized gift that not all share and not all are built to do in terms of running an ashram. The ideal leader takes advantage of all gifts in the group body and sees the body as just the extension of self. The leader will utilize the gifts as his/her own to serve humanity in terms of leadership direction.

One must realize that at this level there is a core group of high-level initiates in the inner-plane ashrams of all ascended masters. As one moves out from the center of the ring, so to speak, the varying degrees of initiation are seen in the disciples. In the core group, however, which ultimately could go as high as forty in the second-ray ashram, a great many of these individuals are ascended. It is here that we can see the sense of equality that comes into play even though one has been given leadership.

Melchizedek said that it has nothing to do with more or less, but with how we are built, or karma, and what we choose as our path of service. The second key principle in this book (after staying clear of the negative ego) is that leadership is the next step after ascension. However, ideally that will come even before ascension is achieved.

Melchizedek said that some paths are to stand out in front and other paths are to support. We each must get in touch with the form of leadership that God would have us fulfill. Melchizedek and Djwhal said that one is not more gifted than another. It is just that there are different types of leadership to fulfill.

I asked Djwhal Khul if he was the one who makes the final decision on all things pertaining to the work of the ashram. He answered by saying, both yes and no, which gets back to this leadership-integrated-with-consensus concept. He said that, yes, his energy signature or stamp goes on all major decisions, but it is through telepathic rapport with the core ashram that group consciousness and consensus is achieved. This telepathic unity among the core ashramic staff is also aided by a type of holographic computer circuit that connects all members.

The core staff would be the forty of whom I spoke earlier, but it might get much larger in time. Djwhal said that there were about 400 individuals on the outer periphery of this group who are also contained within the ashram. This number might also get much larger as time moves on with the renewed interest in this work and during this most amazing period in Earth's history.

Djwhal Khul emphasized again that there definitely are disagreements among masters in his ashram, in the other ashrams and between the seven ashrams. However, in the end, on the fifth-, sixth- and seventh-dimensional levels and up, there is always (and I mean *always*) total consensus at the end of the council meetings.

I think we can see that the Earth and humanity have a long way to go to reach this level of functioning. This is because people are too attached to their egos and are seeing through limited lenses and not from true ascended-master consciousness. In order to keep a clear perspective, the masters of the Planetary Hierarchy also have such masters as Helios and Vesta, the Lord of Sirius, Melchior, Lord Melchizedek, Metatron, Archangel Michael, Sanat Kumara and Lord Buddha to help bring in solar, galactic and universal perspectives if needed.

I was joking around with Melchizedek one day and told him he was like E.F. Hutton. Remember the investment company commercials that used to be on television that said, "When E.F. Hutton talks, people listen"? I told Melchizedek he was the E.F. Hutton of the spiritual world, and we all had a good laugh.

Djwhal Khul went on to say that he was groomed to hold a certain point of leadership and to use his name as a trigger to evoke energy. He went on to say that I have been trained in a similar fashion. I have always known that my name is a trigger. This is not my original name, but the name given to me by spirit at the age of twenty-seven for the full realization of my mission. I always knew that my spiritual name was Joshua, and David was suggested for the full intonational and vibrational completion. When I changed my name I always knew that this was a name that would take time to fully realize, kind of like a larger set of clothes that one has not yet grown into. Over time I have seen the wisdom of this guidance and the name has been almost a mantra.

When Djwhal mentioned the idea of one's name being a trigger for others, I felt the truth in this. It is very important to find a name that totally, 100 percent fits your full monadic and mighty I Am Presence being. Those of you who have not done this might consider making this change, even if it is just with your closest friends. I myself went through the whole legal process.

Having the proper name is also akin to living in the proper geographic location. There is a perfect name that fits each person just as there is a city, state and country that perfectly fits each person. Even though I have not yet moved, I am very drawn to Arizona and the Southwest. This seems to be a power spot for me in terms of being energized and empowered by a city. I also happen to like warm weather, which is why I currently live in the San Fernando Valley and Sherman Oaks in the Los Angeles County area. The weather here is a lot like Arizona. Where you live is another aspect of your leadership mission.

Djwhal Khul continued his discussion by saying that his function as the leader of the synthesis ashram on the inner plane should be considered as different from being a guru. Ashrams in India are often associated with a guru, and he wants to make it clear to the readers of this material that this is not the case with him and indeed with all the inner-plane ashrams.

One other point I would like to make clear has to do with a kind of separation often experienced by high-level initiates on Earth with the masters. A friend who helps with the typing of my books told me a sweet story that relates to this. She was asking for guidance from Ashtar about a potential project involving Commander Ashtar and Lady Athena. She asked him, "What would you like me to do about this?" The reply was, "It is no longer appropriate to ask, 'What do you want me to do about this?' but rather, 'What should *we* do about this?'"

There is no longer a separation between the ascended masters on the inner plane and the ascended beings and high-level initiates on this plane. We are all on the same team. Their challenges are our challenges and our challenges are their challenges. It is now time for this veil of separation between the fourth and fifth kingdoms, the human and spiritual, to be lifted. We are them and they are us. There is no difference. All are one. As Djwhal Khul has often said, "Ponder on this."

At one point I asked the masters about the process of moving into leadership. There are many lightworkers who are moving into advanced stages of initiation but who have not yet fully moved into leadership. I asked Djwhal Khul, Lord Maitreya and Melchizedek what this next step involved for lightworkers.

They said it is through commitment and turning your life over to God and the ascended masters. They said it is a process of putting out to God and the God force: "Here I am. I am willing to serve. I am willing to do whatever is necessary. I hereby make my full commitment to service. I hereby institute the contracts I made before I came into incarnation. I hereby now contract with the masters to take my appropriate leadership position and world-service position." The masters and the God force, I guarantee you, will take you at your word. Ask that this request be written into the soul and the akashic records.

Be aware, however, that once this commitment is made, there is no turning back. This is good, for you don't want to go back. You want to move forward decisively and with full power. Melchizedek went on to say that commitment is the real key. He said that he/she who hesitates is lost. If there is any vacillation, it just won't happen. Leadership is not for the meek at heart. It carries with it enormous responsibility, and it is a movement to the front lines, so to speak. The universe will take you at your word.

If you are ready, then make the invocation and put on your seat belt, for your life is going to accelerate and change radically. The speed at which you move into leadership, realize your ascension and move into planetary world service is all up to your commitment. True inner peace will come only when your commitment is at full throttle. It is time for each and every one of us to take our full place in the grand scheme of things.

It is also important to understand that the form that leadership will take will be different for every person. Not everyone is meant to run an ashram. Not everyone is meant to lecture or channel for 1000 people. God did not build everyone in the same way. Some people's leadership might come through working with individuals, some through writing, some through art and others through teaching children. One is not better than another.

The key lesson here is not to have a preconceived picture of what leadership looks like. What is clear is that God and the masters will guide you if you invoke the form of leadership that it is your destiny to fulfill. It also might evolve and change as you develop and live your full commitment. Do not try and live out other people's leadership puzzle piece. If you try this it will bring nothing but disaster, for as Shakespeare said, "Above all else, to thine own self be true." Stay in tune with your own Tao. This has to do with clearing the negative-ego remnants of competition, envy, jealousy, sibling rivalry, competition, false pride and glamour.

From a personal point of view, leadership on the positive side promotes a lot of accolades and a certain amount of fame. On the negative side it is an enormous responsibility and is stressful at times. The masters expect a lot from you and you are pushed into the front lines. The front lines can at times be like a spiritual war. Large-scale public leadership is not always as glamorous as some people think.

The key here is that the form of leadership you are destined to take is not really up to free choice. It is just built into us, and each of us must do what is our destiny. This is like how an acorn eventually becomes an oak tree. An acorn doesn't turn into a pine tree or a eucalyptus tree. Each human is a different kind of God seed, or starseed. The form of our leadership unfoldment is built into our unique type of seed. The degree of our leadership will be characterized by what stage our unfolding and maturing is in.

The other key point in leadership is that no matter what level of initiation you might be in, you must do your clearing work and psychological work before you will be truly ready for leadership. On some basic level you must become right with self and right with God first. There are plenty of people who move into leadership before achieving this, and they are poor, ineffective leaders who are creating karma. They often misuse their power and authority. If you want to lead people, you must first be self-responsible and self-accountable. All true leaders have an absence of the angry-victim archetype and are well-balanced and integrated in all the archetypes.

Often people have what might be called a strong king or queen archetype. Often people are born into a king or queen lineage with parents holding these positions. The Kennedy family would be a good example. My father is a well-known and respected psychologist, teacher and author. Djwhal Khul told me that I chose to be born into a king line as part of my training in preparation for the leadership responsibilities I now hold.

Djwhal Khul went on to say that leadership is not only connected to the first ray, but in truth is the full integration and unity of all the rays. Timing is also another factor. Using the example of the acorn or seed again here, a seed sprouts in its proper season. It also blooms in its proper season. This is why we must not have any fixed pictures as to how leadership is going to look at any given stage of development. Leave this to God and the masters. Krishna speaks of this in the *Bhagavad-Gita* when he teaches his students not to concern themselves with the fruits of service but just to serve and let God take care of the rest.

There also seems to be steps and stages in leadership. For me personally, spiritual leadership began by doing individual counseling (a counselor or psychologist definitely takes a leadership role in the session). Then it moved to couples counseling, then families, then groups, then smaller lectures, then classes, then larger lectures, then seminars and workshops, then larger seminars and workshops. This has culminated in my hosting large-scale events with from 350 to 1200 people, and it is still growing.

I would not have been ready for this at an earlier stage of my evolution. This gets back to the timing and unfolding process of leadership. It would seem that one is tested at each stage to make sure he/she is solid and stabilized before the next step is taken. It almost seems to be something that is set up by the universe, no matter how hard one tries to accelerate the manifestation. This is probably good, for it allows for a certain maturation process to occur at each level.

The key here is not to be attached to the form of leadership you are given. Live whatever form you are involved with perfectly and more will be given. It doesn't matter if you are helping just one person or 10,000 people. The numbers game is just another ego distraction. All that matters is that you are demonstrating God every moment of your life wherever God, your mighty I Am Presence, the Holy Spirit and the ascended masters place you.

Another aspect of leadership that Melchizedek and Djwhal Khul spoke of is the need to release all of your fears. It is the ability to stand and not be afraid. This is also why the core-fear removal program is so important to lightworkers (see *Beyond Ascension*). It is also why any and all work you do on clearing the negative ego is so important.

Each step we all take in climbing up another spiritual stair, so to speak, we release a little more fear. It will give us the ability to stand in a position of public attention where people look at you and you don't feel afraid or self-conscious.

One can say, then, that leadership is not only about empowerment and commitment, but also about transcending negative-ego consciousness, for negative ego is essentially fear. To really be prepared to take your full leadership realization, negative ego and fear must be transcended. Fear can totally repress your true gifts and qualities.

Once you start releasing fear, you cannot release, say, one-third and then stop. It is like taking a cap off a radiator. Once the lid is off, it becomes an all-or-nothing proposition.

Stages of Leadership

I asked Djwhal Khul, Lord Maitreya and Melchizedek if there were stages of leadership. Djwhal responded by saying that there were, and that they tied into the understanding of first being a disciple, then an initiate, then a kindergarten ascended master and eventually a fully realized ascended master. If we were to continue this into the cosmic realm, we would begin as kindergarten cosmic masters first at the solar level, then galactic, then universal, then multiuniversal and eventually cosmic ascended masters.

Djwhal also said that the stages of leadership on the planetary level could be looked at in terms of the seven levels of initiation, each initiation being a higher stage of leadership. Djwhal Khul said the capability of leadership is really shown at the soul merge, or third initiation. This understanding of the stages of leadership becomes a little more complex when you add to it that many souls come in at a higher level of initiation. The master Jesus came in at the third initiation 2000 years ago, which was an extremely high level at that time.

At this time in history only souls at the third initiation or above are even allowed to come in because of the spiritual evolution of this planet. Now, just because a soul comes in at the third, he/she still has to review or process the previous stages again in terms of gaining mastery over the physical, astral and mental bodies. Everyone who attains leadership must go through the initiations. I will add here that some individuals will move into leadership at a lower stage of initiation than others. In other words, leadership is more than just initiation level. This is part of the definition; however, leadership is also a psychological quality that can be worked on and developed in conjunction with your initiation development.

Djwhal Khul also added that the new-age children who are coming in now are so advanced that they will not forget as much as children who incarnated in the past. This is why proper, well-rounded spiritual and traditional education is more important than ever.

I then asked the masters if leadership was a learned skill, curious to know their response. Djwhal Khul and Melchizedek responded by saying that it was both inborn and learned, which made sense. Djwhal said that leadership also has a lot to do with one's work on other dimensions, lives on other planes and past lives on this plane. They also went on to say that it is also how one is actually built by God. Djwhal said that leadership can even be affected by one's eleven other soul extensions from the oversoul. This is because as one accelerates on his/her spiritual path and begins to become an oversoul or leader for his other soul extensions, the inner-plane soul extensions begin supporting and helping the soul extension (which is probably you who are reading this book) to ascend for the entire group. This added support from one's eleven other soul extensions from the oversoul adds to that individual's leadership power and capabilities.

Djwhal continued by stating that the difference between ordinary leadership and spiritual leadership is that the latter does not use negative control and manipulation as political and social leadership utilizes so often. Djwhal said that one's ray configuration definitely does play a big part in this and that leadership does involve first-ray energy. It must be understood, however, that personal power, or the will energy of God, can definitely be developed on your own even if you don't have it in your ray structure. We are each God and can create whatever we choose. We are not victims of the stars, rays or anything else. True leaders do, however, integrate all the rays and all the signs and are very comfortable synthesizing their power and utilizing it appropriately. Djwhal Khul said, as applied to leadership, that the first and second rays are strongest, which of course include the traits of power and love/wisdom.

Djwhal went on to expound that he wanted people to have a larger understanding of leadership. The first- and second-ray leadership is the classic kind of being on stage and in front of large groups of people. Djwhal was very emphatic in stating that there were other types of leaders of different ray types. For example, a person of the third ray who carries the higher-mind intelligence and works behind the scenes can still have leadership abilities. This is seen through this person's giving of inspiration, writing, inventing something or acting in conjunction with the fifth ray in the scientific field, or in manifesting the seventh ray.

People are meant to demonstrate their leadership in many different ways and through many different puzzle pieces, so it is important not to have a fixed stereotypical image of what leadership always looks like. Djwhal said it must always have a focus of second ray, which of course is love/wisdom. All leaders share this quality. Djwhal said all spiritual leaders will have a component of the first ray; however, that will not necessarily be the biggest factor, which is good.

Djwhal also went on to say that some will have a global-leadership focus, others a state focus and still others the city and community in which they live. One is not better than another. Every kind of leadership is necessary to transform this planet. It is the desire of Melchizedek, Lord Maitreya, Djwhal Khul and all the ascended masters to have all lightworkers on this planet move into leadership now in the form they feel and intuit is right for them and most comfortable, given their individual mission, purpose and commitment.

The second-ray form of leadership, which I personally am most connected to as a second-ray soul and a second-ray monad, is that of world teacher. This is what Djwhal Khul, Lord Maitreya and Melchizedek are connected to also. These masters want to make it clear that this is only one archetypal form of leadership. Each ray has its own archetypal form.

First-ray spiritual leadership is in politics. Third ray is in economics. Fourth ray is in the arts. Fifth ray is in science. Sixth ray is in religion. Seventh ray is in business. This is a rough, generalized theme of these rays; however, one is not held to this, for there are many other factors in choosing a profession besides rays.

So one might say that there are seven great archetypal themes of leadership. It is also possible to blend the types. For example, in this book I have definitely entered the political arena in my writings and have taken on a bit of a first-ray assignment. I have also taken a very scientific approach to many subjects in my books. I am also involved with the business of running an ashram and dealing with the economic aspects of putting on such large events as the Wesak celebration and having people work for me.

Thus, I have to demonstrate leadership skills in some of these other leadership archetypes. The ideal, of course, is to be as well-rounded as possible, but without losing the clear definition of one's puzzle piece as God would have it. All lightworkers will be asked to demonstrate these different aspects of leadership, which ultimately blend into one form of leadership.

Djwhal went on to say that the ultimate leader also blends all the archetypes into the Wise One archetype. This is similar to saying that the ultimate leader integrates all the rays. It is the wise person, or Wise One archetype, who takes such an approach. The true wise leader, however, does not become overidentified with the Wise One to the point of becoming overidentified with this theme and becoming stuck in it.

In other words, the wise leader lives the integrated Wise One archetype without overidentifying with it. To overidentify with it would be to get stuck in the teacher, guru and know-it-all role, which is not good. So no one archetype should be identified with more than another. Each one should be used as appropriate in a balanced manner and then released. Your intuition will guide you as to which archetype is needed at any given moment.

Melchizedek said that the ideal leader is really more interested in guiding, helping and facilitating others to solve their own problems. There is that classic saying that you can give a person a fish to eat for dinner, or you can help the person to learn to fish. One form of help lets one feed the other for a day; the other feeds a person for a whole lifetime. I think that is what is meant here.

The Ascension Buddy System

Djwhal Khul, Lord Maitreya and Melchizedek were also very emphatic about the importance of the ascension buddy system. I spoke of this earlier in this book when I spoke about group leadership. This idea of many leaders working together in group consciousness and group focus is one of the keynotes of the new age.

This in truth is also the ultimate ideal of the United Nations, of leaders of countries joining together in a group leadership. The problem has been, of course, egos creating separation and individual focus rather than recognizing the group consciousness and potential for consensus as leaders. The United Nations will eventually be a model for the ascension buddy system on a global scale. It obviously has not realized this monadic and soul potential yet.

The masters went on to say that this ascension buddy system is the original idea of politics. The ascended masters who helped form the U.S. Constitution and the Bill of Rights envisioned the members of the Senate and House of Representatives and the president working together in an ascension buddy system and group consciousness for the highest good of all concerned. We see how this has been lost because of the contamination of ego. Everyone is out for themselves or their state or their political party or their race or the lobbyists who contribute the most money to their campaigns. There is no global consciousness or ascension buddy system. This is why we have gridlock.

As groups and families, we need to get back to this. This even relates to the breakdown of the family unit in our society. There are so many single parents—and even worse are the deadbeat fathers who don't pay child support and alimony. The masters are not always against divorce. Sometimes divorce is a very good thing. If a mutual caretaking system existed even after divorce, group consciousness would still be maintained, except that the relationship would have changed from life partners to friends.

We as lightworkers must be able to create this ascension buddy system with our closest friends in a personal sense, and in a more impersonal sense with other spiritual leaders in our community, state, country and around the globe. The masters said that the ascension buddy system is the core of spiritual leadership. We're linking buddy to buddy, supporting each other throughout the world.

In *Beyond Ascension* I spoke of this in a more personal sense of the concept, and now I am beginning to speak of it on a city, state, country and global level. Humanity has lost that thread of continuity between these levels and each other, for we have lost our connection to the inherent group-consciousness identity we all share. In my opinion, this is the single biggest blind spot of humanity at this time in Earth's history.

The leadership of our world no longer shares any kind of unified vision. Instead we have millions and millions of leadership egos all seeking to do their own thing and fulfill their own selfish needs. This applies to leaders in the spiritual movement, political leaders, presidents of all the countries of the world, business leaders, world teachers, artistic leaders, economic leaders, scientific leaders, religious leaders and any other types of leaders you can think of. Can you imagine a society where all these different types of leaders shared the same unified group consciousness focused upon God's divine plan?

In my opinion the ascension movement might be a real key to creating this unification, certainly in the spiritual field. Ascension is a concept that all spiritual teachers, schools of thought and ashrams can embrace. It is very universalistic and eclectic, and all ascended masters connect with it. If the spiritual movement is not unified, how can we possibly expect the earthly world to embrace such a unified group-consciousness principle?

Don't live in a fantasy world. The negative ego is as rampant in the New Age movement as it is in other areas. The different spiritual groups around the world are not really working together. Most leaders of their groups are very competitive, or at best do their own thing. I have personally run into this big-time in trying to put on these global, universalistic Wesak festivals. Many spiritual leaders are not able to give up center stage and truly come together in global leadership.

Just because a given spiritual leader is a great teacher or channel and is famous does not mean that he/she has any degree of control over his negative ego and personality. In my experience many leaders are very weak in this area. It is time for the spiritual leaders of this planet to now be willing to take the next step from personal leadership over their own program to global leadership, which embraces vastly different forms, ideas, ideologies and spiritual teachers into a greater and more expanded understanding of leadership.

It is time for the spiritual leadership of this planet to truly come together and work together without competition, ego, jealousy, envy or need for the center stage. It is time for each of us as spiritual leaders to cooperate, network, meditate, brainstorm and work together for the good of the divine plan and not just our individual spiritual groups. It is now time for us all to join together as ascension buddies for the good of planetary ascension, solar-system ascension, galactic ascension, universal ascension, multiuniversal ascension and ultimately, cosmic ascension. In truth there is really only one ascension and all else is illusion. In truth there is only God's ascension and we all share in this together.

Djwhal Khul went on to say that this group consciousness has to do with letting go all differences. It is a telepathic merger. He jokingly referred to the Vulcan mind meld in *Star Trek*. This merge, Djwhal said, is not just mental. It's spiritual first, then transfers down through the mental body, emotional body and eventually into the etheric body.

The ego tells us that we live in a little fence called the physical body and people must understand that this is illusion. This fence is a mental creation of the ego that stems from overidentification with material existence and does not have any reality in truth. You can just as easily identify yourself as God. Now, God has given us an ego (as opposed to a negative ego) to help us function and use this body in service of the divine plan. I bring this up only to point out here the need for integration—in other words, the ability to live in two bodies simultaneously. This is your physical body and your cosmic body, which is your group-identity body, though there are many stages and levels of spiritual bodies that make up one's ultimate cosmic body (planetary, solar, galactic and universal). It is a wonderful thing to live in two bodies simultaneously.

When needed, this group-body identity can be focused to whatever size group you are dealing with at any given moment. For example, at the

Wesak celebrations there is a great focus upon the group body of the 1200 people in attendance. At other times I am focusing on my body. At other times still, I am focusing on the body I have with all of humanity. At other times yet, I am focusing on my cosmic body with all aspects of God and God's creation. Thus there is a focus on whatever body is needed for service at any given moment. At this stage of evolution, however, we are all working with the planetary body and its subgroup bodies most of the time.

Some Eastern masters have been so identified with the group body that they could not take care of the physical body. In my opinion, this is not necessarily good and not an integrated example to set. The devotees of some of these masters had to take care of the master's body. This might be right for some unique master, but it is not the ideal that almost everyone else on the planet is meant to demonstrate. The ideal is to live in both bodies simultaneously, like a dance. Once the group-body concept is firmly implanted and integrated in your four-body system, it is not anything you really have to think about. It becomes automatic to retain both simultaneously. It becomes integrated and has become a habit to identify with both.

Djwhal also pointed out the importance of developing the keen intuition to know when to act out of consensus of the inherent equality of all people, then knowing when to act out of the individual focus of one's hierarchical post and puzzle piece. I personally run into this intuitive process in anchoring the ashrams of Djwhal Khul, Lord Maitreya and Melchizedek in Los Angeles and in knowing when to assert my personal authority in the responsibility I have been given to put on the Wesak celebration. I personally don't find it difficult to integrate the individual and consensus modalities.

An Open-Ended Question

As our discussion on leadership was coming to a close, I asked Djwhal Khul, Lord Maitreya and Melchizedek if there were any other qualities of leadership that needed to be developed that had not been spoken about so far. To my surprise, Djwhal Khul said that one more quality that needed to be developed was that of being "socially savvy."

A leader must really know how to deal with people. He/she must have excellent social skills and must know how to make people feel comfortable, accepted, loved and yet be able to get his points across. This also gets into having appropriate social manners, dressing appropriately and not being personally offensive. This last quality might sound strange, but this can be the downfall of many leaders who might not be grounded enough or developed on the personality level, where they might have eccentric personal habits that offend people.

This could be as simple as not cleaning and vacuuming before a class, or not cleaning the bathroom properly, or personal-hygiene concerns, or knowing what is socially acceptable and what is not. A person could be a great channel, spiritual teacher and psychic, but on a personality level really alienate people. The ideal leader must be well-developed and well-integrated on all levels. He/she must be able to speak on more than just spiritual matters and be able to leave the leader/teacher role and commune in fellowship.

Often one's personal habits, if not checked, can be very distracting or even offensive. This must be closely monitored and appropriate corrections made. This is where being able to receive feedback from trusted friends is important.

The spiritual path is one of refinement and purification on every level. This is just another aspect of one's being and character that must be worked on and refined in order to truly demonstrate God on every level. The true spiritual leader is the Renaissance man/woman who is well-developed and refined on all levels of existence. This could even be something as simple as gracefully excusing yourself in a social situation when you need to protect your boundaries or take care of yourself. It is often the millions of smaller actions of the leader that really form the core of leadership rather than just looking at getting on stage in front of a large group of people.

5

The Pursuit of Excellence

Praise

A good leader is constantly giving praise and compliments to his/her team members. On the other side of the coin, he is also able to give constructive criticism in a loving way when needed, but does it in a way that is uplifting. This helps to create a positive leadership team and positive team members. When team members are getting validated it helps them to be excited about their work and want to do more. So the ideal spiritual leader is, as much as possible, a love-finder, not a faultfinder. The ideal leader is very fair but firm.

Listening

The ideal spiritual leader is a good listener and a good talker and motivator. He/she knows when either role is needed. The ideal leader is also optimistic. When challenges arise, the leader is able to turn the lemon into lemonade. Problems are turned into challenges, spiritual tests and opportunities to grow spiritually. It is an opportunity for the team members to come together, each person in the group recognizing the puzzle piece he or she carries and feeling proud of that part.

Goals

The ideal leader is able to instill a very clear vision of the goals of the team and group. In spiritual groups the goals are to serve God, Sanat Kumara, Buddha, our Planetary Logos, the ascended masters and the divine plan. The goal is to be a perfect instrument of the masters in achieving the objectives your group has set forth for itself. This goal is constantly reinforced from the point of view that it is not for egotistical goals, such as for any one person's personal fame or for power or money.

Money and fame might come, but that is not the primary goal. The primary goal is to serve God and the masters, and all things shall be added unto thee. When the group realizes it is not working for personalities but for the Spiritual Hierarchy, great motivation is instilled along with team unity.

One of the key skills that spiritual leaders need to develop in this vein is to get each team member to commit to reaching the team's goals and objectives. The leader must monitor the team members from time to time to make sure everyone is on the same page and that everyone is fully motivated. For a person to be a team member he/she must verbally or in writing commit to the vision, goals and objectives of the group. It is a good idea to spell this out very clearly, even in writing, so there is no confusion as to the specific focus of the group.

In the group I am in and have leadership for, its focus is to anchor the ashrams of Djwhal Khul, Lord Maitreya and Melchizedek on Earth and disseminate their teachings and the teachings and principles of the ascension movement on a global level. Our goal is to help as many people ascend as possible, to help them achieve liberation and to prepare them for leadership and planetary world service. The people working under my leadership are not really working for me, but as a united force in the ashrams of Djwhal Khul, Lord Maitreya and Melchizedek. In helping me they are helping the masters, for there is no separation, just as the lightworkers who are helping my assistants are also working for the masters. This is the chain of command of the Spiritual Hierarchy.

Visionaries and Manifesters

Another key leadership skill is determining which of your people have the skills of a visionary and which are skilled at manifesting. One is not better than another. God has built every person to do certain things. No job in the ashram or group is better than another one. All are essential to the completion of the divine plan. All are moved along in their initiation process as a wave because of their commitment to do their puzzle piece properly.

When possible, take advantage of the skills of the visionaries and likewise put the manifesters in their proper job position. Often there is a shifting around of personnel to achieve maximum efficiency. It should be stressed that there is no place for egos in your group. Every group is in a sense part of an ashram. Every person on this planet is connected to one of the seven ashrams and often the ashrams of other spiritual teachers like Sai Baba, for example, or Melchizedek. All fit under this umbrella, for these are universal masters.

You might also work for many masters. There is usually a particular ascension lineage to which you are connected. As I have already stated, my personal ascension lineage is Djwhal Khul, Lord Maitreya and Melchizedek. However, I also work for the Mahatma, Lord Arcturus, Sai Baba, the

Lord of Sirius, Vywamus, Buddha, Sanat Kumara, Kuthumi, Metatron, Lord Michael and Lenduce, to name a few. Just because I have an ascension lineage and/or ashram that I work for does not mean that I am limited in my ability to work with other masters at my choosing. I spend a lot of time during the day running the Arcturian energy because I find it is best for my physical body and helps me to get the most possible amount of work done. It is also really good in light-quotient building.

In the evenings I spend most of my time running Melchizedek's energy. Even though this is the case, the master with whom I am most connected in my mission and the one I most reflect is Djwhal Khul. So you see, one is not limited by these titles or labels. I love all the masters and work with them all, and this should be stressed to your team.

This principle also applies to the teachings that are presented. Just because my job responsibility is a leadership one in Djwhal Khul, Lord Maitreya and Melchizedek's ashram does not mean I limit myself to their teachings only. This is just my base of operations; my teachings are totally eclectic and universalistic. This is why Djwhal Khul's ashram is called the synthesis ashram, for it synthesizes the best of all ashrams.

Being Attacked

It is absolutely essential that spiritual leaders manifest absolute integrity and impeccability. This is true for lightworkers in general, but people in leadership positions who are in the limelight need to have the utmost integrity. When you are in the public eye, people look up to you. You are under the microscope at all times, that is, the microscope of team members and the public. If there is any imbalance or lack of impeccability it will be jumped on by the public.

The reason for this is very interesting. Most people are run by the negative ego. The game the negative ego plays is flip-flopping from inferiority to superiority. But as you know, both sides are illusion when you move into the Christ consciousness. This is when you are able to move into a more transcendent philosophy.

When a person moves into leadership, Melchizedek told me that everyone forms an opinion about that person. When the onlooker is run by the negative ego, it will tell him or her that he does not match up to the leader. Then it will tell him to look for discrepancies so that he can attack and criticize the leader, thus feeling good about himself so he can move back into a superior position. This is human nature, but not godly nature. Said another way, this is the nature of the personality and not the soul. Because so many people, including lightworkers and even those of higher initiations, are run by the negative ego, they are constantly competing, comparing and being jealous. Self-esteem is achieved by attack and criticism.

Melchizedek told me that any person who moves into leadership and fame will have to deal with this.

This is why all spiritual leaders need to develop a tough skin and the Christ quality of invulnerability. This stems from the fact that you know that *you* cause your own reality and emotions and no other person should be handed this power. The ideal spiritual leader must learn to respond and not react. The ideal spiritual leader must remain neutral and possess divine indifference. The lesson is often that of humility, turning the other cheek. Often, engaging such critics just makes it worse.

The ultimate lesson here is forgiveness and unconditional love. In extreme cases the person should be reported, in a tough-love manner, to the Planetary Logos, Lord Buddha and the Lords of Karma. As suggested in *Cosmic Ascension,* banns of noninterference should be requested from the Buddha, the Spiritual Hierarchy and Lord Maitreya.

The more impeccable and in integrity you are, the less you will have to deal with this; however, even if you were Jesus Christ incarnate, it would still happen at times. This can be seen in the life of Jesus. All he did is love and heal people, yet look how many people wanted to eliminate him. This was because of the ego sensitivity and unconsciousness of the people of his time. It had nothing to do with any energy he was putting out.

The same is true of the times we are now living in. Even if you are in the Christ consciousness at all times, the negative ego of other people will still attack you. Spiritual leaders must be very strong spiritual warriors. Achieving spiritual leadership and fame is not always what it is cracked up to be. It can actually be a very difficult assignment at times.

Large Groups

When dealing with large groups there are always some very strange and eccentric people. They often try to monopolize the conversation or act as know-it-alls or pontificate and in general disrupt the group energy. I am sure you all know what I am talking about. When I look into the group I often see the other people rolling their eyes and getting irritated, angry and agitated with such disruptive group members.

Part of developing good leadership skills is to know how long to be patient and allowing, and when to move in with tough love and stop the person. If you move in and squash them too quickly, this can create a scene, but waiting too long can be just as bad. Tact must be used and the person must be stopped in a graceful, loving but forceful way. Be prepared for this and have a contingency plan to deal with this sort of thing, for rarely does a large group get together without this occurring.

Djwhal Khul has on a number of occasions asked me to request certain people not to come to class on a permanent basis. This is not pleasant to do, but is a Christ-leadership quality that must be developed. Some would say that this is not being of the Christ consciousness, but I would say just the opposite is true. Letting a person who is being chronically disruptive remain is not of the Christ consciousness. It is one of those unpleasant leadership skills that must be developed.

Priorities

Another aspect of good leadership is to have one's priorities clear. Leaders who are too emotional by nature might focus only on projects and priorities that they enjoy most. This is not good. It is very important in business or in running an ashram or group to take care of business. An example of this might be taxes or going to the dentist. These are not high on the pleasant list for most people; however, if this is what needs to be taken care of, then that is what you must do. Do not leave the unpleasant jobs for last, or they will come back to bite you later.

Good Business Practices

Another important leadership ability to develop is what I call good business practices. By this I mean such things as when people call, return their calls. When you make commitments to people, keep them or do not make them in the first place. Be willing to give certain services away for free to those who have helped you. See every person as part of your team and God's team, and cultivate this in the way you speak to people. Also see yourself as part of their team. Do not procrastinate or be lazy.

Be loving in all your interactions with the public, but also be efficient. Write little personal notes to people when you can. Send thank-you notes or make thank-you calls when appropriate. Put out only good products. If people are not satisfied, give them their money back. When mistakes are made, apologize, and when appropriate offer people a free service as an extra apology. Impress people with how loving, warm and gracious you are and also with how responsible, efficient and in integrity you are in your business dealings. I think you get a sense of what I am speaking of here. This will create nothing but good karma for you and your business or spiritual group.

Personal vs. Impersonal Energies

There are three different leadership styles. One is personal, the second is more impersonal and the third is an ideal blend of both. The third is the ideal, but some people, depending on how they are built, lean slightly one way or the other. One of the things that all leaders will eventually run into is a lot of phone calls and people wanting their time and energy. This can be very draining if you do not have the proper boundaries. This is why the development of impersonality is needed at times. You cannot get into a long personal phone call with everyone.

At times one needs to learn to be businesslike but in a loving way. If a spiritual leader gets too impersonal, people will be turned off and feel disconnected. If you are too personal, you will get drained. Tune into the appropriate balance for each contact. Some people might require a little more time and others a little less. Lovingly give what is called for, but do not overextend to the point where you deplete yourself.

This can occur even on the inner plane while you sleep. One aspect of this lesson is that protection is needed psychically. Another leadership ability here is to be able to shut off your phone and let the answering machine or phone service take messages. Monitoring phone calls and deciding to pick and choose which calls to answer is important. This applies to everyone, regardless of your level of leadership. I have had to learn to delegate authority, which has sometimes been a hard lesson. I have had to allow high-level initiates in the ashram return phone calls for me and answer mail at times.

As a leader, one needs to find a balance between selfish and selfless. Always being selfless will drain you. The key lesson here is to get clear on what your job responsibilities are as the leader and what other people can really do to help. In my own process of moving into larger and larger levels of planetary leadership, it has been hard to let go of a lot of the things that in the past I always did myself. Such things include allowing other people to edit my books once I have written them, returning phone calls and reading my extremely high volume of mail, especially around Wesak celebrations.

When I have tried to do too much myself, as is my style, it has debilitated me physically. This has been a good motivator to let go and delegate authority. Once I have done this, I ask myself, Why didn't I do this a long time ago? This has freed me up to do the things I am really supposed to do, like write new books and plan large workshops and planetary events.

This brings up another leadership quality of allowing myself to trust people. The negative ego, of course, wants to control everything. I have had to learn to be a hands-off instead of a hands-on leader. There is just too much work to do to continue in this old style. So learn to find the balance between personal and impersonal energies. If you are too impersonal, lightworkers will turn on you even if you do good work. If you are too personal, they will drain your energy and time. This is a leadership skill that takes some practice and can be quite tricky at times.

Manifesting Good People

This is one of the most important lessons of spiritual leadership. As I was in my kindergarten stages of leadership, I had a great number of people around me I would rely on. However, many of them were very unclear, especially psychologically. They would have great gifts in one area, but because of their psychological and personal problems, I could not always rely on them. I would give them a job to do and they would procrastinate, be lazy or simply lose their focus. Instead of being in mastery, their emotional and desire bodies held too much control over them and their life. I would constantly have to call them, coddle them or walk on eggshells around them. I could not rely on them to be responsible. When they finally finished the project they were given, they did a great job; however, I had to psychically pay in blood, so to speak.

As I evolved and moved into higher levels of leadership, I finally had enough of this. I did spring cleaning in a loving way and let go of the people in my life who were psychologically and emotionally draining. I felt I had paid my dues and did not have to put up with this anymore. By the grace of God, I have now manifested a group of people who are all high-level initiates who are service-oriented and totally dedicated to the work of the masters.

I now require love, devotion and efficiency. I am also much clearer about what I need done. I set reasonable time limits for a given project. I have the person agree to this time limit, or I politely tell them I will have someone else do it if it is not acceptable to them.

Leaders must realize that lightworkers all over the world are looking for a way to serve. In my case, to be connected to a high-level ashram and serve as part of a core group running the ashram is a great honor. There are great spiritual benefits that come from this, even if it is mundane work such as stuffing envelopes, answering phone calls or opening mail. I do not think there is any feeling in the world that is better than working in an ashram or spiritual group in a project directed by the ascended masters and spirit. In such an environment, everything one does becomes completely energized and on fire with the spirit of God.

Spiritual leaders should ask in their prayers and state in their attitude, affirmations and visualizations that they want loving, selfless, efficient, service-oriented people to become a part of their service group. If people are found to be too unclear or damaged psychologically, then remove them lovingly and politely and command from the universe that the right people now be manifested to help in the group work.

Spiritual leaders must humble themselves and not be afraid to ask for help. Good intuitive decisions must be made about compensation. Some might need to be paid. For others it will be the honor of having the opportunity to serve the masters. Others might be compensated through free workshops, books, personal sessions or the like. Your intuition will guide you about what is appropriate for every project and person.

In stating this, my goal is that spiritual leaders allow other people to help in the great work to such a large degree that these leaders are free to do the creative work that only they can do. In my own case, I have delegated responsibilities in the ashram to the point where all my energies are now freed up to oversee everything that goes on, which allows me to write new books in just eight or nine months and plan the Wesak celebration for 1200 or more people. I can do this, for I am now allowing high-level initiates to take care of a lot of the logistics that I formerly did myself. This is the difference between running an individual business and running an ashram or spiritual group in service to the masters.

Achieving Goals As a Team

Another essential element of leadership is to instill the attitude that the achievement of goals is a team win, not the win of any one individual or personality. The entire ashram wins. The divine plan wins in service of Lord Maitreya and Buddha. Melchizedek and God win when goals are achieved. More and more is one's identity seen as a group. Your group then is seen as just one of many groups, which are still larger puzzle pieces in the big picture. As in sports, every person on the team gets a championship award, whether the team captain or one of the players.

How to Become a Leader

The first step is to become a leader over yourself, which means owning your personal power, self-mastery and becoming a cause of your reality in service of love and of God. The second step is to simply claim this within yourself, not out of ego but out of love for God and a sincere desire to serve. It was stated in *A Course in Miracles* that all are chosen, but few choose to listen. Once you achieve some level of self-actualization, soul merge and monadic realization, you are then ready to step out and lead others with the gifts God has given you.

The first step is simply to make that decision in your own mind and heart. This will draw to you ideas and guidance about how you might implement this in service of the divine plan. This will then magnetize and attract opportunities for you to share your wisdom with people whom God would have you lead. Becoming a leader is a natural byproduct of being a teacher of God.

Detachment

Every leader must have detachment. The group of people you lead is like a body. The leader must hold the position of third eye, crown, throat and heart chakras. Team members carry these also; however, in the larger body some might focus on being the hands, feet, arms or legs, in terms of their job position. The third eye allows detachment, objectivity and being a witness.

The larger body is like a personality. Just as you must have objectivity and detachment from your own personality with all its thoughts, feelings, emotions, images, subpersonalities, instincts and intuitions, so too must you maintain detachment from the other parts of this larger body. The larger body or team carries many voices made up of qualities similar to these. The ideal spiritual leader must not be knocked off balance by all these voices and energies. Once you have learned to do this within self, it is not that hard a leap to then do it with other people.

You cannot have mastery without having detachment and maintaining a separate identity. The leader is like the third eye of the group body, who receives guidance for the group from the crown and communicates this through the throat, always in a loving manner from the heart. The leader also needs to be grounded and integrated in the lower chakras; however, often the team members help out with many of the basic day-to-day responsibilities of the group body. The leader must hold the overall vision for the group body.

As one evolves through the initiation process, one is given larger and larger levels of responsibility of leadership. I see this process in how the masters have guided me in putting on these Wesak celebrations. Originally it was just a small group. Then it became 50 people, then 350 people and so on. The festivals have grown to include more than 1200 people, and in the year 1998, the masters have projected that 2500 people will attend. In the year 2000 they want us to go for 5000. Each level of leadership and responsibility must be proven before the masters will allow the next step.

Everyone who moves into the higher levels of initiation and on into the sixth and seventh initiations is expected to take on leadership responsibilities. It is the natural evolution of the ascension process. It is the next step after ascension, along with planetary world service. Some will take on this mantle of leadership at earlier stages, and this is good. Others will wait for the right timing.

The lesson is always to remain in the Tao and not get ahead of the wave, but to not go too slowly either.

Creating Ownership

It is an essential quality of an effective leader to help the group and team members create a feeling of ownership. In Japan, a small island that has become such an incredible economic success, the employees own the company, which is a natural motivation to work and succeed. The same principle can be applied to spiritual groups. In the synthesis ashram that I am involved in, everyone owns a piece of the company. I have certain leadership responsibilities in this company, but other people also have key roles.

Every leader serves the level above. Djwhal is subservient in a spiritual sense to Kuthumi, and Kuthumi to Lord Maitreya. Each person involved in the spiritual group or ashram can be proud, for they represent the ashram in everything they do. In a larger context, we are all part of God's ashram and all represent God, for we are all pieces and parts of God. I emphasize again that everyone is a part of God's ashram and many other ashrams.

When I use the term "ashram" I am not using it in the same sense as the ashrams of Eastern masters in India. I am using the term as a unifying principle that ties many lightworkers together in a specialized, focused work under the specific guidance of a certain ray. Each earthly and/or ascended master on the inner plane works under a certain ashramic influence. You are also not limited to just one. You might indeed switch around a lot, and that is fine, too.

In my experience, however, the higher you go in your initiation process, the more specific and focalized your specific mission will become. It is usually your monadic ray that determines this; however, this is not always the case. Sometimes it is up to the individual as to which masters you are most devoted. Everyone on this planet works in the ashrams of Lord Maitreya, Buddha, Sanat Kumara, Helios and Vesta, Melchior, the Mahatma and Melchizedek.

You might also work for specific ashrams of certain individualized masters as well as for one of the chohans of the seven rays. Those in initiations one through four might work under the influence of the ashram of their soul ray. Those in initiations four through seven are under the influence of the chohan, or lord, of their monadic ray and of the master(s) of their choosing.

Claim this affinity, and this will bring around you people of like mind. The most important thing to remember is that no ashram is better than another. All are essential to the full implementation and completion of the divine plan.

The thing I enjoy absolutely the most about the Wesak celebrations is that they represent all ashrams, all masters, all mystery schools, all spirit guides, all archangels, all religions, all schools of thought and all spiritual texts. All come together under the unifying principle of ascension and planetary world service. These yearly festivals are hosted on a spiritual level by Djwhal Khul, Lord Maitreya, Lord Buddha, the Mahatma and Melchizedek, but all planetary and cosmic masters and guides are invited and involved.

At the last Wesak festival Djwhal Khul told me when it was over that he had never in all his days of service work seen so many diverse planetary and cosmic masters focused so intently on one weekend event. The reason for this is because this was the vision for the event and thus they were invoked. This creates a tremendous feeling of inclusiveness and unity in diversity. It allows leaders in the field to come together in equality, brotherhood, sisterhood and fellowship. It allows all leaders to come together and unify into one group-leadership being.

To meditate with 1200 spiritual leaders in total unity and group consciousness on Wesak at the full moon in Taurus, to activate the next set of waves of mass ascension, is an amazing thing. Please consider coming to the next event. They usually occur every year at the full moon in May or occasionally at the full moon at the end of April. Nothing will catalyze your full realization of your leadership abilities like coming together with 1200 to 2500 spiritual leaders such as this.

Benefits

Another essential quality of leadership is to be able to demonstrate to the team members the benefits of reaching your group's specific goals. This applies to business and to spiritual groups as well. If the team members know the benefits, they will be more motivated to work. In business if they know they are putting out a good product that helps the planet, this provides motivation. If they know they will get a bonus if a certain selling point is reached and if they know praise and gratitude is forthcoming, these too will encourage productivity.

In spiritual groups the benefits are multifaceted. It provides an opportunity to serve. It provides an opportunity to be a part of a spiritual team. It provides the opportunity to work directly under the ascended masters' guidance and vision. The work helps people to ascend and achieve liberation. Serving in such a manner will greatly accelerate their own ascension and initiation process. There might be financial benefits. There are benefits of friendship and companionship. There are benefits of serving God and one's brothers and sisters.

It is essential for an effective leader to keep his or her team aware of these benefits and let them know that it is a blessing to have the opportunity to serve in such a manner. As stated in *A Course in Miracles*, "True happiness is serving God."

Negative Manipulation vs. Clear Communication

Another one of the lessons of effective leadership is to learn to communicate with team members in a very clear, loving, calm, rational, objective, powerful, concise manner. The negative ego tries to use negative manipulation to influence people. This might have short-term success, but it will always fail in the long run. Honesty is always the best policy. Communication skills might be one of the most important qualities of an effective leader.

Make sure that each person knows his/her part to play. Another very important part of effective leadership is to make sure that each person on your team has a very clear understanding of his/her role in the divine plan of your group project. It is essential that each knows his or her specific part and also have an overall vision of each of the other people's parts. Each person needs to know that his/her part is essential to the completion of the divine plan, no part being seen better or worse than any other. All are seen as special and essential. This leads to an attitude of egolessness and selfless service for the good of the whole. Personalities are deemphasized and group consciousness is constantly reemphasized.

Sharing in the Benefits

Another very important leadership skill is when your objectives and goals are achieved, make sure you gather the team members and share in the joy of completion. This might be a gathering at the end of certain major projects where there is a celebration and party. Often in groups there are certain people who get recognition. It is essential for a leader to acknowledge the team during the major events and later as well. The idea here is to share the recognition with the team.

The danger for the leader is the negative ego, which will try to get you to claim all the fame and attention for yourself, when in truth the team did much of the work. The celebration or party at the end gives the group a sense of positive completion. If people are going to work hard, they need to have the emotional release and feeling of completion as a team.

It is also a way for the leader to give gratitude, thanks and acknowledgments. It is a time for all to share in joy before the next project begins. It is an acknowledgment of the emotional body and the group body. This is a time to share in some of the deeper insights, guidance and reflections about the process, something that often is not shared with the team members because everyone has been too busy.

No Such Thing As Failure

The attitude that failure is a false concept and that it does not really exist is an essential quality of an effective leader. Failure is an attitude of the negative ego based upon judgment. The soul sees only mistakes and lessons and opportunities to grow and improve. No one ever fails at anything; they just learn lessons.

Occasional meetings should be held to examine what the group and team is doing well and where lessons need to be learned to do even better in the future. An attitude such as this is guaranteed to be a success. Adjustments are constantly made until success is achieved.

Long-Term vs. Short-Term Plan of Action

An effective leader must first have a very clear vision of the long-term plan of action. This must then be broken down into a short-term plan, with each person being given his/her specific assignment.

My long-term plan is to fully manifest Djwhal Khul, Lord Maitreya and Melchizedek's ashram on Earth as it exists in the spiritual planes. Because it is an ashram of synthesis, the energy of the Mahatma, who is the avatar of synthesis, is also a fundamental part of this work. The plan is to learn as much as I can between the years 1995 and 2012, which is the end of the Mayan calendar, to externalize the inner-plane ashrams and spread the ascension work. My specific long-term plan is to write as many as fifty books, many of which are already completed and published. Melchizedek has asked me to write about literally everything in the vein of the *Easy-to-Read Encyclopedia of the Spiritual Path.*

My long-term plan is also to be the main coordinator for the Wesak celebrations each year and build them each year until I reach my ultimate goal, which is hosting an event for 50,000 people in a large stadium by the year 2012. Can you imagine doing this kind of ascension light-activation work with 50,000 people? The long-term goal I hold most steadfastly is to sell millions of sets of books and have them translated into every language on the globe, and this has already begun to happen.

I attribute the large-scale attendance at the Wesak celebrations to the books. Those in the leadership field might consider writing books to advertise their programs.

The short-term plan is of course the individual writing of each book, and all the work that goes into putting on the Wesak celebrations for from 1200 to 2500 people and so on down the line. The short-term work is where all the disciples and initiates in the ashram come into play in helping with all the various projects with which I am involved. I literally could not do all of these things without their help. As I have already stated, I have twelve people helping with Wesak, others helping with books, others helping in research and other key people around the globe doing similar work who represent the Melchizedek, Lord Maitreya and Djwhal Khul synthesis ashram.

Social Skills

To be an effective leader you must be like a master psychologist, even if you do not have a degree. You must be able to deal well with people not only in the ashram or group you are involved with, but also with the public. You might be the best channel, psychic, teacher, healer, doctor, counselor or whatever, but if you do not deal well with people, your program will not hold together well. One must not only deal well in public speaking, but also in leadership meetings, in friendships, on the phone with people, in meeting strangers and at parties. This is where a lot of leaders fall by the wayside. They have great spiritual gifts, but on a personality level enormous problems are created. This is why the ideal leader is balanced, integrated and has mastery on all levels, not just spiritual or in a specific gift or profession.

Setting Positive, Reachable Goals

Another very important leadership skill is to set positive, reachable goals. There is the tendency to get excited and carried away in one's visions sometimes and not be realistic. Do not try to expand enormously immediately. That is not in harmony with divine law. One must move up slowly and prove him/herself worthy and competent at each level. Setting up unrealistic or unreachable goals will just create disappointment and frustration. It is better to start small and build successes and team spirit. Do not buy into the ego's game of needing to go big. If you help one person, that is significant. If you help twelve, that is even better.

I personally spent an enormously long time paying my dues before success came my way. To be honest, I was never looking for fame. I was so immersed in my sincere and devoted desire to just serve that I was very surprised when public recognition came. I am actually very glad that it did not come sooner in my life, for I would not have been ready. It came after many, many years, when I had had time to ripen and mature.

Do not go for numbers; go for service. Whether you are helping three or fifty people, always put out the same effort and leave the rest to God and the masters.

Customer Service

The most important thing in leading a spiritual group or business is that the customer, client or student comes first. All other considerations are secondary. The whole purpose of your business/ashram/spiritual group is to be of service. Prosperity comes as a byproduct of giving yourself completely to this principle. Focusing completely on service will draw clientele and students to you. There is nothing wrong with charging a fair price for your service, but do not put money before service.

When I wrote these books, I literally gave everything and held nothing back for myself. It is because of this that I believe God has given me everything. In truth, I have given it to myself. In whatever service situation you are in, give 100 percent. If you are seeing a person for free, give the same effort as if he/she were paying you $150 an hour. See every person you speak to or who walks in your door as God. This is not just a trick you are playing with yourself; it is literally the truth.

All Leaders Are Also Students

It is very important for people who have moved or who are moving into leadership to also see themselves as students. No matter how big one's leadership responsibilities are he/she will always be a student also. Life is always teaching us something, as are other people. Djwhal Khul is a student of Kuthumi. Kuthumi is a student of Lord Maitreya. Even Melchizedek is still a student of a higher being above him. We are all students of God.

One of the dangers of leadership is where the negative ego uses leadership to try and lock the person into being a know-it-all or the guru all the time. He/she becomes overidentified with the Wise One archetype. One of the signs of a good leader is his/her ability to step out of leadership when she needs simply to be a person, or to let others lead when appropriate. Again, a good leader does not always need center stage.

Creativity

It is an essential quality to not only be creative as a leader but also to encourage people on the team to be creative. This will empower your leadership team. You do not want machines working for the ashram and for you. Since we are dealing here with spiritual leadership, most of the people will be channels, intuitives and telepaths. Take advantage of this.

As Djwhal Khul once told me, even though he runs the synthesis ashram, a great many of the people have knowledge equal to his. The powers that be have given him the leadership position. This is much like the president of the United States. Even though the president is in charge, that does not mean he is necessarily the smartest person on every subject.

Take advantage of the creative ideas, intuitions, psychic perceptions and channelings of the people with whom you work. Do not let your ego tell you that you had to come up with the idea. You are beyond such pettiness. In dealing with such a group or ashram, you are dealing with a group mind and group intelligence. Do not limit yourself to your own.

I would say that the number-one reason my personal evolution has occurred so quickly is that during the past five years I have merged my evolution with other people, such as those in the core group. This ascension buddy system and merger of group consciousness has also greatly enhanced my leadership abilities.

Allow the people working for you to run with the ball and do not be a control freak who has to make all decisions. In truth, the other members of your group are actually running *with* you. Seeing your work through this lens will also create much more job satisfaction among team members. I have had to learn to do this with my books. I write the books very clearly and distinctly. From there, Djwhal Khul has guided me to let go of them and let other people input them on the computer and do the editing. I do not have time to spend years going over my books in endless perfectionism.

This was a hard lesson to learn and let go of; however, once I did it I was incredibly relieved. The publisher's staff editor then edits my books again and I don't even look at it now. All I care about is whether the information I wrote is in there. Instead of redoing the book over and over after each editing, I can write two more new books. This is a better use of my energies, abilities and time. It allows other people to use their creative abilities who have skills in those areas.

Do not be a negative perfectionist, having to have things always go a certain way. Let the group create, not just your individual mind. It always comes down to letting go of the negative ego and its self-centeredness.

Consumers

Another important task of spiritual leadership is to be able to tune in to what the disciples, initiates and consumers really need and want. If the leader is not tuned in to this, he/she might bulldoze his own program or agenda onto the public and it will fall flat on its face. The leader might be interested in this subject, but the consumer might not be. Another aspect is that the leader must be able to tune in to the level of development of the group he is dealing with. Many leaders fail in their work by making their program too advanced or, even worse, too childlike, not recognizing how advanced the group is. The leader must be sensitive to the energies of the group and to spirit and guidance on this matter.

It is also very important to encourage audience participation when possible. This creates an energizing effect. It is also better never to simply read a speech. It is okay to have notes or an outline, but do not merely read a speech. It will kill or flatten the energy.

Public Speaking

Another skill that all leaders must develop is public speaking. I always liked Paramahansa Yogananda's prescription for effective public speaking. He said to make an outline, but do not fill it in. Have more information

The Pursuit of Excellence 207

available than you need just in case you run through the material quickly. Tell a few jokes or funny stories and always pray right before you go on stage, asking spirit and the masters for help.

The outline helps you relax and calm and organize the mind, but the fact that it is not filled in allows spirit to fill in the space. Be sure to have plenty of breaks in a longer workshop. Try not to present either too much or too little material. A great talk that takes ten minutes too long can lessen its effectiveness.

On the other side of the coin, make sure to give them their money's worth. It was stated in *A Course in Miracles* that to have all, one must give all to all. In other words, give 100 percent energy to helping people as best you can and the public will see, know and recognize your sincerity. Try also to find a balance between didactic information and experiential exercises. Too much of either one will have a negative effect.

There is an old adage that the first twenty minutes of every speech either hooks or loses the audience, which I think is true.

Being a Gracious Host

Another important quality in terms of leadership is being a gracious host. There are some leaders who have little personal contact with the people they work with. This is usually a product of negative ego and being aloof. Some boundaries are obviously important. As people arrive, it is important to make them feel at home, welcomed and loved. If the leader cannot do this, then people in the core group should be assigned this task.

As we know, people often make snap judgments about people and things. To be welcomed, loved and received in a gracious manner can positively color everything that happens the rest of the day or night. It is even better if the leader is willing to participate in this. The same applies at the end of the event. People want to make personal contact with those who are in a position of spiritual leadership. Everyone needs to be welcomed with the consciousness of innocent perception.

Every leader will have different boundaries in this regard; however, a little time and energy spent doing this is very important. The public is not just looking at the product you are presenting, but also at you as a personality to see if you are walking your talk on all levels. One of the biggest problems I have often seen among leaders is that they are great when they have their professional hat on; however, when you get them back to their personal lives, they can be living terrors.

The ultimate ideal here is always to be the same. This is a quality that many leaders and lightworkers have not developed. They hold the energy when they have to, but let go of the mastery when they do not have to. I personally strive to be exactly the same whether I am in my psychologist role, public workshop role or in my house visiting with friends.

When people go to work they often keep their personalities together, then when they get home they feel it is okay to let down. It is obviously okay to let down and relax when you get home, but it is not okay to lose your spiritual mastery over your personality and negative ego. This would be a false indulgence. A true master is a master all the time, even while sleeping.

God vs. Money

This is another spiritual test for the true spiritual leader. Many of them pass all the tests, but when it comes to the spiritual money test, they fail. They fail first because they do not realize that it is a test. Spiritual leaders are most often extremely nice, gracious and spiritual as long as they are getting paid. Take away the money, and they can be holy terrors. An even bigger test is when they are not paid what they are owed. I am not saying here that the money is not important, for it is. The key question, however, always is what comes first, God or money?

Spiritual leaders must develop a good business sense. The key question here is, how do you respond when someone rips you off, which is a lesson all spiritual leaders will have to deal with. Do you respond from your negative ego or from the Christ consciousness?

This lesson was firmly in my mind recently when a woman owed me a large sum of money for books she had ordered. She was unable to pay me for the order that I had originally sent her on the honor system. After a year of waiting I finally responded with tough love, which was appropriate. However, I had a very clear choice as to whether I was going to put God or money first. I actually liked this person and wrote a second letter telling her that even though I felt it was time to get paid, I valued our friendship more than money and that I did not want our business dealing to create any separation between us.

I think my letter touched her soul, because she immediately called me to share what had been going on with her, which I had not known. Once I heard her story, I felt great compassion and we became closer than ever. We agreed to a payment plan she could work with. In the long run she will be a great advocate for my work and the masters' work.

As another example, I was in a business deal with a person who turned out to be a full-blown sociopath. A sociopath is a person who has no conscience. Such people's only concerns are their own selfish needs and desires. They are often pathological liars.

In this particular lesson I just had to report this person to the Spiritual Hierarchy and hand this whole affair over to the masters. The masters said that they would take over the whole process and make sure no limitations would be created. They said I would be fairly compensated, but in a different way than I originally expected. God often works in mysterious ways. I had to let go and surrender it, just love and forgive.

Spiritual leaders often look at some of these experiences as unexpected tithing. Another lesson regarding leadership and money is that when you move into a position of power, do you become greedy and money-hungry? What are your true motivations? Is money your true goal or service? Are you willing to give scholarships or free passes to some people now that you have the power and fame? Are you still willing to give your time and energy to people now that you are a big shot?

Ask yourself if your personality will change, or if it has already changed after power, fame and money came your way. If it has, then the negative ego needs to be checked. Another big danger here is being sure you are making good, sound business decisions as leadership, power, fame and money come in. The sense of power and leadership can go to your head like a drug, and you can spend too much money on a given project that ends up falling flat on its face. If this happens, you could go bankrupt and end up alienating a great number of people and developing a bad reputation in the community. The lesson here is to build your program slowly and gradually.

The ego always has grandiose ideas and they often are not well-grounded in reality. It is always better to move upward slowly but surely before any large financial risks are incurred. Never let money problems with people create separation, lack of love or lack of forgiveness. As the Bible says, "For what is a man profited if he gain the whole world and lose his own soul?"

Individual and Team Goals

In the ideal vision of spiritual leadership, individual and team goals are achieved simultaneously. This is because there is within the vision an honoring of every individual and the group-consciousness body simultaneously. Within spiritual leadership, when an individual member can give him/herself selflessly to the group endeavor, the masters perceive this as individual achievement. This is the sign of the true spiritual master, one who can surrender the negative ego for the good of the whole. A good spiritual leader always makes sure that each person's individual needs as well as the group's needs are being met.

Constant adjustments are always being made in a continual revision of the group vision. The key here is to keep the lines of communication always open between leadership and team members and between all members of the group consciousness. Communication is the key that makes everything work.

Service Is the Reward

The true reward of spiritual leadership and group consciousness is the opportunity to be of service. There is no better feeling than this or greater joy. Money, although important, is secondary to service. By being of service you are fulfilling your mission and purpose for being here. You are making yourself useful to the ascended masters and to the divine plan. It is in truth through service that you evolve. The higher you go in the initiation process, the less you focus on your own individual spiritual growth and the more you immerse yourself in service. I hardly ever meditate or do individual spiritual practices anymore, for I have too much service work to do. Service work is the ultimate sadhana, or spiritual practice.

Courage

It takes great courage to move into leadership. It is much easier to remain in the background. Leadership requires you to be responsible for many people and many job responsibilities. Being in the public eye is not always as glamorous as it seems. You often have to deal with a lot of people, letters and phone calls that are very strange.

Leadership is often being out on the front lines, so to speak. One must learn to be a master of psychic self-defense. It has its perks, but it also has its hardships. The ascended masters are very appreciative of those who are willing to step forward into mass consciousness to make changes. They have it a lot easier, for they do not have to deal with physical bodies. It is in the mass consciousness that the changes really need to be made.

When you are in the public eye, everyone has an opinion or judgment about you. This is why it is so important to keep the highest possible standard of personal ethics. Often potshots are taken at you because of the ego sensitivity and inferiority complex of many lightworkers, who need to criticize to make themselves feel cool.

Courage is the theme for our entire universe for this cosmic day. It is a quality that the ascended masters greatly admire and appreciate, for God and the masters know how hard this school is. This is why Lord Maitreya has held back his declaration. He is waiting for the climate to be right; otherwise the negative backlash of ego-driven people will be too great. We, as leaders and lightworkers, are paving the way for his externalized leadership that is soon to come. Taking on spiritual leadership and being in the front lines is often experienced as a spiritual war, and that is why all must become spiritual warriors in this work. There are often enormous amounts of negative energy that must be faced and overcome. If God and the masters are with us, who or what can be against us?

Goal and Process Orientation

Another facet of spiritual leadership is to create an atmosphere where goals and purpose are clearly defined and strived for; however, there is also time to smell the roses and enjoy the process of service. If service is not a joyful process, what is the point? Many lightworkers get way too serious. There is great work to do and it is a serious business at times; however, true masters have detachment and thus a sense of humor. It is important to be immersed in the details of the little picture, but not overidentify with it. Often certain goal-oriented meetings must be interrupted to care for the process-oriented needs of the team members. This could also be seen as a need to balance the mental and emotional bodies and give them equal value and time.

Perseverance

Given that the spiritual path is most often experienced as climbing a mountain or fighting a great spiritual war, the qualities of perseverance and tenacity are ones that every spiritual leader needs to develop. The spiritual path is like running a marathon; you do not want to burn out in the beginning. I see this often in many seekers. They are enthusiastic in the beginning, but they are not able to maintain the divine enthusiasm and perseverance over the long haul. This is because they are too anchored in the emotional body and not enough in the mental and spiritual body.

True spiritual leaders are unceasing in their efforts. They know when to rest, but nothing can stop their efforts. They are literally unstoppable no matter what the obstacle. They do not coddle themselves, and whatever the obstacle is, they find a way to make the appropriate adjustment, prayer, affirmation, visualization and take the action that is needed.

They know how to take care of business and are consistent spiritually, mentally, emotionally and physically in their efforts. They know how to give clear, practical instructions to team members so they are not overburdened themselves. They are constantly enthusiastic even when others might interrupt the situation with warnings of impending doom. Their faith, trust and patience in God are unwavering. They are levelheaded and practical within this divine enthusiasm. Their efforts are like the ocean waves, which just keep coming until victory is achieved. The ideal spiritual leader will not take no for an answer, yet knows when to change course and direction when this is the divine guidance.

Care for Disciples and Initiates

The first concern of the spiritual leader is the service mission in relation to the general public. Spiritual leaders also have within their care fellow disciples and initiates. The ideal spiritual leader knows when to intervene and personally help fellow team members and also when to remain silent. Such a leader is aware of the sins of omission and commission and chooses wisely when to act. There is always a fine balance between taking care of your own four-body system and the four-body system of the team/group, and serving the public. When getting involved in a spiritual service group there will be a great acceleration of all members' spiritual evolution. This acceleration is guaranteed to bring up a lot of stuff. This must be taken into consideration by the group leader and by all members of the team.

There is always a fine balance that must be achieved in taking care of your individual four-body system, the group-body system and then the service work of the public. The effective spiritual leader must care for, consider and monitor all of these aspects. As disciples and initiates are perceived to be ready, more responsibility can be given to them. Every member of the team must always be willing and ready to help fellow team members deal with their personal matters.

Having clearing sessions where gripes or constructive criticism can be shared is a good idea. A time where team members can share anything on their mind to clear the air each week helps to maintain the group body. This might be considered preventive medicine for the group. Team members need to know that they can also talk and communicate with the leader without standing on ceremony. This can be done privately or in the group.

The effective leader must also consider the spiritual and evolutionary needs of each member under his/her care. There might be suggestions about how individuals can accelerate their initiation process and ascension realization, which you must be responsible for in addition to the service mission. You as leader must also be aware of the emotional and relationship concerns of spouse, children and family in making decisions. All must be balanced and integrated for the ideal service group.

Detachment

This is one of the most important qualities that all new-age leaders must develop: an attitude of detachment, invulnerability and thick skin. The ideal is to be like a rubber pillow that things gently bounce off of. The ideal is to let things slide off you like water off a duck's back. The ideal is to own that as a master you are mentally and emotionally invulnerable because you cause your own emotions and thoughts. This quality necessitates cultivating a strong sense of self, a well-developed sense of self-love and self-worth and unceasing mastery and personal power.

This will take an *inner* direction, not an outer direction. It is essential that all leaders develop this quality, for no matter how clear you are, attacks will still come. These attacks are really spiritual tests to see how strong and ready for leadership you are. If you are truly immersed in your mighty I Am Presence and ascended-master consciousness, they will have no effect. All lightworkers must be prepared for this, for it comes with the territory.

Unity

The true test of leadership, according to the ascended masters, is the ability of any given spiritual leader to create unity consciousness within the team and the group of people he/she is serving. The ideal leader is a master at removing separation consciousness or, in other words, removing negative-ego consciousness at all levels. If there is one goal and one key that all spiritual leaders should strive for, it is this one.

Advertising

As you move into leadership and full empowerment, your service work will undoubtedly expand to larger and larger levels. In some cases it will mean taking your work to a global level. One of the important facets of this expansion has to do with advertising. Most lightworkers do not have a lot of money, so they are very conservative about advertising, which of course I have great compassion for. The problem is, however, if you do not advertise your service and/or product, how will it get known?

The key is to take the risk and advertise, but to put great care and conscience into using your advertising money wisely. When I first started advertising, the smallest amount of money seemed like a lot to me. After I got into the swing of things and became responsible for putting on the Wesak celebrations each year, I began to spend enormous amounts of money on advertising. I was shocked to see how much money I was spending. However, the masters and spirit kept telling me to go for it.

I consider proper advertising to be one of the real keys to success. One must write an advertisement that really catches the heart, the soul and the emotional body of the reader. The advertisement must be filled with divine energy so that people notice it. It must be well-written and aesthetically designed. When you do not have a lot of money, I know it is hard to take this risk. But this is when you need it the most. I would keep telling myself that if I spent $1000 on an advertisement, all I needed was for four people to sign up for the Wesak, which would pay for the ad. In truth, each ad would bring in one hundred people if it were a global magazine.

I suggest looking at it this way: Ask yourself if this ad will bring in the one or two clients or five to ten people that would pay for it. If it does, you can see clearly that it is indeed worth it. For global events I have had good success with *The Ascending Times* and *Sedona Journal of Emergence!* For local events find your local spiritual and holistic newspapers. Advertising also helps get your name out there. Another aspect of effective advertising is to have a really good phone message on your phone service or answering machine. I use mine to advertise my workshops.

As a leader you have to be willing to sell yourself. If you are not willing to sell yourself, who will? If you are no good at this, then hire someone or make a trade with someone to do it for you. I have bumped into some light-workers who, in a noble attempt to be humble, manifest what I would call negative humility by not sharing with people how good their service really is. Do not be afraid to let people know you believe in yourself and in your work. Qualify it if you like by saying, "I don't mean this to sound egotistical," then put your full self-confidence and belief in yourself out there. Talk about your work with everyone, and you will be amazed by all the unexpected ways you will find clients and students.

The last key to leadership and advertising comes with what is called a prayer, meditation, affirmation and visualization program, which is essential to make your advertising program work.

Your Prayer Program

As just mentioned, I consider this an absolute golden key to making your advertising work. This can be done by yourself or with the group of people you work with. I will use the Wesak as an example. In putting on the Wesak celebrations for 1200 to 2500 people, I was guided to write up all the flyers and materials, get them into the magazines and newspapers around the country and then begin a massive prayer program.

In so doing, I wrote up a Huna prayer (see *Beyond Ascension* for details on how to do this). I began by having the core group and myself do this together. Then I requested about nine other people to commit to saying this prayer every day out loud for six straight months leading up to the Wesak celebration.

I gave a free ticket to Wesak as an added incentive for those people who did this for me. I wrote up one of the best Huna prayers I had ever written, calling upon all the masters of the spiritual and cosmic hierarchies. The prayer I used I have enclosed here for you to use as an example. As you read it, you will feel its power. Imagine twelve core high-level initiates and ascended beings in the synthesis ashram saying this every day out loud around the country. As time went on I began giving it to more and more people in the united ashram.

Huna Prayer for Wesak

Beloved Presence of God; Cosmic Council of Twelve; Twenty-four Elders who surround the Throne of Grace; Mahatma; Melchizedek; Metatron; Archangel Michael; Elohim councils; Archangels of the Tree of Life; Hyos Ha Koidesh; Paradise sons; Melchior; Lord of Sirius; Lenduce; Vywamus; Lord Arcturus and the Arcturians; Sanat Kumara; Atlanto; Adonis; Archangel Sandalphon; Helios and Vesta; Ashtar and the Ashtar Command; Archangels Jophiel, Chamuel, Gabriel, Raphael, Uriel and Zadkiel; the elohim Hercules, Apollo, Heros, Purity, Cyclopia, Peace and Arcturus; Mahachohan; Allah Gobi; Lord Buddha; Babaji; Sai Baba; the lady masters Helena, Virgin Mary, Isis, Quan Yin, Pallas Athena, Goddess of Liberty, Portia, Vista and Lady Nada; Horus; Osiris; the Great Divine Director; the six Buddhas of activity; Lord Maitreya; Djwhal Khul; the ray masters El Morya, Kuthumi, Serapis Bey, Paul the Venetian, Hilarion, Sananda and Saint Germain; the mountain of Mount Shasta; the Earth Mother; Ganesha; Lady Helena; and the Manifestation Council.

We now call forth the entire Planetary and Cosmic Hierarchy on behalf of his holiness Lord Melchizedek for the prayer of all prayers. We hereby pray with all our heart and soul and mind and might for your combined planetary and cosmic help to attract and magnetize the 1200 high-level Melchizedek initiates and ascended beings from around the globe who form the planetary leadership group, to come to the Wesak celebration in Mount Shasta May 3-5 [or appropriate dates], 199–.

The advertising for this event has already begun to hit the newsstands and will go into full force in October. We ask that this event spread like absolute wildfire, that people begin signing up in droves and that the phones begin ringing off the hook with people lining up to get in. We ask that the excitement for this event be greater than for any event in this century, with all credit going to Djwhal Khul, Lord Maitreya, Lord Buddha and Lord Melchizedek, who are our gracious hosts.

We now put forth the clarion call to all the masters we have called forth and to the entire Spiritual and Cosmic Hierarchy to help us manifest this unique group of people and help us sell out as soon as possible.

We also request that the series of books Joshua has written spread like absolute wildfire around the globe in conjunction with this celebration to lay the foundation and groundwork for this event. We invite you all to attend the actual event and ask for your help in all ways and all things to help it come about in divine perfection. We thank thee and accept this as done. Amen.

Our beloved subconscious minds, we hereby ask and command that you take this thought-form prayer with all the *mana* and vital force that is needed and necessary to manifest and demonstrate this prayer to the source of our being through Melchizedek. Amen.

Beloved Presence of God, Cosmic and Planetary Hierarchy, let the rain of blessings fall! Amen.

This Huna prayer specifically spelled out exactly what was desired and called on all the masters for help in achieving it. Then I would also suggest to the core manifestation group that they visualize it throughout the day as being sold out, then affirm it to be sold out in an unwavering manner. Finally, I suggested that they each then take all physical actions and steps within their personal power to make it happen, so all three minds—superconscious, conscious and subconscious—are being utilized.

This process can be done by you, the reader, as an individual or in a group. If you can have more people helping, even if it is just one or two, it will be even more powerful. Did not the master Jesus say "where two or more are gathered in my name"?

Now I am going to share with you the next golden key and secret I have utilized to gather such large numbers of people at Wesak. After doing the Huna prayer, I would then to go to individual masters on the inner plane and personally ask them for help as a favor and prayer request. I would always begin, of course, with Melchizedek, Lord Maitreya and Djwhal Khul, who are my personal teachers. However, I would not stop there. Every day I would call in another master.

I would often do this with someone else, for it was more fun when doing it with a friend. It can be done by alone, however. For example, I would ask his holiness Lord Sai Baba for help. When I asked, he would wave his hands and thousands of rose petals would fall from the sky, or he would move his arm and hand in an omnipotent fashion pushing crowds of people my way. Remember that commercial: "When E.F. Hutton talks, people listen"? When Sai Baba makes a command, it is as good as gold.

This is where we come back to advertising. How can the masters and spirit help you if you have no advertising? You must put yourself out there in every way possible to give spirit a catalyst that connects with you. The masters and spirit will guide people to see your advertisement and they will call you.

Each day I would ask another master for help and request that all the initiates in his/her ashram help also. Look at the Cosmic Map in *Beyond Ascension* and *The Complete Ascension Manual*, then pick out the masters you want to ask for help. Also look at the masters I have listed at the beginning of the Huna prayer.

I would not necessarily go through them all, but I would focus on the ones I felt intuitively guided to make personal contact with. You have to realize that these masters, even Melchizedek, are just people like you and me. They are actually honored that you have thought of them and called upon them for help. Most of them do not say a lot after I ask. Most of them just say, "So be it."

Then what I do is tell the core group about all the masters I have spoken to, not for ego purposes but to build excitement and faith. This helps all members recognize that they are part of something much bigger than their individual selves. This creates great motivation, and no one wants to get left out. Everyone feels honored to be involved. Do you see the wisdom of this approach?

By doing this I am taking advantage of the group-body potentiality. I am taking advantage of the group mind, the group prayer, the group visualization, the group personal power and the group action. This creates an enormous vortex of energy, each individual and each group being like a radar antenna on the inner plane. The key is to keep the enthusiasm, excitement and expectation up for instant manifestation.

One of the biggest lessons I have had to learn as a leader is to not try and do everything myself. This is what I did the first forty years of my life. I have now shifted my consciousness in recent years and take advantage of the group body, mind and spirit in everything I do.

I have had to do this recently because of the amount of mail that I receive. I cannot possibly answer all the letters. Many of the letters are heartfelt, ten-page letters from people I have never met. I am so busy I do not have time to respond to all of them. Recently I have enlisted the help of high-level initiates and channels to help me. Instead of simply not responding, I finally was guided to simply ask the ashram for help.

Do you see the shift that I suggest people make? The negative ego tells us that we have to do everything ourselves and be independent. This is true during a certain phase of the evolutionary process. There comes a more advanced stage, however, when this is transcended and group consciousness is entered into.

First, I am not afraid to ask the masters for help. Second, I am not afraid to ask questions of the masters. Third, I have not been afraid to ask people for help and to delegate authority. Once I have gotten into the flow of this shift of consciousness from trying to do everything myself, I now ask for help in everything I do. Disciples and initiates in the ashram and all over the world are honored that I ask them for help.

As I said earlier, I ask every person I talk to on the phone or in my letters to tell his/her students and friends about the books and about Wesak. We are all a part of God's ashram and as a spokesperson for the planetary ascension movement, I call on all initiates of all ashrams, all spiritual teachers, all religions, all spiritual paths for help. This approach is reflected in my Huna prayer, in which I called on a diverse group of masters.

The concept of ascension seems also to be a unifying principle that all initiates and disciples on planet Earth can relate to regardless of their spiritual teacher and orientation. Even though I have been given certain leadership positions in the spiritual government, I had been practicing the same principles before this occurred. The leadership I have been given by the Spiritual Hierarchy really has nothing do with this. I am suggesting that everyone practice such principles, for all are God. All are spiritual leaders in truth. And we are all on the same team. I am as happy to help other spiritual leaders in their work as I hope they are or will be to help me.

This is why I invite guest speakers to come from other ashrams to have a more universal representation at Wesak. This is why I allow a large group of the major spiritual leaders to have tables at the festival to sell their products. I do not want to hog the wealth or fame. I want to share it. This is why each year when Wesak is over, I put together a leadership group meeting for about 50 to 100 people to bring all the leaders together to cooperate in an equal fashion, brainstorm, meditate, network and see how we can help one another. The time for people doing only their own thing is over. The time for universal, eclectic fellowship and cooperation has come.

The Midas Touch

The key to leadership success is developing what has been called the Midas touch, where everything turns to gold. The formula for developing the Midas touch is very simple. Stay in your personal power at all times. Remain unconditionally loving and forgiving at all times. Stay attuned to God, your own mighty I Am Presence and the ascended masters at all times. Remain balanced in everything you do. Remain the cause of your own reality at all times. Most of all, strive to become completely free of ego. Never give in to fear, separation or self-centeredness.

Take the vow of the bodhisattva and dedicate yourself completely to the service of humanity. Develop unchanging self-love and self-worth. Be attached to nothing and have only preferences. Pray and meditate constantly. Recognize that you are maintaining an individual body and a group body simultaneously, and nurture both. Claim your leadership and do not wait for the ascended masters to acknowledge you as one.

Purify your physical, emotional, mental, etheric and spiritual body of all physical toxins, negative emotions, alien implants, negative elementals, astral entities, negative thoughts, etheric mucus and imbalanced energies. Remain in the Christ/Buddha mind at all times and never interpret reality from the negative ego or lower-self mind.

If you will strive to maintain these simple principles in your daily life and hold on to them like a drowning man wants air, never giving in no matter what the spiritual test, I personally guarantee you that you will have the Midas touch, and everything you think, say and do will turn to gold and to God. Everything you do in your personal and professional life will be successful because you will have attained full merging with your soul, monad, ascended masters and God.

This takes enormous commitment, self-mastery, self-discipline, great joy and great focus. You are here to achieve greatness and grandeur in God's eyes. Do not waste this incarnation on lower-self, impermanent side roads. You were created for a much greater mission, purpose, destiny and fate than this. Claim your empowerment, claim your leadership, claim your commitment to fully achieve and realize your ascension, and let nothing in this universe stop you ever again no matter how great the spiritual test.

How to Become a Leader

There are many things you can do to accelerate this process. One is to read autobiographies of people who have been great leaders in the spiritual movement, in politics and in sports. Learn from their lives and emulate their examples. Pray for God's and the masters' help in moving into your full ascension and leadership status. They will be happy to oblige you. If you do pray for this, put on your spiritual seat belts and get ready for the ride of your life. As the saying goes, be careful what you ask for because you just might get it.

The next principle is to act as if you were a leader, or fake it until you make it. The same applies to being an ascended master. The best way to achieve this is to pretend you are one right now in your every thought, word and deed, and never veer from this commitment. No spiritual sadhana will accelerate your ascension evolution more. When I took my ascension it was not that big a shock, for I had been practicing being an ascended master for fifteen years before I took this initiation. If you want to be with God in heaven, the way to get there is very simple: Act like God in everything you think, say and do.

The Leadership Team and the Inner-Plane Ashram

It is very important as a spiritual leader that you recognize that your leadership team is set up just like the inner-plane ashram. Everyone is actually running an ashram of one of the masters here. This is the same as saying that we are all externalized members of the Spiritual Hierarchy. The Spiritual Hierarchy is not just in the fifth, sixth and seventh dimensions; it is also on Earth. We are it.

This has always been the case, but we have not always recognized it, just as we have not always realized how we are all connected to the seven great inner-plane ashrams of the ray masters. The externalization of the Spiritual Hierarchy that Djwhal Khul wrote of in the Alice Bailey books is now happening. We are it. Claim this and share this with your students and friends.

The ascended masters are not going to do this for us. We, the disciples, initiates and ascended masters on Earth, are meant to do this for ourselves. We have looked too much to leadership outside of ourselves, and it is time to see that it has always been waiting to be claimed within ourselves. The inner- and outer-plane ashrams are one. They blend and merge and integrate perfectly together.

Set up your team as you imagine the inner-plane ashrams of the great masters are set up. Sense the cooperation, the freedom from ego, the commitment to service, the team unity. Call on the inner-plane ashram that you are most connected to for help. I believe that each inner-plane ashram has at least 400 core members and many more peripheral members. Ask to merge and blend completely with this ashram and become one with its purpose. Ask for this not only for yourself but also for all team members.

The idea is for your externalized ashram to become an extension of this inner-plane ashram, just like the seven ashrams of Lord Maitreya and the chohans are extensions of Buddha's ashram in Shamballa. Buddha's ashram in Shamballa is an extension of the Lord of Sirius' ashram in the Great White Lodge on Sirius. That ashram is an extension of Melchizedek's ashram. Melchizedek's ashram is an extension the Cosmic Council of Twelve at the 352d level, the Mahatma. The Cosmic Council of Twelve is an extension of God. Do you see the chain of command?

The people helping you in your leadership work are extensions of you. The people helping them are continued extensions, down through animal, plant and mineral kingdoms. This is the great evolutionary chain of the spiritual and cosmic hierarchies. The ideal at whatever level you are on is to become one and completely subservient to the level around you. This allows the flow of divine intelligence and energy to come directly from the heart and mind of God to all aspects of His creation no matter how infinitesimal.

As we evolve in our leadership we will slowly but surely move up the chain of command and others will take our place. This will continue until all eventually return to God. All we need to focus on now is doing our piece of the puzzle, whatever it might be, as perfectly as we can. When that is complete, the next phase of leadership, service and initiation will be given.

The Group Body

One of the keys to effective leadership is to see the group body and team, or ashram, as an extension of oneself. The leader is like the head of a larger body. The key is to take advantage of the potentiality on all levels of this larger body.

Leadership moves in stages. It begins with self, expands to two or three and then slowly but surely expands larger and larger. This can occur in a spiritual group or business, in sports or volunteer work. Taking advantage of the group body takes a shift in your perception and identification. In the stages of evolution we can see this shift from identifying first with oneself as a personality to ourselves as a soul, then as a monad or mighty I Am Presence, then as a grouping of monads. After this we evolve to a more complex grouping of monads on the solar, then galactic, universal, multiuniversal and, finally, at the ultimate cosmic levels.

It is important to understand that in the ultimate sense of things there is only one monad and only one soul. This is similar to what Jesus meant when he said that God has only one son or daughter. We are all a part of the sonship/daughtership. In the same vein there is only one monad.

Moving into full cosmic leadership is to recognize and own that fact. Again, this requires a shift in identification. There are many stages in between of greater and greater identification to fully realize this level. In the ultimate sense of leadership, every being in the infinite universe is a part of your group body and you are a part of theirs.

Begin seeing life more from this fluctuating consciousness of shifting back and forth from individual to group consciousness. Individual consciousness still needs to be maintained. It is not egotistical to have an individual consciousness. The lesson is to maintain both simultaneously, and to shift back and forth as needed in identifying with these larger and larger levels of monadic consciousness through the 352 levels of the Mahatma. At this stage of development, one is not afraid to call and ask for help.

The keynote of the new age and Aquarian Age is group consciousness. We limit ourselves in the most unbelievable manner by not calling upon the group consciousness and group body for help. This group body can be seen in a personal or impersonal sense. On a personal level, for example, my leadership is focused in the Djwhal Khul/Kuthumi/Lord Maitreya/Melchizedek synthesis ashram and in the planetary ascension movement. On an impersonal level, I share leadership with everyone as you do, because we are all one, and God has in truth one son, or one monad.

The key lesson for leadership here is to call on the group potentiality of those you lead personally and also on the help of those you lead impersonally. When I ask people around the country and globe to share my books with their students and friends and to turn people on to Wesak, I am calling on the impersonal group body for help. I can do this in a sincere manner, for I recognize them and you as my brothers and sisters in a much larger family, all working on the same team.

I call on help in a more personal manner in the ashrams of high-level disciples and initiates because of a more recognized personal leadership. Again, people are not working for me, because there is no me, for my identity is completely immersed in Djwhal Khul, Lord Maitreya, Melchizedek and my own group-monadic consciousness. When people help me they are in truth helping the masters, for I retain nothing for myself. I want nothing for myself other than to be one with God and an instrument of the masters.

People, I believe, recognize this on some level and feel inspired to help by the grace of God. The spiritual path is always a greater and greater process of removing and releasing greater and greater levels of negative ego and separation consciousness. Another way of saying this is that my subconscious mind and body serve me. I completely serve my monad, as my monad completely serves the cosmic monad, thereby integrating all levels in my consciousness and making me one with all individual monads because of my progressing consciousness toward complete identification with the cosmic monad. This is similar to the trinity of God.

God is a trinity of the Father, Son and Holy Spirit, which function as one. The idea is for the Father, Son and Holy Spirit and God's sons and daughters on Earth to function as one. To achieve this is nothing more than a shift in perception and attitude. When you think with your Christ mind, this is how it is. When you think with the negative ego or lower-self mind with its lack of integration and separation, then fear is created. When you are one with God, you are automatically one with all your brothers and sisters, for God *is* your brother and sister.

More and more as you evolve, begin to identify yourself as not just the individualized monad but as the cosmic monad. For more information on this, read *Cosmic Ascension.*

More Leadership Qualities

The ideal leader is always fair and respectful in dealings with people. He/she is not afraid to question or be questioned, to challenge or be challenged. This is always done, however, in a spirit of love, respect and friendship. The ideal leader welcomes new ideas and perspectives from spirit, the ascended masters and fellow team members. Total group intelligence is emphasized and cultivated. The ideal leader has a strong sense of self, self-mastery, inner confidence and self-love tempered with humility. The ideal leader is not afraid to take risks and be creative, for failure does not exist in her vocabulary or thinking.

Most of all, the ideal leader has an overwhelming desire to help others. The only desire of the ideal spiritual leader is to realize fully his/her ascension and remain on Earth to be of service to the Spiritual Hierarchy and humanity. The source of strength of the ideal spiritual leader is God and the masters and his own personal power and commitment. The ideal spiritual leader is a good problem-solver who knows when to ask the masters and other people for help.

The ideal spiritual leader welcomes adversity and sees everything that occurs as a spiritual test and opportunity to grow. He/she is very organized, but is not neurotic or an extreme perfectionist. The ideal spiritual leader returns phone calls, writes thank-you letters and considers other people's time and energies as important as his.

Contamination by Negative Ego

When leadership is contaminated by negative ego, it can take many forms. Negative-ego contamination in a leader can manifest in these ways: hunger for power and money, self-inflation, drive for fame, competitiveness and comparing, jealousy, power struggles, ego battles, lack of team unity, judgment and criticism, grandiosity, negative manipulation, materialistic ambition, sexual misconduct, self-centered isolationism, too much selfish desire, inability to take feedback, inability to integrate group consciousness, making money more important than service, superiority complex, lack of universalism in leadership, self-absorption, anger used as a means of control, elitism with team, concern with self rather than team members and personality issues that contaminate leadership. This list could go on and on, but these are some of the basic ones to watch out for.

The Concept of Kaizen

The word *kaizen* is a Japanese word that means "constant improvement." The ideal leader cultivates this attitude of kaizen, which means to do your best and then try to do better than your best. The idea here is to appreciate the achievements of yourself and your team, but on another level never be satisfied. This is the true pursuit of excellence. The lack of kaizen is what allows some people to achieve some level of success and then remain there as if this were the ultimate goal.

This concept can be applied to the spiritual path. You can reach, let's say, the seventh initiation and be satisfied, not continuing your cosmic ascension with the same level of intensity you had in pursuing your planetary ascension. The ideal spiritual leader enjoys accomplishment, but will never be satisfied until cosmic ascension is achieved by all. To strive for perfection and work hard becomes a lifestyle no matter how much success or how many spiritual achievements you attain. I personally can relate to this in how I have lived my life. This quality is a sure sign of an effective leadership group.

Making Clear Contracts

Another very important leadership skill is making very clear contracts with team leaders. This can save much future misunderstanding. For each job that is given be very clear about what the rewards are and the timetable for completion. Also explain any other ground rules. I have made the mistake of not doing this in the past, and a job might end up taking many, many months longer than expected. This was my fault, for I did not give a time limit in our contract. One of the biggest mistakes a leader can make is to think that other people operate on the same parameters he/she does.

Without trying to sound judgmental, I think that as a rule most people are run largely by the subconscious mind. The nature of the subconscious is to follow the line of least resistance. It operates much like the inner child, who does basically only what it has to. I have made past mistakes by thinking that other people are as disciplined and work-oriented as I am. Nothing could be further from the truth.

I have learned to make contracts with all major projects now so there is no confusion on this point. Part of the lesson here is to have the best possible people working on your team. There are many lightworkers who are very spiritual, but also very damaged emotionally and/or psychologically. In magnetizing and attracting the proper people, this should be watched out for, but of course not judged.

In meditation make it part of your prayers to attract the right people to help. This might be in the form of volunteers; often they are the best workers and helpers. When a contract is not made and agreed to, the leader might constantly need to call and motivate people to do the work. The negative ego, subconscious mind and inner child come up with a million-and-one different reasons for not taking care of business. This is probably one of the biggest lessons I have had to learn in the school of hard knocks.

My personal style is that when I have a job to do, I take care of business and just get it done. I have clearly learned, however, that this is not how most people operate. When by the grace of God I find lightworkers who know how to work and are not damaged emotionally and psychologically, I treasure them like pure gold.

Part of the lesson here is for leaders to let go of the people who are not of the highest caliber. New lightworkers cannot be brought in if the deadwood is not let go of in a loving way. Find a balance between not pushing your team members too hard but not coddling them either.

I have coddled some workers too much and let them get away with murder. This is always a tricky business. One of the key lessons here is tuning in to the ego-sensitivity factor of team members. When a person is ego-sensitive, the slightest bit of feedback is interpreted as criticism. As a matter of fact, he/she interprets almost everything as criticism even if none was given. This type of person needs to be let go of in a loving way. Usually this stems from lack of personal power, self-mastery and self-love.

In dealing with this type of person and others of an even more disturbed nature, I have learned to resort to prayer to God and to the masters. I ask Djwhal Khul, Lord Maitreya, Melchizedek and often Sai Baba to motivate them to take more responsibility. In cases such as this it is the best solution possible, other than inviting more-integrated people into the core leadership group. I like calling the team the core leadership group, for all at this level *are* truly leaders.

Look for team members who have what I call saint consciousness. These are people whose sole goal in life is to serve the masters and humanity in total joy and mastery. They are selfless in nature, and this is what I look for. They know how to work and do not complain no matter what the job. They are not lazy and do not procrastinate, yet they are extremely loving and transcend negative-ego consciousness.

By the grace of God I have a number of such souls working in the Los Angeles ashram. I cannot tell you how grateful I am to have found such souls. They make my job literally a million times much easier. One such soul is my dear friend and spiritual brother Mikio, who is my right arm in putting on the Wesak festivals. Another one I would like to acknowledge is Janna Parker, who is my left arm in the ashram, helping me with the enormous amount of deskwork.

When I have people such as these and many others not mentioned here, running the ashram is much more fun. I also try to have people I like on the team and who I consider my friends. At the highest levels of world service, work and socializing seem to blend together.

Friendship and Authority

There is certainly nothing wrong with being friends with your leadership team. This is totally appropriate but not required, of course. The only lesson here is that when it is time for the leader to assert his/her authority, she needs to be able to do this and switch hats in a loving way. It is never appropriate for a leader to talk to a team member in either a bossy or derogatory way. No matter what level we operate from, we must remember that in truth we are all God communicating and working with God. If it is a group leadership, there needs to be a slightly different approach. There is a hierarchical chain of command in the Spiritual Hierarchy and in business, and even though many lightworkers do not like this idea, it is a fact of life. As long as hierarchical leadership is not contaminated by the negative ego, this does not have to be an issue and should not be one.

Positive Qualities of Leadership

In summarizing some of the notes I have put together, here are some of the ideal qualities of an effective leader: stable, tactful, patient, tenacious, trustworthy, tolerant, understanding, upbeat, flexible, precise, professional, impersonal and personal, punctual, quick-thinking, reliable, resilient, resourceful, reputable, responsible, self-starting, self-assured, self-confident, self-mastered, self-disciplined, service-minded, sincere, friendly, hard-working, honest, interdependent, industrious, innovative, intelligent, harmless, kind, knowledgeable, likable, logical, intuitive, mature, motivated, open-minded, organized, poised, polite, positive, assertive, articulate, attentive to detail, calm, cheerful, civic-minded, conscientious, consistent, courteous, dependable, determined, dynamic, efficient, compassionate, extroverted when needed, discerning, forgiving, joyful, detached yet involved, even-minded, self-loving, self-confident, centered, balanced, inner-directed, faithful, trusting, prosperity-minded, successful, accepting, nonjudgmental, nonaggressive, group-oriented. He is a leader yet not superior, competitive or self-righteous. She is authoritative, tolerant, assertive yet never aggressive or intimidating, harmless, discreet, honest and has integrity.

Daily Tasks

Another ability of an effective leader is to be able to break down team leadership responsibilities into doable tasks in an appropriate manner. The group might have a great vision, but how does this translate on a daily basis in terms of what needs to get done and who is going to do what? This is where many groups fail. The vision might be great, but it translates into earthly manifestation on a daily basis as chaotic. This is where the group consciousness is important. No one person has all skills and abilities.

The group body must be examined to see who is best fitted for what skills and jobs. Where a piece is missing, these people need to be manifested or magnetized from outside the core group. The leader must also recognize his/her own limitations and replace self with the appropriate people. Once proper people are in place, exacting guidance as to each person's mission and assignment must be clearly delineated on a daily basis. Goal objectives for the week, month, quarter and year should be clearly defined.

Good Judgment

One of the most important leadership lessons is for the leader to make good decisions on how he/she uses time and energy. The leader should not do work that other people can do. The ideal leader should focus on those activities that only he can do. This can be a difficult lesson for leaders, for they are used to doing many of these other things. One example of this for me personally is opening all the mail that comes in during Wesak celebrations.

I am used to opening my own mail. This takes an enormous amount of time, especially when I am trying to put on a workshop for 1200 to 2500 people. I can spend at least three hours a day just dealing with mail, book orders and letters. The fact is, I like doing this. The key lesson for me, however, is that it is not a good use of my time. I could be writing new books, seeing clients or taking care of business and phone calls that only I can take care of.

Another example is how people put off the big jobs they have to do and instead focus on the unimportant little tasks. Using good judgment in this matter has been a letting-go process for me. Now, having let go and really being clear on this lesson, it is an enormous relief. This has freed me to do the creative endeavors that God and the masters really want me to do and for which I have a gift. Team members are happy to help, for they clearly see the wisdom in this decision.

Saying No

Another very important lesson for those in leadership and for those moving into leadership is the ability to say no, to be spiritually selfish and set boundaries. An effective leader must not be worried about what other people think or about hurting the feelings of people who are too ego-sensitive. There is a time in life to say yes and a time to say no. Just as one must say no to all negative-ego thoughts and impulses in one's own mind, the same applies to the outside world, like when someone calls on the phone or comes to the door to sell you something, or when a street person asks for money. At least 50 percent of the time a person solid in his/her leadership needs to say no and not feel guilty for doing so.

How many of you who are reading this section have given money or time when you really did not want to? This was because you were reluctant in that moment to say no. There could be many reasons for this, including guilt, fear, being on automatic pilot and so on. The reasons do not matter; the lesson is to give yourself permission from now on in all situations to say no in a tough-love manner. In truth, you are doing the other person a favor, for you are not wasting his/her time.

Another example of this is when someone tries to sell you something over the phone and you know you are not going to buy that service, yet you listen to the speech anyway. You have just wasted his time as well as yours. The ideal leader needs to have the keen intuition and discernment to know when to step in and say no and stop negative or irrelevant things from going on within self and in interactions with other people. This is part of empowerment.

Fostering a Sense of Accomplishment

Another important leadership skill is the ability to convey to the leadership group a sense of accomplishment on a continual basis. There is a very close relationship between motivation and a sense of accomplishment. We all know what a good feeling a sense of accomplishment really is. The danger here is for the leader to be continually focused upon the unlimited amount of work that needs to be done without conveying to the team members that short-term goals are actually being achieved. A little praise and sense of accomplishment goes a long way toward maintaining morale.

Another aspect of this lesson is to be cognizant of the jobs that individuals as well as the group are doing. When a given individual has done a job beyond the call of duty, which is quite often the case, it is important to acknowledge him/her individually in front of the team and when appropriate at larger events in front of the general public and the masters. Being gracious is infectious. It brings out the best in people.

I have noticed a joyful phenomenon of "battling" in friendly ways as to who can be more selfless and giving. This is good. People speak of colds and flu as being infectious. Well, I have news for you: saintliness can be just as infectious. Let the spirit of saintliness and selfless generosity and giving be the energy that is transmitted among team members.

Self-Knowledge

The premiere quality of an effective leader is a continual commitment to work on self and to correct character flaws. Do not fall into the negative-ego trap of thinking just because you are a leader, are well-known and have achieved your ascension, you do not have to work upon yourself as hard as always. Being a leader, you have to work on yourself even harder. Always strive to achieve greater self-knowledge, for this is the ultimate key to your success.

Leadership Must Be Earned

Anyone can claim to be a leader, but this is really only the first step. True leadership, however, must be earned. It is earned through long years of self-service and commitment to your ideals. It is also earned by demonstration among your peers. When you have truly earned it, people will give it to you, for people will sense this quality within your aura and being. By continually demonstrating the christed qualities of leadership rather than negative-ego leadership, you will earn the admiration and respect of those you lead.

Building Relationships

Building relationships is a skill that all leaders need to develop. Begin by building relationships with your team and top business members. Then expand to building relationships with colleagues, families of team members and fellow leaders in the field. This is one of the jobs of being a leader —acting as an ambassador for the work you represent.

Most people are successful, not because of their résumé, no matter how impressive it is, but because of the relationships they have built with people. This involves the development of good social and networking skills. Nothing will help build your business or leadership goals and achievements more than the good relationships you build. Most decisions are not made for intellectual reasons but because of how people feel about you. It is very important for spiritual leaders to network in person, on the phone, by mail and by fax machine. The time spent doing this is worth its weight in gold and will open many doors for yourself and your friends.

Do not be a leader who lives isolated from team members and separate from the world community. Take risks, make phone calls, send free products and give your professional information and advertising materials away at every opportunity. Do not be afraid to sell yourself. Make trades where appropriate. Do joint workshops, conferences and seminars with leaders of differing backgrounds and orientations. You will never know when you might need to call on these relationships in the future. I have been amazed at how open, gracious and generous many of these relationships are. In return, this has encouraged me to reciprocate. Very often it is these acquaintances and relationships, which at the time did not seem to mean a lot, that turn out to be the keys to your success. The more relationships you build with people, the more that spirit and the masters have an opportunity to work. Building relationships is in truth a leadership imperative.

Self-Motivation

A leader needs to be self-motivated and self-actualized. The leader does not have anyone to give him/her strokes or pep talks or all the other things he is trying to give the team members. This is the nature of the beast, so to speak. The whole idea of being a leader is that these qualities are contained within self and do not need to come from an outside source. The paradox is that credit and honor usually come when you no longer need it. A leader can certainly enjoy it, but the nature of being an effective leader is that everything you need you give to yourself.

Effective leaders are excellent parents to their own inner child. Self-validation and self-empowerment are abilities firmly built into their psyche. Hence, they are totally inner-directed and do not need outer direction.

This self-actualization allows leaders to lead effectively.

How to Deal with Ego-Sensitive Personalities

One of the most important jobs of the team leader is to facilitate the healing and the freedom from ego among the team group. Every business, team group and spiritual community, no matter where, will have personalities and ego sensitivities as well as negative-ego feelings and emotions come up. Petty jealousies, competitiveness, comparing, anger, irritation, impatience and judgment often arise. There is no group on the planet that does not have this operating, because there is no group on the planet that is totally clear of the negative ego, including mine.

When stuff comes up within the core group, we often speak of it as our inner child acting up, which is a nice way to frame it. In the larger ashram, this issue has constantly to be dealt with and monitored. No group can get rid of negative ego completely; however, the lesson is to minimize these reactions.

The first way to do this is to communicate clearly to the group and to everyone who enters the business or team that this is one of the main philosophical principles by which the organization is guided. You might even write up some kind of philosophical doctrine and read or maybe even have people sign before joining the team.

When things come up, communication is the key and things should be worked out as soon as possible. The negative ego is like a cancer. If it is allowed to grow, it can contaminate the entire group. When certain members do not have a handle on this, they should be called aside privately by the leader and/or core leadership group and in total love but firmness be told that this type of consciousness and behavior is unacceptable.

In my case, Djwhal Khul has told us that negative-ego consciousness is not allowed in his inner-plane ashram or in the externalized ashram. Counseling, books and support are recommended for that individual, and if he/she continues to cause great decisiveness and separation, he will have to be removed from the ashram in a loving and forgiving way. Everything possible must be done to help that person first, however. In some cases that might not be possible and the team leader must have the mastery and power to remove the person.

When personality issues arise and people do not have control of their negative ego, I recommend that they read *Soul Psychology* as well as Marianne Williamson's and Jerry Jampolsky's books, which are based on *A Course in Miracles*. I also recommend John Bradshaw's book *Homecoming: Reclaiming and Championing Your Inner Child*. It must be realized that most lightworkers are much more developed spiritually than psychologically.

The Ability to Motivate

Another quality of good leaders is the ability to motivate. They are usually passionate in their appeal and have the ability to inspire people to action. When this ability is merged with the soul and mighty I Am Presence rather than the negative ego, we have a great and inspirational spiritual leader. Leaders with this ability can not only engage people's minds, but also their spirit and emotional body. John Kennedy had this ability and Jesse Jackson, regardless how one feels about his politics, has this ability. Martin Luther King was a classic example. Some of his speeches are legendary.

When a public speaker uses the full potential of the emotional body by using all of his/her passion and enthusiasm in combination with a brilliant mind in service of spirit, the effects can be electrifying.

Conflict Resolution

Another skill of an effective leader is his/her ability to resolve conflict. This conflict can be in-house or with outside people or leaders. Conflict is inevitable and unavoidable once you step into leadership. It comes with the territory. One of the most outstanding leaders in the world who exemplifies this quality of leadership is former president Jimmy Carter. He has set up an institute for the purpose of conflict resolution. We are all aware of the success he has had around the world. Foreign dignitaries continually ask for his help when unsolvable conflicts have arisen. President Carter is more loved now for the work he is doing than while he was president. It is basically because of this extraordinary ability. This is the president who helped broker the peace agreement between Israel and Egypt.

Resolving conflict has to do with letting go negative-ego barriers and attachments. It has to do with finding common ground instead of differences. Another great leader in conflict resolution was Mahatma Gandhi. When conflicts arose in India's movement for self-rule, his incredible spirit of selflessness and commitment to nonviolent protest inspired others to resolve conflict peaceably. His extraordinary example touched a deep, soulful chord in India, Great Britain and the whole world.

Those skilled in conflict resolution are trustworthy, honest and can be objective. They are expert at unifying rather than separating. They are experts in spiritual forms of communicating rather than negative-ego forms. They are able to facilitate compromise and a spirit of integrity. They are in truth peacemakers. They are adept at helping others release fear and embrace love and forgiveness. They are able to show the people involved that they can disagree without creating separation and disrespect.

Conflict-resolution experts are skilled in inspiring soul and Holy Spirit consciousness rather than lower self, negative-ego, attack/defense consciousness. This is a skill that all effective leaders should strive to develop. Leaders with skills in conflict resolution first establish all the areas in which there is agreement. They then resolve the areas of disagreement that are easiest to resolve. At this point the two parties involved see that two-thirds of their problems are already resolved, which lays the foundation to resolve the last third, often the most difficult. The two-thirds successful bridge-building has opened the door and created a light at the end of the tunnel, and compromise and communication is now viewed as possible.

Now, in some cases the leader might be part of the conflict, but the same skills and ideology are used. There are many wonderful books available for those who would like to study more about this. Conflict resolution has much to do with effective communication skills and learning spiritual rather egotistical forms of communication strategies.

Considerate Supervision

The ideal leader in business or spiritual organizations has a quality that has been called considerate supervision. In other words, he/she takes care of business and gives the needed direction, guidance and orders; however, it is done in a very loving, friendly, kind and considerate manner. Though it is forceful and carries the strength of an effective leader, it is also loving, warm and has the harmlessness of a saint. This inspires team members not to resent this authority. It is the proper blending of first-, second- and third-ray energies. The supervisor demonstrates a genuine and sincere caring while still supervising. The supervisor is not so goal-oriented as to treat team members like machines or exploit them simply as a means to make money.

This could manifest by taking time away from work to help them with personal problems, by sending them home if they feel unwell or by a kind touch or word. Overall, this involves creating an atmosphere of efficiency, love and fellowship. This helps build an empowered, well-balanced, well-integrated work force where all members truly care about each other and have a sense of community and team spirit even though they might not all be personal friends. So an effective leader can also be seen as a coach and role model, not a cold, impersonal businessperson who simply gives orders.

Benefits

Another essential quality of leadership is to be able to demonstrate to team members the benefits of reaching your group's specific goals. This applies to both business and spiritual groups. If the team members know the benefits, they will be more motivated to work. If business employees know they are putting out a good product that helps the planet, this provides motivation. If they know they will get a bonus if a certain selling point is reached and/or if they know praise and gratitude is forthcoming, productivity will increase.

In spiritual groups the benefits are multifaceted. The group provides an opportunity to serve and to be a part of a spiritual team. It provides the opportunity to work directly under the ascended masters' guidance and vision. The work helps people to ascend and achieve liberation. Serving in such a manner will greatly accelerate your own ascension and initiation process. There might be financial benefits. There are benefits of friendship and companionship as well as benefits of serving God and one's brothers and sisters.

It is essential for an effective leader to keep the team aware of these benefits and to impart what a blessing it is to be able to serve in such a manner. True happiness is serving God.

Negative Manipulation vs. Clear Communication

Another quality of effective leadership is to communicate with team members in a clear, loving, calm, rational, objective, powerful and concise manner. The negative ego tries to use negative manipulation to influence people. This might have short-term success, but it will always fail in the long run. Honesty is always the best policy. Communication skills might be one of the most important qualities of an effective leadership.

Another important part of effective leadership is to make sure that each person on the team has a clear understanding of his/her role in the divine plan of the group project. It is essential that team members know their individual parts and also have an overall vision of each of the other people's parts. Each person needs to know that his/her part is essential to the completion of the plan. No part should be seen as better or worse than another; all should be seen as special and essential. This leads to an attitude free of ego and that promotes selfless service for the good of the whole. Personalities are deemphasized and group consciousness is constantly reemphasized.

Hard Work

Leaders must explain to the new team members the hard work that is often involved. I remember the great spiritual teacher from England who used to call much of the spiritual path donkey work. Hard work is actually fun when you are working for God and the masters. Any work done for God and the masters, even if it is stuffing envelopes or stapling, can realign and energize. There is much hard work to do, but the joy of completion, the feeling of a job well done on all levels and knowing that the masters are pleased and grateful is worth it a thousand times over.

Effective leaders are not afraid to work, and find great joy in working. They also know how to relax and enjoy themselves. However much of their joy, friendships and companionship stems from the work. I personally tend to be a workaholic; however, I do not find what I am doing to be work at all. For example, I do not find writing books drudgery. I love to do it. I cannot wait every day to get up as early as I can to start working. I literally cannot wait to begin. Even though I am probably a total workaholic from an objective point of view, in my personal experience I do not feel like I am working at all. I am simply doing what I enjoy doing and find most meaningful.

Leadership Can Be Learned

It is most important for all who read this book to understand that leadership *can* be learned. It begins with leadership over self, which will naturally expand to leadership of others. The ideal spiritual leader often has to wear many hats. This might be as spiritual teacher, channel, prophet, psychic, psychologist, marriage counselor, accountant, financier, minister, politician, artist, scientist and ambassador. The ideal leader moves through these as appropriate with no ego involvement.

The ideal leader is fully empowered, yet filled with compassion, empathy and love. He/she is able to set up programs and procedures for the team where needed, yet knows the appropriate balance of creativity and spontaneity in team function. She has the ability to translate intention into reality through inspiring committed group action. The ideal leader is able to take risks and is open to change.

Even though leaders do lead, they are not separate from those they lead. Leadership does not mean separation, superiority or egotistical aloofness. They are one with those they lead, yet command respect and loyalty because of their self-mastery, their love, their success and their vision. All people are destined to be leaders on the spiritual path in some capacity. It begins with self and extends to their personal family, extended family, children, neighbors, community, business, friends, professional peers, acquaintances and humanity as a whole.

Leadership is a natural byproduct of being God in your daily life. It is something you learn over time because of your complete commitment to your spiritual ideals and service to humanity. Just as we learn to become leaders over ourselves, we also learn the skills and wisdom to be effective leaders of and with other people.

Leadership can come before ascension; however, it is also the next step after ascension. The next step after ascension is planetary leadership and world service. It is the vow of the bodhisattva. You have achieved your liberation from the wheel of rebirth and you have now chosen to remain on

Earth to lead and serve others. There are many forms this can take. Some do it through words. Others do this through running big organizations, businesses or ashrams. Others do this through seeing individual clients. All do it through their example every moment of their lives.

Call forth to Sanat Kumara, Lord Buddha, Lord Maitreya, Lord Melchizedek, the Mahatma and your own mighty I Am Presence. Now call forth the anchoring and activation of the mantle of leadership as God would have it be. Let this permanent mantle you now have been given not separate you from your brothers and sisters, but make you closer to them. The purpose of your leadership is to help lead others back to God. If at times you do not know the words to say, then ask the Holy Spirit and the ascended masters of your choice to speak through you.

The only way this world is going to change is if the common people like you and me change it. This is our world, and this is our change. The masters are not going to do it, for they are long graduated and are either off to their cosmic evolution or will soon be going there. We are the externalization of the Spiritual Hierarchy. The masters help us on the inner plane by teaching and showing us how we may do this. They might guide us, but it is our job to *do* it. Do not wait to claim your leadership until everything feels perfect. You just might end up waiting forever.

Leadership is empowerment. Once you claim it, never let go of it again and be absolute steel in terms of your commitment. Never forget that true leadership is earned. Just because a person is in a position of leading people does not make him/her a good leader. Spiritual leadership is really what you are striving for, embodying and practicing it every day. It is now time to fully claim the rod and mantle of leadership, and in this moment dedicate your life to serve humanity and exemplify God to the best of your ability.

Consistency

One of the marks of a truly effective leader is that of consistency. An ideal leader is in mastery and personal power all the time. In truth, he/she never leaves this state of consciousness. He is, in a sense, locked in because of his complete devotion and commitment. An ideal leader is also completely consistent in his unconditional devotion to the ideal of balance, spiritual leadership and freedom from ego. A model leader is unwavering in his commitment to these ideals and does not give in to the lower self or to self-indulgence in weak moments or when he is tired. The ideal leader is also really not trying to be a leader; he/she just *is* a leader. This is simply a natural expression of the essence of his being.

An ideal leader never holds leadership as a means of separation or superiority but just the opposite. Leadership is consistent manifestation and expression of oneness and equality. Consistency in leadership is achieved through complete, 100 percent commitment. When this is achieved, positive leadership then becomes a positive habit in the subconscious mind and takes very little effort to maintain. The ideal leader is always the same in all situations. All archetypes blend and integrate into one consistent, ongoing manifestation.

Anyone who strives for self-mastery is a leader. Once self-mastery is achieved, it is the natural evolution of things to become a leader of other people. Your mastery and love automatically put you in this role and will draw people to you.

Leadership will be manifested in different ways, depending on each individual's mission and purpose. A leader leads others by his/her example and works toward a specific ideal. Ask to be infused with the leadership qualities and energy of Sanat Kumara, Lord Buddha, Lord Maitreya and the Holy Spirit. Ask that they imprint their leadership wisdom and knowledge upon you. Ask that all light packets of information in the spiritual archives of the Hierarchy and Shamballa be programmed into you at night while you sleep. Always remember that leadership is really the next step beyond ascension.

Task and Relationship Orientation

The ideal spiritual leader has a very fine balance between task and relationship orientation. Task orientation focuses upon achieving his/her goals and purpose. This unceasing drive to accomplish what she has set forth is an essential quality to develop. However, the ideal leader has a very strong relationship function. She focuses on goals but does not trample the emotional body of the fellow team members. Love, friendship, spiritual fellowship, spiritual community and true caring about team members are just as important as achieving the goal. This might be considered one of the aspects of achieving the proper yin/yang, or feminine/masculine, balance. It is also an aspect of the personal/impersonal balance.

Leadership Dreams

I had three personal sleep-time dreams that speak of this process of leadership development for myself that you might find interesting. In the first dream I was learning to drive a very large bus. In the beginning I was having a hard time controlling it, but after a few days I began to get the hang of it.

If you think about the difference between driving a car and a bus, a car is more individually focused and a bus carries many, people I would be driving/leading. This is the difference between having just an individual body and having an individual body *and* a group body.

In my next dream I was on the Enterprise with Captain Picard, the bald captain in *Star Trek: The Next Generation.* In the dream he comes up to me and tells me he is my father. My guidance on this dream from the masters was that being the captain of the Star Trek Enterprise is like running an inner-plane ashram. On the Enterprise there are anywhere from 400 to 2000 crew members. This is similar to Djwhal Khul's ashram. I am now in the process of training or growing into the leadership of a starship ashram. Captain Picard, whose character I like a lot, was the image that my mighty I Am Presence and subconscious mind chose to reflect this movement and development process.

In my next leadership dream I was in an auditorium of people and a man came up to me and asked me what my name was. I told him my name was Djwhal Khul. When I asked Djwhal Khul about this dream, he told me that this had to do with the unfolding process within my inner psyche to take over the ashram. Needless to say, it was a wonderful dream.

As you read this book and work with the process of leadership, track your own leadership dream process. Ask for a dream or channeling from spirit and the masters before bed regarding how they see your leadership development.

Invocation and Prayer for Leadership

Call forth the Mahatma, Melchizedek, Lord Buddha, Lord Maitreya and the seven ray masters. Stand before these masters and the Spiritual Hierarchy and give your vows of leadership and service to them. Share with them in normal language your current plans and commitment in this regard. Ask for their blessing and for the full anchoring of the mantle of leadership and service upon you. Ask and pray for their help in becoming the most effective leader and servant you possibly can. Ask and pray for their help in fully achieving your ascension so that you may lead and serve better.

In this moment you have died and been reborn. You have taken the vow of the bodhisattva, which means that you have dedicated your life to achieving your full ascension and will remain on Earth to lead and serve humanity and all God's kingdoms home. Be at peace, my friends, for you have come home and fully joined the army of high-level initiates and ascended beings who are going to transform this planet and all its inhabitants into a shining star. Victory is assured. The outcome is inevitable. It is just a matter of time. One more cell and ascending being in the body of God has now fully taken his/her place.

Kodoish, Kodoish, Kodoish Adonai Tsabayoth (Holy, holy, holy is the Lord God of hosts). Namasté to you, my fellow brothers and sisters and leaders in the light.

6

Leadership Gems

Bridging Traditional Religion and
the Ascension Movement

When looking at humankind throughout history, specifically (although certainly not exclusively) spiritual or religious history, we usually find ourselves standing agape at the new, feeling fearful, doubtful and mistrusting. When Jesus Christ lived and walked the soils of Jerusalem, there were no churches or popes and certainly no great cathedrals. Despite the success of his divine mission on Earth, there was so much fear among those living in his time and so much mistrust within the hearts and minds of Roman and Jew alike that the crowd yelled to crucify him. What they were really saying is, "Crucify this new revelation, for we are comfortable in our discomfort and have made a home of our beliefs. We are afraid!" There were others, as there always are, who welcomed the new revelation, for their souls had been anticipating it for a long, long time. We now have Christianity firmly established in its many and diverse forms, and there are churches, popes and great cathedrals. It was not an easy journey, though; revelation seldom is.

When a new religion or wisdom teaching springs forth, in the past it has been generally based on one man's vision, inspiration, light and love. Thus you have Judaism, Christianity, Buddhism and the like. Now we are in a new age, a new revelation, and this time one in which many are inspired. Where before the vision was basically given to one great soul, we are now realizing that we are each great souls and have access to Source, to inspiration, to higher beings.

I wonder sometimes why so many traditionally religious people find the concept of the ascended beings so hard to accept—or the concept of reincarnation, for that matter. Reincarnation is mentioned throughout the writings of traditional religious material. For example, Tibetan Buddhists search over the centuries for the rebirth of the Dalai Lama into his next embodiment. In the Eastern religions reincarnation is accepted as simple fact. Native Americans have gone on vision quests to find their spirit guides. People in his time wondered if Jesus was the reincarnation of John the Baptist. Jesus, who communed with the angelic kingdom, as did the Virgin Mary, spoke with beings from the other side who aided him through his mission and crucifixion. What of the saints and angels that many a Catholic prays to? Could another name for them be ascended masters? Could this also apply to Shiva, Vishnu, Rama, Ganesha and so forth of the Hindu and Eastern religions? I earnestly believe it does. A rose by any other name . . .

We are now in the age of Aquarius, which by its very nature is group consciousness. This unique period in history gives conscious access to humanity as a whole to communion with the Father/Mother God and thereby the many rooms Jesus the Christ spoke of that were in the Father/Mother's mansions, to gain the wisdom, guidance, love, light and grace of beings who have overcome the Earth. These same beings have achieved their liberation and dwell within those lofty regions.

So now we have an abundance of people accessing these frequencies, claiming their own mastery and being their own channels. It is really not such a great leap from traditional religion, simply one small step for humankind. Those who have attained a certain degree of light and wisdom are now doing what few people before them did.

Do not misunderstand me, there is plenty of room for mistakes that the negative ego can misinterpret (and I have written extensively on this matter). My main point is that this step up in consciousness has occurred and these divine beings who before were basically only believed in by the masses are now being contacted and communicated with. It is indeed a giant step for humankind, a great and wondrous new revelation. Once again the bulk of humanity is reacting with fear and doubt, staring agape into the unknown, annoyed that there is a new territory to explore that will challenge old belief systems.

However, if we were to take a good look at our so-called traditional religions, we would find that these seemingly unfamiliar new concepts have been written about over the centuries. The main difference is that what was theoretical in the past is now becoming actual in the present. I urge all Doubting Thomases to have the courage to take up this challenge. You will be relieved to find that although we are in the group consciousness of Aquarius and a giant step for humankind is unfolding, it is really only one small step—that of theoretical knowledge, communing and knowing. We are all on the path of ascension, on our way back to the godhead. I promise you this day that you will be with me in the kingdom of God (Jesus Christ, New Testament).

The Leadership Role of the United States in the Global Community

Living in America with the onslaught of noise pollution, air pollution, drive-by shootings, the national deficit, political craziness, a growing rate of unemployment and a lowering self-esteem as so many find themselves literally out on the streets, it can be somewhat difficult to hear the finer tones emitted by America. Amid all this chaos it can be nearly impossible to tune in to the fact that she has a unique and wonderful part to play in the global community. America was founded on the axiom "In God we trust," and despite the seemingly messy state we find the U.S. in, there is a divine hand at work in the development of America (as there is in the world community). Additionally, the United States of America has and is playing a key role in the world at large.

When looked at side by side with other world powers, two things about America are immediately noticeable. One is that America is not unique in her messy struggles—and is, in fact, in far better shape than many (though not all) other countries. There is more freedom here than in most other countries, and although we still have quite a ways to go, when placed next to the sheer barbarism of some of the Third World countries, America is indeed the land of the free.

The second point of note is that America, when compared with other countries and civilizations, is at best an adolescent. She is young, with no great culture to speak of, such as in Italy or England. America's history does not go back very far; in a certain sense, she is newly born. Looked at in a certain light (and I mean this literally, for I am speaking of the divine light that sees into the true nature of things), America is the melting pot of the world. She has taken in the tired, the poor and the huddled masses from a vast array of lands. She has also, as in the case of the African Americans, thrown some of her people into the pot by force; the analogy of tossing a live lobster into a vat of boiling water comes to mind. Nevertheless, here we all are during this most potent time of planetary transition, comprising the strongest and most powerful nation in the world.

Power rightly used is divine. Combined with love and wisdom, it is the manifestation of God Him/Herself. America must watch her power and look back to the founding fathers for guidance, as the people who formed our country were overlighted by the masters and guided to form "one nation under God." And so they did to the best of their ability. God's name is on the face of the dollar bill, as is the pyramid and the symbol of the third eye, which pierces through the veil.

People came here to escape tyranny and create a world of freedom. In a short time America has evolved into the land of the free, relatively speaking.

Being young, however, America must watch herself lest as an adolescent she runs amok with ego power, ignoring issues of health, education, the plight of the poor and so forth. Another aspect of this land is not so young and has much wisdom to offer. It is culture of the Native American people, who graced this soil for a long time with love, devotion, understanding and unity with Mother Earth—wisdom that Americans as a whole would do well to learn. Those who were called here were brought with a divine plan in mind. As young as America is as we know her, it does us well to remember the roots of the land and the great culture that begs to be incorporated into her. Our strengths are many indeed. The entire world looks to us for aid, some seeing us as a threat, but as a nation we have a high profile.

We would do well to look back to our ideals of our founding fathers and the basic Earth wisdom of the Native American. Then, hopefully, we can take our great assets and bring them into full maturity, fulfilling our true place in the scheme of things to the best of our ability.

We must learn to use the materials we have without being lost in materialism. We must remember that the homeless people are ourselves only a couple of paychecks away and not see them and us as two separate species. We should see that this is our mutual trouble and do what we can to help correct the situation. We cannot personally solve every problem of this great nation, but we can pay attention to what is going on in the world and nation and do our utmost to help put the people of greatest light into the leadership positions of government.

We are now moving into a higher dimension, the new millennium, and it is time for America to grow up and acknowledge her position, working to fulfill her unique calling in the global community. She is, after all, at the forefront of the global community and possesses many advantages that other countries only dream of. As has been stated, when much is given, much is expected. This is true of the United States of America, with its unique position.

A Look at Russia and Other Aspects of Nations

It is not our intent to get too specific or detailed in this chapter that takes a higher-dimensional view on leadership positions. These gems or gifts of wisdom are given forth to broaden the readers' view that all positions, events, movement and the turning and transforming of and upon planet Earth be viewed from the highest, most inclusive and divinely humane position possible. We are not here to represent a specific political platform, but to guide each to the most expansive place possible from which to make all choices, political and otherwise, and from which to develop leadership qualities. The one thing that can and must be specifically stated, however, is that no nation can flourish under totalitarianism or dictatorship, as that is directly counter to hierarchical intent.

Each person and indeed each nation as a whole, with its many peoples, have as their birthright and divine destiny to find their connection with Source, freed from all tyrannies within and without to pursue their unique course of evolution within the whole. With that in mind, we will say a bit about Russia.

Taking into account her historical background, Russia has achieved a wonderful victory in her evolution in the abolishment of the Union of Soviet Socialist Republics (USSR) to a more freely based, independent-functioning government. Freedom from totalitarian control is now being experimented with in the various smaller countries that comprised the USSR and in Russia herself. However, it must be understood that these countries are still in a very precarious position. If we were to look at our own personal life and in a broader sense society in general, it would easily be established that we are often more comfortable with the known, even a known evil or negativity, than a venture into the unknown.

The only way to overcome this tendency is to supersede the negative ego with the higher self. That, of course, is a process. There are also those who comprised (and still do) the underbelly of the former USSR society, those who feed off control, ruthlessness, fear and terror and who seek desperately to reestablish that control at all costs. This danger is not unique to Russia's specific situation, although it is certainly something to watch out for. Those in whom the negative ego reigns supreme are bent on selfishness, greed, materialism and feed on fear and confusion. They will always, and most definitely in this situation, seek to regain that control using the changes and upheaval apparent in the societies of Russia and the former states of the USSR.

These same people will work by subterfuge, taking advantage of times of apparent peace when the guard is down to make their moves. Therefore I give you a word of caution in this regard. Those upholding the light in any and all areas must always keep vigilant and watchful lest the power-hungry find means to corrupt that light. Those candles burn bright in the new freedoms of Russia and the surrounding countries, so this word should provide ample food for thought and vigilance.

Seen from a hierarchical standpoint, the issues remain global and intrinsic to humanity as a whole. The divine plan is that each person on Earth grow increasingly free—free within and free without.

Any government using any sort of coercion, force and, above all, fear and fear tactics to control its people is running counter to the winds of evolution. Every nation is guilty of this to one degree or another, so each must work from where it is at to cleanse and uproot these negative qualities and align itself with purity and love. Under the communist regime, the Soviet Union with its KGB has run rampant in its use of fear and terror, and the individuals involved in carrying out those deeds have much to answer for. Those aligned with light have much work to do to see that such forces do not gain a foothold again.

On a different note it might surprise many to know that from the hierarchical standpoint, communism per se is not negative. It is only the negative ego that makes it so. This is equally true of democracy. Both in their purest and most evolved forms have much to offer. Contained within the word *communism* is "commune," and from that comes "community." Is it not community that those who are pulsing to the beat of the age of Aquarius are seeking in abundance?

Democracy focuses on divine independence and freedom that in its highest development, freed of the entrapments of materialism, negative egotism and the division between the haves and have-nots, has a great and glorious destiny. There is potentially great good within these two apparently different forms of government. It is the Hierarchy's intent to aid humanity to develop societies that operate from a soul and monadic level in order to bring to glory the human potential.

At this time the democratic nations are way ahead of all types of regimes of oppression, to be sure, but until humanity is freed from the oppression of the negative ego within itself, it will not be able to bring that forth in any of its nations.

We remind you that we are not speaking specifically about political platforms and ideologies, but about soul/monadic evolution, the abundant use of goodwill or the will-to-good operating at its highest level so that the form of any government will represent that of the good, the beautiful and the true. This applies to all nations and all peoples. There is not one way, but there is only one One. The unique manifestation of the One is channeled through the various ray qualities of a nation similar to the way the rays work through and within a person, soul and monad. The goal of a nation is to access its ray's highest qualities. I give more explicit details on the rays of various nations in *Cosmic Ascension.*

The individual, the nation and the planet itself contact their respective highest potentials, seek to be and act from that highest level. Remember that the will-to-good is of light and ever strives to manifest that. Let man give to man, nation give to nation and both man and nation give to themselves the freedom to pursue their highest levels of self-expression, never having to hold another or themselves in the grasp of fear or fear tactics, but only grow and evolve on a foundation of mutual respect and spiritual values.

The Bombing of Hiroshima and Nagasaki

A vastly complex issue cannot be answered on a simple level. I have asked the masters their view of the nuclear bombing of Hiroshima and Nagasaki and this was the first clear answer I received. The second was simply looking at some footage or photos of those bombings and see what came up for me. The third answer, which leads to this discourse, is that such an occurrence is not an isolated issue but is woven into the core and choices of humanity over a vast period of time.

The soil and the climate of a world that breeds or opens the doorway for such a horrific expression of negative ego and evil as that which manifested during the Nazi regime and World War II is the climate that led to the culmination of that evil in the devastating bombings of one group of humanity upon another.

What I am being told is to look to humanity itself for the answer, to look at the world as a whole and then to the various nations that opened themselves up to the lowest aspects of their rays and potentialities, which allowed for this evil. If that word seems harsh, please note that it is not directed against a particular nation, but the climate of all nations that allowed the few representatives of true negativity to gain sway and take hold over the planet.

Once evil or negativity of such magnitude takes hold, it invariably runs amok. It had to be stopped. There is no doubt that it had to be stopped in what seemed the only way possible. There is great doubt and much predictability insofar as things breed things of a like nature. So, says the Hierarchy, the question should not be whether we should have dropped the bombs, for the very nature of the question contains the answer. When havoc is rampant, there is no wisdom. The question should instead be how to create a climate where such questions become unnecessary.

If this seems trite or seems to avoid the issue, pause for a moment and look around. Pockets of light are arising all around the globe, to be sure, but the world at large is in crisis. It is a crisis of transformation, but it is vital that we who are representatives of the light get out there and shine our light into each and every arena of life. We each have a particular calling, a path, a ray we operate from, and some of these rays give us a nature that will take us into the political arena itself. This is very much the seventh ray, which is the ray coming into full manifestation at this time. Each of the rays offers opportunities for each of us to do what we do and live and manifest the godliness that we are within the world.

There is no doubt that we each have a part to play that is a vital contribution to the whole. It has been stated by beloved Djwhal Khul through Alice Bailey many times over (and I paraphrase), all it takes for the negative ego to triumph is enough men and women of Christ/Buddha consciousness (or goodwill) to do nothing!

Therefore, I am told the answer to my question regarding the past atrocities on all levels is to be found in the *now* by each and every one of us leaving no stone unturned in our personal cleansing and by moving into the age of love/wisdom revealed and by having the courage to play our part.

Was it okay to drop such a weapon as the atomic bomb on two cities? No, it was not okay. However, was it okay for leaders to manifest such extreme negativity as was the case in World War II, to gain the power they did and to commit crimes of the highest magnitude with pure evil intent? The answer can only be a resounding no!

Preventing a repetition of that scenario becomes a very personal, meditative, love-embracing, cleansing and healing from within and is embodied in the courage to manifest the light outwardly within the arena of the world in the way you are best suited. It is the soil, the climate, the pulse beat of humanity itself that must shift from a negative-ego-based personality and even nationality to an all-inclusive global unity. That is another reason why, my beloved readers, I am so strongly urged by the Hierarchy to make the Wesak celebration a global event.

The transformation that the turning of the divine wheel seeks to bring forth is on a global scale, yet it must (and this is vital) arise sincerely out of the hearts, souls, minds and spirits of each person individually through meditation, self-examination and right service to the whole in which we all live, move and have our being.

The final answers to my questions come to me in the form of guidance. We must all stop being inwardly dictators, manipulators and racists. We must heal the cleavages in our very own natures and thence take an active role in healing the cleavages that divide our planet. We must seek ever to grow and expand, but in an organic manner. We cannot take the kingdom of God by force, nor should we ever try to force our views or seek control.

The outer invariably reflects the inner, so we must be steadfast in the light, love and gentle divine power of God. Let us learn not to beat ourselves up in the process, for that serves no purpose to growth but instead is like dropping bombs upon our own tender and precious selves daily—and for some of us, hourly.

The kingdom of God lies within and is manifested without in accordance with our inner worlds. So let us till the soil of love divine that we might so manifest that divinity that we will not need to ask questions regarding past horrors, but rather say how to do the greater good.

Thus the masters have answered my inquiry.

Terrorism

There are really no two ways to look at acts of terrorism, for the word contains the description and very meaning of these terrible and horrific acts being unleashed against God and humanity. There is, however, a way to understand terrorism in the context of the world in which we live, and we must vigilantly work to transform it both within ourselves and in the outer world at large. We and our world are operating out of a base of fear rather than a base of love.

This problem of terrorism is multidimensional in that both outer and inner measures are called for to bring it to an abrupt halt. If one were to take just one more step in looking at these devastating and horrific acts, one would see that part and parcel of the cause of terrorism as it operates on the scale and in the manner it is now, is based upon the fact that the planet is moving into the light, and those who still hold fast to the darkness within themselves must fight with every ounce of strength to keep that darkness alive and functioning. So terrorism must be addressed from various angles and must be dealt with likewise from various levels of being.

The highest way is of course to keep on transforming oneself and one's world into a love-based world. When all are resonating to the keynote of love, then fear and terror will have no place. When we do not do this, we terrorize ourselves daily in seemingly little ways, but the cumulative effect is to be put into a state of shock not unlike the shock of a moment during a terrorist attack.

Years of living in fear outside a love-based reality will wreak as much havoc as a moment of terror. However, the highest way is the path of evolution/ascension into the love/light itself, a process that takes time. The best we can do is to take the time we need and be as aware as we can in each instant to overcome fear by love.

The next step is to teach this to each other. Let friends be mirrors one to the other to wash away negative patterns of fear and terror and replace them with love. A word to the wise: Do this lovingly and with patience, or do not do it at all. Otherwise you will succeed only in creating more fear, apprehension and fear of failure. By all means teach the children self-love and the love of the whole. Help them see the world as it is in all its magnificent madness of transformation and teach them to be part of the solution, not the problem. How? By love, not fear; by direction, not scolding; by encouragement and teaching self-esteem. Bring this to the schools, to camp, to playgrounds and sports arenas, but you who have influence over the children, in heaven's name, bring them love!

These vile acts of terrorism shatter a person's physical, etheric, astral and mental bodies and lead him/her down the road to more fear and mistrust, which is exactly what these acts are designed to do. The question remains, how do we deal with the acts and the perpetrators themselves? We cannot stand idly by nor should our government. However, we should and must each act from our highest level, for we each have our puzzle piece. Let the meditators meditate on love and invoke God's and the masters' help in overcoming fear with love.

On the other side of the spectrum, let the earthly protectors protect and use every means available to prevent these acts from happening. This is no easy task, but a task force should indeed be operating at peak preventive level, investigating possible and potential target points and keeping alert on the physical level to stop any possible acts of terrorism that can be even remotely anticipated. The trap here is that it inevitably breeds fear and mistrust. Even the scanners at airports can give one a sinking feeling. Unfortunately, with the great acceleration of light is the darkness revealed, and therefore efforts must be made at every appropriate level to keep that darkness in check.

There is one further factor. The Earth is out of balance between the haves and have-nots, be it neighbor to neighbor or country to country. This inevitably creates a ripe soil for discontent among the have-nots, and into that discontent, darkness and negativity find ample opportunity to take hold and, in extreme cases such as terrorism, run rampant. The work of bringing the world into a more balanced state is not an overnight process and each of us needs to do our part from our level. The causes of terrorism are vast, as is the cure, but to get to the core of this problem and many another is to see that we can choose either fear or love. Perfect love must and shall cast out all fear. The steps on this arduous journey must be taken by each of us according to our point of evolution. But take steps to make the effort, whether in meditation, in politics or in the heat of the fray, and be ever mindful that ultimately a world built on love and light will abolish these terrible crimes as well as a host of other problems. It is up to each of us to examine our own part and perform them in the best and highest way possible.

The Olympics

It is vital to understand that from the Hierarchy's point of view, each rung on the ladder of evolution has its place. Though it would not be appropriate for a group of masters to get together for a bit of the healthy competition, setting out to prove their personal best, the grand Olympic competitions carry an enormous positive force for growth, unity, development, the cultivation of group consciousness and extreme discipline. These competitions bring out much in humanity, and that is why they are so exciting and pull so many people into the heart and rhythm of the events.

For one thing, let us consider the discipline needed, the hours of train-ing and dedication that each person who makes the Olympic team must put forth. This teaches the soul much and brings one into a point of focus that is not normally called for. This quality of discipline and focus will eventually come into play in the subtler realms of meditation. It is a quality that every chela on the path will need in moving up the ladder of evolution.

The Olympics demands the development of such dedication, discipline and focus that it is permanently imprinted on the soul of the participant, an imprint that can be called on in future endeavors, useful for bringing focus in meditation, thus avoiding many a laborious struggle that they who delve into the higher realms so often have, not having had this background of dis-cipline.

A great sense of unity is also cultivated because each member stands with pride not only for him/herself but for her country. The realms that the trailblazers, the initiates, are moving into are global; the realms of the mas-ters are universal in ever more inclusive degrees. Let us not forget this. The ideal of group consciousness must start somewhere, and a magnificent way to experience unity of country is through the Olympic games. A far better show of devotion to one's country than war, would you not say? Here in these games each one stands for him/herself in his own individuality with all his hopes, dreams and desires—and likewise for the country he repre-sents. On a higher turn of the spiral, each of us also stands in our own indi-viduality, merging that individuality into the plan, purpose and being of ever greater wholes, such as global, planetary, solar and cosmic.

How beautiful is the passing of the lighted torch from one to another! So too the masters pass their flame from one to the other as they move on-ward and upward. The beautiful fluidity of motion expressed by the many athletes reflects the fluidity of the movement of life. Notice how the first ray is invoked, which is that of will, the will of each and every participant to do his/her best. The second ray of love/wisdom is expressed in the love of that particular sport and the understanding of the tools needed to develop the required skill. There is a science to each sport (fifth ray), a struggle and an art (fourth ray), a demand for intelligence (third ray), the understanding of each particular skill and much devotion (sixth ray) to the sport itself, the trainer, the team goal, the country represented and, of course, to the great event of the Olympics itself.

As all this is put forth in a tremendous ceremony (seventh ray) the likes of which has seldom been seen, we can note that all the various rays play their part in splendor and intense application.

So the Olympics provides an organism through which the players as well as the watching world are brought into a kind of miniversion of God It-self at play. This is why such excitement is generated and also why negative forces will often spring up and attack, struggling to grasp at a world transforming into light and reaching in desperation to squelch that light. This can be seen in the various acts of terrorism throughout recent Olympic history.

It must be mentioned, however, that there are still a couple of areas where there is room for growth within the Olympic arena. It is the Hierarchy's vision that those participating in the event, be they athlete or spectator, transform their personal pride into group integrity, love and devotion to one's country and even more, into a global sense of love and devotion. It is their hope that eventually the focus and discipline for a particular sport will grow into the focus, discipline and dedication of that sport performance to God.

The hierarchical intent is to see humanity move away from the focus of ego consciousness, even if that is the ego of a particular country, and into the Olympics focus of a global competition. It is true that the vehicle of these events has moved forward and has grown more inclusive and expansive, but the time is at hand when an even greater expansion of consciousness is ready to occur.

If we move the Olympics one more step up the ladder, imagining these great games taking place just one rung higher, then we would not have country against country but rather each country contributing its own unique gifts, talents and skills to what would be a global victory. With this approach everyone participating would already feel victorious in the level of mastery they have developed. Competition would still play its part, urging each nation and each individual to do his/her very best, but each athlete's ego would not be so much on the line.

The athletes, having brought to mastery a particular skill, would then reveal that mastery in their performance and dedicate it to God and the global community rather than solely to the country they represent. True, they would be on teams, but the attitude would be one of national best for the glory of God rather than nation against nation. This attitude would likewise eliminate the desperate need to earn the gold medal, so much so that silver medalists are often distraught at having come so close to the gold. This need not be the focus. If the focus of the Olympics were to change, the participants would find that on the next step up the ladder, the event presents all humanity as the divine golden child, each in our own way polishing that gold to a shimmering luster.

Let the light of the Olympics shine forth and the flame burn brightly. Let each participant gain the value of all seven rays as he/she exercises, runs, swims and so on, her way through the Olympics. Let all participants and spectators alike continue to grow within the arena that the Olympics provides by becoming a more universal whole, shining with ever greater brightness the light, love, power and unity of purpose that is humanity's destiny.

In summary, how one sees the Olympics depends on which lens he/she is looking through. When looked at from the level of the personality, the Olympics is definitely a movement toward greater soul consciousness. When looked at from the lens of the soul and monad, the Olympics are moving in the right direction, but still retain too many negative-ego concerns such as preoccupation with being the best, egotistical competition and patriotism, lack of sportsmanship and winning a gold medal to the extent that a silver or bronze medal is interpreted as failure. The Olympics are definitely soul-inspired events. The next step is to bring forth complete soul and monadic infusion, and the Olympic Games will become even better than they are now, allowing more and more of the higher aspects and potentials of humankind to shine forth.

Affirmative Action

You must realize, beloved ones, that when the planetary and cosmic hierarchies are asked to speak on worldly matters, we do so from an entirely different point of view or lens than if a human functioning within these three-dimensional systems were to speak on such matters. This is so because the broader perspective is always held within our range of vision, and it is most difficult to speak from a more limited perspective when the whole vista of unfolding evolution stands revealed to our unclouded vision.

With this in mind, however, we will seek to answer this question regarding affirmative action and relate to you our view from the vantage point of the Hierarchy. We understand that this is a most delicate issue at this time, for it is a time when the blending of the races must become fact. In order to do this humanity must by necessity put some restraints upon its conduct and means of functioning, for to effectuate the necessary changes requires affirmative action. Therefore, this period in history still requires a certain setting of boundaries and laws, which will provide for the necessary changes.

The way in which we view the quota system of insisting that a certain number of your planet's more subjugated members find equal opportunity in the workplace is this: We would retain the line of demarcation that calls for a certain number of ethnic peoples in any given job market, but the line would be drawn with an elastic band rather than a steel grid. That is, we would still prefer that the door be opened to individuals of various cultures and races for various positions that have been in effect via affirmative action. However, we would replace that steel grid of quotas with an elastic band wherein the exception is as often as great as the rule and that no qualified person be excluded.

We mean that although we suggest you try to fulfill certain quotas in order to swing the pendulum of discrimination into a point of proper balance, those equally or better qualified, regardless of race, creed or color, should be allowed into positions they are qualified for regardless of a given quota. Thus no one would be discriminated against, but rather a greater opportunity would open for those individuals and races that are as yet being held in discrimination. They would be given the best opportunity wherever appropriate and possible. On the other hand, this would allow those who are better or equally skilled to move through the elastic boundary of affirmative action to take their rightful place as well. Such a plan would allow for the best of all possibilities for all concerned.

Superstition

Many a spiritual leader will put down the idea of superstition, calling it the vague and nebulous imaginings of a human's mind. If we take a moment to look a little deeper into this statement, we will find a key word, "imaginings." Imagination is one of the primary tools of humanity's evolution. How often in spiritual literature do we find such phrases as "As a man thinketh, so he is" or "What you think, that you are"? More profound still is the scriptural, "I say unto you, if you have faith the size of a mustard seed and say to the mountain move, it shall move."

What then do we have? Imagination, belief system or a type of superstition, if you will. At the core of superstition lies the awesome power of thought. Thought is the thing, many wisdom teachings tell us, and superstition is basically thought power with a strong force and history behind it. It is so strong indeed that by the power of our belief do we make things so.

The key to superstition is to keep the positive and throw out the negative; in that way we can make it work for us. I recently saw a swimmer on the Olympic team who will race only with his lucky penny. At first this seemed ludicrous. Then I thought more about it. If the swimmer believes the penny will bring him luck, will make him swim faster, then that belief deep within the reaches of his subconscious mind *will* actually make him or help him swim faster. It is his confidence-builder. Why in the world should he discard it? True, a full master, a yogi and so forth, who has over lifetimes programmed his subconscious mind, would not need the help of such a belief system. Yet if the belief system itself helps one to develop confidence and positive imagery, why not?

More superstitions than one might think are based on folklore or are ancient observations. Some of these are actually fact-based, although many come from a misunderstanding of observations and events. However, these thought forms have been built up over centuries and can be very strong. So we are left with both baby and bath water. Although ultimately humans will come to rely upon their higher self, soul, monad and God, humankind is at various stages of this process and the masters take everything and all stages into account.

We, even those of us with mastership and high-initiate standing, who walk the Earth tend not to take into account or allow for each stage of evolving man/woman to have its place. The masters out of incarnation, unfettered by physical limitation, have an unbounded sense of compassion and an unfettered understanding of human nature. They know how crutches can help us reprogram our subconscious in ever higher ways if we so choose, and they support us along every step of the process. They have pointed out that if one can choose one's superstitions, the positive superstitions that reprogram the subconscious to higher ideals should be chosen. However, we must be mindful to reject from our thought worlds the patterns of superstition that work against our evolution and those that are fear-based. We must become selectively superstitious.

This positive side of superstition (the lucky penny and so forth) will key us into the power of belief. The ideal, of course, is to transcend superstition altogether and program our subconscious minds via our love/will and divine intent. Yet just as we work with astrology until astrology, as it works for the average man, is transcended and stepped up to a higher frequency, so too can we healthily work with the power of the mind and thought-form creation via the positive use of superstition and the group thought form that empowers it. The goal is to transcend the tools, but one can use every available tool to get to the transcendent place.

I know this is a different look at superstition, for it is from another vantage point that disciples and initiates usually view it, but it is nonetheless a valid look at one of humankind's most common practices.

How many of us have worn the same clothes to an interview that got us one job in hopes of gaining another? Of course it is not the clothing, but a subconscious confidence that might get us that job. It will at least increase our chances. How many of us have avoided driving down a street where we have previously gotten a ticket or had a minor accident? We might even take a more complex and dangerous route just to avoid the feeling that that street holds those particular perils. In this latter case I advise transcending your superstition and reprogramming your subconscious so that you can calmly drive your regular route. It is, however, noteworthy to mention that before the subconscious is reprogrammed, the fear itself might invoke the feared outcome. In this case I highly advise throwing out the bath water (the superstition), but first look well and see the power of the subconscious mind.

The ideal is the transcendence of superstition either positive or negative, but since most of us have these beliefs to some degree or another, why not use the positive ones to help build confidence in positive ways, such as to run faster, swim harder, get the desired job and so forth? Superstition in the most positive sense is the raft, and when the other side of the river is securely reached, the raft is discarded. However, while we are traveling the river and reprogramming our subconscious minds to the highest, why not use the raft of our positive superstitions and belief systems to move us swiftly to the hallowed shore at the journey's end?

The Mayan Calendar

The spin of the Earth, the turning of Terra, is intimately connected with the rate and frequencies of her vibration. The Earth being evolves as do all in and within the multiplicity of the universe. Time, which is the moving of cycles, is tracked in relationship to Earth and Sun and extends to the furthermost reaches of the cosmos. The Mayan calendar was created (or discovered, if you will) based on the relationship at a given point in time of the Earth and her frequencies and the Sun and its frequencies and the levels of those evolving in these particular frequencies. Much like a heartbeat or a pulse beat, these heavenly and earthly relationships (found everywhere, as all things exist in relation to each other, being divinely related one to the other) have a certain pulsation. This pulsation and rhythm, following certain patterns, created a specific way to format, track and count days and cycles of our personal lives and that of the heavens.

Now, when there is a shift of vibration and frequency, so too must these inevitably follow a shift of relationship and way of measuring that relationship. Vibrations move into another pattern and must be counted and measured in harmony with these new patterns and levels. Thus as the Earth herself begins to vibrate differently and finally stabilizes at a new higher frequency, so the measurement of time charted on the calendar is called to shift to match these new frequencies.

Here is a complex matter stated simply. We might say, inversely, that a simple matter of moving from one rate of frequency and dimension to another is made complex by the confusion within the human mind. This need not be so. What is happening is that new frequencies create new relationships, and a new relationship calls for an understanding of the cycles of that relationship. Thus new measurements are being computed and/or revealed.

This also must affect astrology, as it naturally follows that from different frequencies and relationships spring forth different and higher energy patterns. So again, the new age reveals itself in the calling forth of new manifestations, and those new manifestations will ultimately be a calendar more reflective of present frequencies and cycles. The year 2012 marks the stabilization of these new frequencies and the official beginning of a new calendar cycle of relationship. The new calendar will reference these adjustments, which more accurately reflect the relative relationship of Earth, the Sun and the heavenly bodies as well as cosmic shifts. All is relationship and we are speaking of the birthing and stabilization of new vibrational frequencies.

No Leader Is an Island unto Him/Herself

The unseen hand of the Creator absolute taps the invisible baton upon the podium of the yet-unformed heavens, and the highest of the angels begin to tone. The vast choir or heavenly host bursts into song and the music of the spheres is now in motion. From that flow forth the vast universes of form. Somewhere upon this little world a musical conductor stands. The first violinist sounds forth a resounding E, or the oboist sounds the note of A and the rest of the orchestra follows his lead. Then the conductor taps his baton on the podium and there is a moment of silence. A wave of his hand sets the players in motion and the symphony begins.

There is no doubt that the conductor is the so-called leader, setting the pace and rhythm that all may follow. Yet without the musicians and the composer there would be naught but the mad flapping of an arm with a baton at the end of it, for each part together with all other parts is the functioning whole.

When we assume the leadership of anything, be it an organization, a business, a spiritual community or a nation, it is vital to realize that although in the leadership position, we are but playing one role, fulfilling our puzzle piece, and that the group as a whole is the thing. All too often leaders can get caught in a trap of leadership, and in the glamour of their position forget that they are as much a part of the whole as is each and every one of the orchestra players.

Continuing the analogy, by simply taking the violin out of a violin concerto, or even a violin out of a flute concerto, we will not have the music divine. We will have just so many instruments searching desperately to find their place in the scheme of things. The leader, like the conductor, is the trailblazer, the pacesetter, who holds in cohesion each separate part; yet in that role let him/her not forget that she too is but part of the whole. Be mindful leaders and conductors in various positions of life's enterprise. Try not to be just the cellist, drummer, flutist, pianist and so forth. Learn not to hoard your position or power but how to delegate it amongst other parts of your particular whole. Do this with utmost discretion, because judgment or, better said, criticism rolls uphill and the work of the group will invariably be reflected upon you. Do not let this be cause for fear or trying to do it all yourself, for that is itself a trap and will bring to a halt the goal you seek to achieve. Simply be cautious, seek out those best suited to certain duties and delegate, delegate, delegate.

The singer looks to the accompanist, the accompanist looks to the singer and together they look to the conductor. As the conductor, forget not to look toward them, to your whole, or you put yourself and your goals at risk in having no one to conduct.

The role of leadership is not of negative ego but that of humility. He that is first shall be last. The saying goes that if you are to lead (and the world surely needs its leaders), be cautious not to invoke followers, but use your position to create and develop appropriate cocreators and co-leaders. In the orchestra all other violinists take their lead from the first violin. The first violin takes his/her lead from the conductor.

Yet the symphony is not complete if the triangle whose job it is to ring out a single tone fails to sound. Remember always to think of the whole and of yourselves in your unique leadership position as part and parcel of that whole. So it is with the universe down to the smallest grain of sand and into the heart of the electron and smaller still. Therefore the leaders stand, not with pride, but with integrity. Seek not followers but fellow participants and cocreators. Do not try to be or do the whole thing yourself, for that would be based on either negative-ego pride or negative-ego fear. Play your part by helping and encouraging the other members of your team, your band, your orchestra to play their own parts to the best of their abilities and by delegating responsibility to responsible people. Indeed lead, but as glorious trailblazers and conductors be ever mindful that you are simply and gloriously part of the whole.

Please, oh beloved trailblazers, those who tell good tidings of Zion and are up onto the high mountains, compete not one with the other. Give up competition amongst yourselves utterly and completely. There is a place for competition, but this is not it. At certain stages of growth a competitive spirit gives the person the needed impetus to make great and rapid progress. Once you have assumed the position of leadership, particularly spiritual leadership, all that must be cast aside. This is the time for cooperation and co-leadership. It is these qualities that move you and the whole ahead in the process of evolution. So please do a self-examination on a regular basis and throw into the violet flame any residual competitive qualities. Cooperation and moving at your own divine pace is the key to the perfect rhythm. The pulse of your own monadic and group rhythm is the key to higher leadership qualities. Follow this path with heart and group intent, and each group comprising the even greater wholes will proceed forward in perfect divine time—and the music will be magnificent!

Another Look at Leadership within the New Age

In this book on leadership it is of vital importance to look and look again, to examine and reexamine the idea of leadership in the new age.

This being the age of Aquarius and of group consciousness, it is by its very nature a group unfolding, whereas in the previous ages, and in particular the preceding Piscean era, looking to a leader was a natural outgrowth and manifestation. Now what we are dealing with is group consciousness, which is the awakening of the inner Christ, the inner Buddha, the inner God-self en masse. From this new and hallowed place we have group awakening, but those who are in the forefront of this awakening, by virtue of their own spiritual evolution, are the natural leaders of this new era.

The unique group awakening and the position of leadership within this awakening group is a subject for careful consideration. Humanity is now in the process more than ever before of moving forward en masse, awakening to the I Am Presence by direct experience and by tuning in to the very fact that humanity indeed moves forward as a whole. Whether this whole is in a small organization or in the realms of the soul, the monad and the cosmos itself, leadership takes on a new meaning. This is rightly so, as it is a new age.

Leaders will find themselves functioning in a very different fashion than previous leaders, especially in the spiritual arena. Leadership will take more of a role of guide, wayshower or, even more appropriately, way-sharer. The inner teacher will be revealed in each individual and more and more people will come to hear and follow the guidance of that inner teacher. The place of the leader will remain, although under a different guise.

To examine this point let us slow down a little and take a quick look at the evolutionary process itself. As man evolves, he is first under the dictates of his lower nature, the instinctual nature, the negative ego and the like. As he progresses he becomes more and more under the guidance of his own soul and, eventually, his monad. In the realm of soul/monad into which humanity is quickly moving, the realm of group consciousness is entered into in greater and greater wholes. Thus the role of leadership must, by the very nature of humanity's evolutionary standing, take on a new coloring. (For detailed information on humanity's evolution please refer to *The Complete Ascension Manual, Beyond Ascension, Cosmic Ascension* and *Revelations of a Melchizedek Initiate.*)

The leader finds him/herself the guiding force by virtue of the spiritual qualities developed at the apex of a particular group movement. The role of leadership in the new age has a great and important place. It is, however, a different place than in ages past and holds a different role. Leaders will find that they cannot blithely give orders that their group will blindly follow. And this is rightly so. Their place is to shine their light of love/wisdom with all its brilliance, to guide and to set an example. Leaders have an important and new job, and it is well to pay attention to this fact. To try and lead in any sort of dictatorial manner will not bear the desired fruit, for as previously stated, with more and more humans getting in touch with their souls and monads humanity must find its ultimate guidance within.

However, as there will invariably be others who are, for lack of better wording, further along their spiritual journey into the whole, those will by their very nature fall into or be called into positions of leadership. To them we say with loving wisdom, tread this path with utmost caution. Encourage but do not demand; give counsel and guidance but do not order; be the wayshower and trailblazer but never set yourself apart. The group moves forward, onward and upward as a whole. Souls are in groups, monads in greater groupings and the entire evolutionary thrust brings one more and more to function within the group whole. Therefore do your part, leaders, but realize that within the energies of this new age, leadership takes on a new and unique role. Lead by who you are and by a deeper and greater merging within the light and love that God is (which is also who you are), but tread lightly. Remember that what you are leading or way-showing is how to merge more fully within the whole of God and the whole of oneself, and how each may play his/her divine part within that whole to the fullness of one's capability.

So to you at the apex of various group movements, by all means shine your light and state your truth to its fullest. Guide, hold nothing back and do not shrink from your position, for it springs forth from your evolutionary status as well as your particular calling/work on the path of evolution. Remember also that it springs forth out of group need and the part you are playing within the group. Keep ever vigilant watch over yourselves that it is to the group that you offer the service of your unique positions, never the dictates of the negative ego's personal power.

You leaders are in truth trailblazers and wayshowers within a vastly expanding group consciousness and group evolution within the whole of God. Therefore pick up your mantles and wear them well in the roles that you are graced to play, but remember, ever keep in the fore of your mind and heart that leadership in the new age is not what it was in ages past, and that in your role you are as much a part of the awakening and expanding group as anyone else. More aptly stated, you are more group-aware, and it is your very surrendering to the greater whole of soul, monad, God and oneness that has put you in your positions at the apex of a group movement. Therefore guard well against any form of negative egotism, pride or separation. Assume your position and work within the whole, ever at one with the group you lead or, more appropriately stated, guide with the wisdom of your divine being.

Gossip

Regarding gossip or judgment of others, the Hierarchy puts forth a resounding, "*Stop it!* Let it not be." This comes through clear and resolutely, for they point out that the times we are living in call for, above all else, a cleansing of self, a focusing on the work and a clearing away of the personal and planetary contamination. "To judge," they continue to resound within me, "is to contaminate and not to cleanse."

Discriminate, always discriminate, or else you let yourself into the victim mode and can blindly be led to places you do not want to go. Keep alert to what is happening. Choose your right and highest path, then quietly go about your business. There is never a need to gossip, create or indulge in rumors or fragments of truths. You are only and always called upon to see your highest truth and live it to the fullest.

In these times where channels or prophets of sorts are in abundance, there is ample wisdom, light and love being revealed through them (us) to the planet. There is also room to critique, to judge, to compare and to gossip. Let us keep on the watch that this does not ever overtake us. Truths are revealed through many a voice, and one is not necessarily better than the other. The fountains, streams and rivers of God flow abundantly, and it is for some to drink from one fountain and for others to drink from another. Groups are springing up like flowers in the spring. Various centers of light are being formed to reflect and refract various aspects of the light.

We must definitely discern Christ consciousness from the negative ego and, yes, we must follow the call of one's particular spectrum of light, but that is all. We must not sit in judgment or join in gossip about a particular aspect of truth or light just because we are not called to pursue it. Perhaps you have already been down a particular path and another is first coming upon it. What value then to put down a particular teacher or aspect of light in the pits of gossip and destroy what should freely shine forth for other pilgrims whose very next step to awakening lies at the foothills of that particular teaching? Do not do it. Simply go on your way. If we each shine our light at the absolute brightest we can at a given time, then the darkness will be overtaken by our brightness and no harm will be done. But if we start picking at each other, we can do much damage.

Most lightworkers are sensitive to one degree or another. Some of us are very sensitive, for that is in the very nature of the work we do. While we work as well to develop our personal power to the utmost, we must also remain open to the energies, for that is how we receive and give. Gossip among our community is not simply a house divided against itself, but it is also a planet and cosmic purpose divided against itself. We simply must not judge, only discriminate and turn our concern to the work at hand.

I must again go back to the puzzle piece. Each being has his/her own part to play. The ladder has many steps, and it is vital that as we each awaken we are able to find assistance on those various rungs of the ladder. I try to cover everything or mention at least all stages of the path in my work because no step can be omitted and no rung of the ladder bypassed.

So if you find yourself looking at a brother or sister struggling with the rung just beneath you, offer him/her your hand, not your gossip. If you meet with a teacher or a book that is bringing light to that particular rung of the ladder, be glad and remember how it was when you struggled to reach it. Offer that person your love and support, not your gossip, for he/she is perhaps making an even greater sacrifice than you by coming down from the mountain to reach the hearts of her divine family that is climbing up. Who knows? I only know that the ascension movement should steer clear and remain clean from gossip and take into this new millennium the blessed words of Jesus, "Be not concerned with the speck in your brother's eye, but remove the beam from your own eye."

Let us proceed to shine our special lights, traversing all the rungs upon the great cosmic ladder with love and humility, not gossip and judgments.

The Glamour of Words

I find myself in the uniquely precarious position of being guided to share with you, my beloved readers, many, many words. Yet am I also guided directly from the master Djwhal Khul himself to caution you against the glamour of words.

I love words and the wisdom revealed through words. I speak them, I read them and I drink in the wisdom teachings of various wonderful channels, prophets of old and the masters. Now I am being told to hand you my gifts with a warning label that cautions you about all the glorious and incredible pearls of wisdom written and spoken by the various teachers through the ages. This warning is put into my mind through the remembrance of guidance given by Djwhal Khul through Alice Bailey: "Words tend to hide the truth rather than reveal it."

So I wonder what am I doing telling you this through words. Herein lies the paradox revealed. Although the medium of words and thought itself, when stepped down into the three-dimensional world, cannot possibly convey the energies tapped into from the higher-dimensional worlds, words act as a bridge between these worlds and propel us into ever finer vibrations. Words are sound and sound is energy. Energy carries with it various frequencies. The frequency varies with the word spoken. Some words, mantras and tones put us immediately in touch with the angels, with some of the highest and most glorious spheres. Other words (and we all can imagine what they are) plunk us into the gutter. Some words do far worse; some heal and some hurt.

This strange push I am getting from Djwhal to write about writing mainly has to do with one thing—to use the inspired word to propel you and carry you into the meditative stillness of your own I Am Presence, monad, group monad, inner being and your godliness itself. Words are like seeds that sprout within us so that we may come to full bloom in the indescribable. They are not to be discarded, for they are also like rafts that carry us to ever more divine realms. Yet these realms themselves are beyond description, and the silence is the greatest teacher of all.

Here is another interesting analogy. Suppose a book is like a lover. You talk, you laugh, you find out about each other and then simply get lost in love itself, in making and/or expressing it, in gazing silently into one another's eyes. So too the words reveal much, open much, take us to places that we have never dreamed possible. Eventually we then stop and meld with those divine places. We meditate, sit in the silence and gaze into the wonders of the word revealed.

It is my calling to offer you words and teachings, just as it is the masters' calling to offer these words and teachings to me and in other cases directly to you if you are telepathic, intuitive or a channel yourself. This is a most precious, precious gift and calling. The guidance, however, is this: Use the words to get to the place yourself. Take a seed thought and work with it; see and feel where it takes you. Even as I write this I am being shown two streams. They flow side by side up the great mountain of God (or the 352 levels of the Mahatma). At times these streams merge and become one bigger stream, then separate again, always moving in a constant flow one beside the other.

At the very apex of the mountain, at the godhead, at the 352d level of the Mahatma, the streams merge fully into a glorious crystalline pool. One of the streams is the word through various books, lectures, revelations, channelings, teachings, prophecy and guidance. It is the voice of God at various levels of the mountain, as the sound current at the top of the mountain.

The second stream is the silence, the meditation wherein the word, the thought, the idea, becomes the reality, the experience, the beingness. Man travels by both streams simultaneously, eventually to merge fully, totally and completely in the silent crystalline pool where all wisdom and love is contained. In the beginning was the word and the word was with God and the word was God! The two are *one*.

So, my beloved readers, you who seek the wisdom teaching of many revelations throughout the ages, I am guided to ask you only one thing, and that is not to forget to incorporate these precious wisdom pearls that many masters, prophets and channels have brought forth over time within the silence of your being. Take time to simply be, to live the words, to explore the glories that the written or spoken word attempts to reveal. Swim equally in the stream of revelation and the stream of silence, for they both course through your veins and are your very self.

Remember, it is that place where you become love, wisdom and being-ness—where you float in the heavenly pool at the top of the mountain or in the smaller pools where the two streams merge along the way—that you become the truth you seek, then reveal and transmit the knowledge and wisdom you know. For God is at once both the silence and the word, the doer and the deed, the journey and the journey's end, the eternal silence and the eternal sound. *Om Shanti Om.*

The Glamour of the Ascended Master

My beloved readers, this little gem is as important for me to write as it is for you to read and imbue within your consciousness, for it deals with a subject matter of great import. The ascended planetary and cosmic masters come forth to us upon Earth to reveal the light, love, wisdom and power and various other attributes of God. They in all their magnificence come forward; they step down their vibrations and raise our vibrations and frequencies to reveal God. Know that we are gods.

They come with various gifts, all of God. They come revealing various aspects of God such as light in the case of Lord Metatron, protection through Lord Michael and love and faith through the Christ energy of Jesus/Sananda, Lord Maitreya and his holiness Lord Sai Baba. But it all boils down (or rather up) to one thing: They come to reveal God and the glories thereof and to help us unfold the same within ourselves.

They do not come, my beloved readers and fellow pilgrims, to be celebrities. They do not come so that we may glorify ourselves through using their holy names or by the glamour of our missions. The son of man comes to serve, not to be served, said Jesus. So too the ascended beings come to serve, and like Jesus/Sananda, Lord Maitreya wants us to know that these works that they do, we too can do—and even greater works, for we go unto the Father.

The very purpose of the masters is to help us in our ascension process, and a core part of that process is to help us serve, to glorify God in man upon this planet and to bring glory to the Earth herself. The masters seek our devotion, it is true, but what they do with our devotion and reverence is twofold. They send it back to Source for the glory of God, then they magnify it and send it back to us for the glory of humanity and the raising up of the Earth. The masters are well aware of the fine line they tread in revealing themselves, yet this they do as part of the natural order of the merging of heaven and Earth. However, we the leaders who are in the forefront, at the cutting edge of this spiritual turning point, must guard vigilantly against being caught in what they have so aptly termed "the glamour of the ascended masters."

We must remember (and they tell me that they are pleased, as many of us are on the right track) that they have come forth to us in their infinite love and wisdom so that we can go forth into the world carrying within us their messages and our own incorporation and integration of that infinite love and wisdom. We must be ever mindful, however, that that love and wisdom, light, power and revelation not be tainted with any pride on our part, but rather filled with humility and gratitude for our purpose and the part we play. We must each recognize the various and diverse gifts of each other and by no means *ever* be in competition with each other.

As do the masters, so do we each have our particular puzzle piece to add, flesh out and embody. We should embrace that piece with love, joy and humility. There are wonderful leaders who work from inspiration and who neither see nor hear the masters consciously, yet are merged in the energy flow of the divine, simply doing the work. They are neither less than nor lower down than those whose puzzle piece it might be to consciously channel the masters. Some masters' work is behind the scenes and not to be known, even as it is the work of other ascended masters to work in the forefront and demonstrate the love, wisdom and powers of mastership.

All are part of the puzzle, and the *work* is the thing, not the glamour of the work or the masters.

Let us be careful and cautious then, we whose work is public and on the cutting edge of new revelation. Let us not even for a moment get sidetracked in the glamours of the work we do. We are here to work and bask in the glory of the presence and revelations of God and the masters, but never to make celebrities of ourselves or the ascended masters. Our holy communion with them is not notches on our spiritual belts, but through divine self-centeredness we are expanded into ever greater group consciousness and group centeredness. From planetary to solar to cosmic realms, our divine journey takes us, expands us and glorifies us, the sons/daughters of the whole, that we in turn might glorify the whole God.

But watch out for the pitfall of these realms. Be mindful not to miss the entire point in your revelations and exaltations. We liberate ourselves so that we might simply *be:* God is, we are. In fact, at every point on the journey we would be wise to remember this. Whether we till the soil to grow a single rose or mind-create worlds and all the vastness of God's glory that lies between the two, remember to simply be and embrace where we are. We can stumble upon a small stone, twisting the ankle, and fall to the ground with a thump if the vision ignores the road—the very path that is itself God. I am not saying not to keep your sights on the highest, but to remember also to be where you are.

One can likewise trip over the masters, and this is not their blessed intention. They come to us as beacons in the night, heralds of the dawn as Earth and heaven blend. They are indeed our elder brethren, sisters and friends, even as they are exalted lights. They want us to grow, to blossom into the splendor they are even as they expand beyond, for all moves onward, upward and becomes more inclusive. But how glorious the tender spring bud, pure in its green or white or violet or pink tender beginnings!

Do we not enjoy this wonderful sight even as we enjoy the fully opened flower? This is the essence of this little and potent revelation. Appreciate each step on the road, which is God, and the masters whose light illumines the road, which is God. Do what you do, the work at hand. Welcome the magnificence of the masters into your heart, mind and soul, but lose not yourself in the garden of higher revelations and make the masters a roadblock. All is God—all—and if your puzzle piece is to till the fields, type a manuscript, chop the wood or carry the water, let yourself be in that, and you will know that in that being you are God even as are the masters in their varied and glorious ranks. That thou art, and all is already one.

When this is known and fully embraced, when your beingness rejoices within yourself, you will look around and see yourself standing side by side with the masters. By the light and love of your being is revealed the knowing of God and in beatific humility you will find that you have become the master. It is by embracing the all and the work at hand that we cannot fail but to become in essence that which we already are—and that is God.

The Glamour of Initiation

It is a spiritual fact that humanity is part of a great evolutionary process. To elaborate on this subject in this little chapter would not be appropriate, but please read *The Complete Ascension Manual* for a detailed description. For a concise mental picture of the process I highly recommend Annie Besant's book *The Ancient Wisdom: An Outline of Theosophical Teachings* and also Djwhal Khul's channeled books through Alice Bailey, *Initiation Human and Solar, Letters on Occult Meditation* and *The Rays and the Initiations*.

Suffice it to say, then, that the monad putting down parts of itself into the causal world via the soul and into the four lower bodies via the personality through a process called initiation through the denser worlds, the monad evolves back into God, bringing with it the great expansion from its rounds of birth and rebirth. This is stated so simply that it barely does justice to the process. *Beyond Ascension, Cosmic Ascension* and *Revelation of a Melchizedek Initiate* go into this in as expansive a manner as possible. The point is that on our upward journey back to Source we go through a process of initiation, each one taking the personality/soul and then the monad itself into greater groupings, expansions and the love/wisdom realms of God Itself.

For centuries the Eastern traditional religions have honored that fact, and the people living within those cultures had a sense of working toward liberation from the wheel of birth and death to eventually return back to the unity from whence they (we) first came forth. Ancient mystery schools taught this in secret to certain initiates and disciples of high standing. Now the process is being recognized around the planet and is being called the ascension movement, which is the process of becoming more and more light, uniting with our monads and transforming into our God-selves.

At the dawn of the new millennium a vast number of people are awake to the initiatory process of growth, and under the banner of the ascension movement they are making great strides in their own initiation process and taking their guide or leadership positions, if that be the specific calling. This is a most wondrous and glorified time to live in, as the doorway to the kingdom of God is swung wide open and many of us are advancing past our wildest dreams at a rate that was virtually impossible only a short time ago. Of this I have also written extensively, and many of you know this information through other channeled material and your own connection to Source.

What the masters en masse impress upon me now is to speak of the glamour contained within the process of initiation itself and of the personal race it has become for many, if not almost all who work so diligently on their evolutionary process. They tell me the vantage point of initiation must not be seen through the lens of the personal self or lower ego at all, and that while most of us see almost clearly, we give way to a sort of contact lens, a minute but active lens of negative lower-ego perception of this process. They emphatically state that that lens must be cast out completely and utterly. To view initiation and ascension with any other faculty than the soul/monad is to corrupt its very purpose and purity.

We are not in a race. We are all part of an expanding group body. The vast group body itself expands as we travel the pathway of the higher initiations. Nevertheless, to be initiated means to expand with awareness into a greater group, the soul group, the monadic group, the ashramic group and so forth. It has nothing to do with personality or personal achievement, although it is a process that requires utter personal commitment and dedication. Therein lies the paradox.

We are each called upon to bring in the light, expand the light-and-love quotient, grow and find our place in world service, purify, cleanse and pass through the ranks of initiation. Yet to paraphrase beloved master Jesus the Christ, He (God) must grow greater and greater and I less and less.

If we begin comparing our own initiation levels one to the other, if we find ourselves competing against each other either personally or in a group, such as thinking that because we follow one teaching rather than another we are higher, better, more advanced, we are completely missing the mark. We should look at humanity itself as holding hands and forming one great circle. In circle formation do we ascend the mount of initiation. Those who are at the higher mark upon the mountain serve but to propel the entire group forward.

Ascension and initiation is a planetary event, not a personal competition. If you are made aware of your status of initiation, know that that is a gift given to you so you may greater serve the whole and see with more clarity the next step of your journey. It is not an Olympic gold medal you have won. It is a revelation that you have been given for the greater good. You are not better than another based on your level of initiation. If at a higher level of initiation you are, hopefully, consciously *more* at one with another and all others, that is all.

Those who have gone before us are our elder brethren and sisters. Although in higher planetary, solar or cosmic realms, they are still part of the circle. Everything is connected, and if anything should be focused on, it is that our higher initiations bring us deeper and more fully into this cosmic connectedness.

This needs to be brought out into the open because even high-level initiates and certainly disciples can fall into the trap of seeing their initiation through the negative ego. If this is done even by the tiniest of lenses in our eye, it distorts and leads away from true seeing. Do not compare. We say again, *do not compare*. Be ye not proud if you find out you are further along than you thought, nor be hurt and feel less than if you have not stabilized at a certain level you thought you had.

Initiation and ascension, while calling each and every one of you into ever higher realms, really has nothing to do with you. It is the letting go of the little I that propels us forward into the greater I—the eye of the needle, the eye of the cosmos. It is in forgetting yourself in the work that you do (and we are speaking specifically to disciples and initiates here, although the constant truth remains that you gain yourself) and in fulfilling your particular puzzle piece to your absolute best that the self is transformed into the greater self—the I Am, the monad—and you find yourself an initiate of great standing.

But remember, you are all great children of God, sacred parts of the whole, and it is to that whole that the attention should be focused, and to the work at hand. We who have achieved a certain high level of initiation embrace each and every one of you with our love. We say to you, the journey homeward is a glory unto God even as it is the reaching of home called ascension. Even we are called to ever greater spheres of inclusiveness. Home itself is ever expanding, so relax as you work diligently and know that you are sacred and cherished and needed right where you are even as you move upward.

Never forget that you are part and parcel of the evolving whole of humanity that is holding hands, and the heights achieved by one serve but to move the whole forward. All we ask is that you do the best where you are and drop any and all ideas of competition like a hot potato, so to speak, for the process of initiation and ascension is not a race but a journey. It is not the journey of the individual but the movement of the whole. And it is not a competition but rather a humble honor and glory, a glory that touches all parts of the whole simply because God is whole and God *is* the Whole.

So do what you do where you are, and do it to the best of your abilities. It will take you far. But relax in your process, for you are all ever blessed. We, your elder brothers and sisters, who remain at one with you have spoken. Namasté. *Om Shanti Om.*

7

God's Law vs. Man's Law

Throughout time, laws have been given forth to provide certain defini- tive structures through which humanity can function and evolve. Some of these laws were brought forth through the initiates, who were enabled to access the divine guidance of spirit, Source or God. Other laws were set forth by humanity itself. Such human or civil laws range from the noblest aspirations of those individuals who are or have been connected to their higher self to those that stem from the negative-ego mind. We as lightwork- ers have a deep responsibility to explore the laws that have been set before us in order to use our discrimination and discernment in their application.

I am by no means suggesting in any way, shape or form that we think ourselves above or outside the law. In truth, it is by the highest law that the cosmos itself functions and flows. I suggest that we examine the disparity that often lies between the inner law of God and the outer laws of humanity. In this transition period from one age to the next, many of us will undoubt- edly feel compelled and guided to be the instruments of this transition. Just as old forms will give way to newer, more refined forms, so must old, out- dated laws give way to the laws of this next millennium. The golden age cannot help but require golden laws.

Therefore, as lightworkers it is our responsibility to explore this sub- ject and to find the proper point of balance and understanding within our- selves. This subject is vast and multifaceted. There are many lenses through which we need to look at law, the two most outstanding being the civil laws made by man and the higher laws brought forth through the di- vine. We must, however, be aware that almost all forms of law are meant for the specific period of civilization when they came into being. This is much easier to see when looking at civil law, but it is equally true when looking at divine law.

In the days of Moses one injunction (law, if you will) was that dairy products must not be combined with meat or eaten from the same plate, and that a certain amount of time had to pass between eating these two foods. This was quite valid and spiritually directed at the time, for to mix the two without our present means of cleansing and purifying would invariably lead to bacterial contamination. Many people who follow a kosher diet observe this same law today even though the reason for the law is no longer valid.

In our exploration of laws in this chapter, be careful to remember that all laws are subject to transformation and transmutation. Beloved master Jesus himself was confronted with breaking the law of the Sabbath, for he healed a man on that day of rest. When accused of breaking this law of God, he said, "Verily, verily I say unto you, man was not made for the Sabbath but the Sabbath was made for man." It is with this lens of Lord Jesus/Sananda that I shall venture into the sanctified realm of law. It is likewise with this lens, as well as the wide-angled lens of the Mahatma and all his 352 levels of existence, that I invite you with me into this arena of exploration.

Civil Laws and the Negative Ego

Looking at the laws that govern various civilizations, states and nations, one can see that the governing laws come forth from many different levels of God attunement. A quick survey will reveal that some laws come from a soul level and are truly meant for the betterment and safekeeping of a given community, while others spring from the devious negative-ego mind. One such negative-ego law that immediately pops into my mind is the one that called for all African Americans to sit at the back of buses. There is no way in the universe to view such a law except from the vantage point of the negative ego's most self-deluded mode. That fact, however, did not stop it from becoming law, one that at the time had to be obeyed.

On the other hand, the laws against murder, rape and vandalism are soul-inspired. They have been created and are maintained as law so that humanity can live in peace and function without fear. This civil law is actually a manifestation of the spiritual laws to "love thy neighbor as thyself" and "thou shalt not kill" of the Ten Commandments. Unfortunately, our civilization often chooses to obey the laws that have come into being from the negative ego and disobey the laws that have come from soul inspiration. Although the bulk of humanity usually takes the higher road, there is much to contend with from those drawn to the negative ego.

The interesting thing is that all laws demand a full investigation via the Christ/Buddha mind. If we fail to do this, we will be unable to discern from what level a particular law is coming from or even when a divinely inspired law, such as that which prohibits stealing, might not be appropriate to follow. Consider the countries that chop off a person's hand for stealing a loaf of bread for a starving child. One would do well to question whether the robber or the law enforcer was acting more in accordance with true spiritual intent. Most would view the enforcer of this law as the true violator of divine intent.

Often throughout civilization, laws were created as much to glorify the negative-ego based rulers of the day as to offer protection to the people. Basically, such laws were mandated to keep the population in line that they might better serve the rulers. We have to look no further today than to these countries ruled by dictators to see the vile and inhumane laws that are put into effect so that the populations of these countries live only to serve and further the purposes of the dictators.

One of the most obvious examples of this is that of Hitler and the Nazi regime. It is a horrific and amazing reality that so many followed Nazi law, doing the most vile and horrendous deeds while functioning under this belief system, then later excusing their behavior with the words, "I was only following orders." Laws, my beloved readers, must be looked at through the eyes of our own God-selves. There it is clear what is out of alignment with the highest good, which is the highest law. Fear of physical consequences will bring the response, "I was only following orders." Almost all readers are in a country where most laws stem from a place of soul attunement. That is not to say that any of us should be puppets of any laws, but that the basic flow of our lives and the law of the land provides us with an environment where we can mostly be in the knowledge that we are not drastically out of harmony with God.

We are, however, in the transition period to a new age and dispensation when we are required to examine some of the intricacies of our laws in order to see from the Christ/Buddha lens. After such an examination we will be able to see where they need adjustment and refining in order to be in harmony with the newer frequencies.

One final note as we proceed. Within all subjects that we shall examine the negative ego versus the Christ/Buddha consciousness will be involved. Varying degrees of the negative ego will come into play, from the grossest and vilest level to those that barely brush the law that streams forth out of the Christ/Buddha mind, heart and spirit. I ask you all to keep this in the fore of your consciousness as I explore the multifaceted and various laws that humanity is enjoined to obey.

Freedom of Speech

The fight for free speech, one of our most quoted amendments, is a prime example of a law subject to multifaceted interpretations. This particular amendment, in the masters' opinion as they have made it known to me, is often used to justify distasteful and even highly debauched verbal and physical actions of humanity. I say "physical" because there are many instances when freedom of speech used to excess builds up such a mass of energy that it cannot help but explode into physical reality.

We need look no further than what is presently occurring at abortion clinics. Looked at from the viewpoint of the first amendment, everyone indeed has the right of free speech. No one holding any viewpoint on this delicate issue is dissuaded from speaking his/her mind. Self-expression and various opinions are intrinsic to human nature, which is why this amendment came into being.

The problem that this creates, however, is twofold. The first is the simple fact that most people functioning from the negative ego will not be content in the mere expression of their particular viewpoints. They will cling to them with such conviction that they will close off a true soul and spiritual assessment of the situation. This energy builds and builds, feeding upon both itself and those of like viewpoints until it cannot help but reach critical mass. This is what is producing the dire situations occurring all too frequently at abortion clinics throughout the country.

We thus have the dual problem of closed-minded, highly opinionated people taking freedom of speech to such excess that a physical manifestation follows, and clinics are bombed and doctors shot. Both actions result in the taking of lives—the very thing the crowd has gathered for and protests against!

Then there is the issue of racism, which is unfortunately still a real and tangible part of our society. The freedom of speech amendment tells us that we do have the right to speak our minds. Yet I ask you, my friends, does this give us the right to verbally attack and debase a race simply because it is not our own?

Fortunately, we as lightworkers see with a full-spectrum lens and know one another as brothers and sisters, souls forming part of the one spirit. But this is not the attitude held by society en masse. What then of the first amendment? It is there as law, there is no doubt of that. But should it not be tempered by the greater laws of soul, spirit and godliness? The masters tell me that indeed it should, for words in and of themselves carry their own unique energies and frequencies and have wrought far greater damage than the masses of humanity can even remotely consider.

We have countless examples of the force of emotionally charged words and thoughts manifesting brutally upon the physical plane. This can easily be seen when it hits a leader in the public eye such as Martin Luther King. Yet it is happening daily and hourly, claiming precious physical lives in all races. This affects even those who hold no race hatred in their hearts, for this is a group and world karma that lays its dense fog and astral miasma around the entire planet.

Discernment

The new millennium calls forth our utmost discernment regarding all laws, but let us focus a little longer on the freedom of speech. With the coming of new and higher frequencies, humanity in general is becoming aware of certain truths previously not accessible. For example, people are now generally aware that fur coats involve the painful trapping and killing of animals. The trade exists for the glamour and glorification of humans. Furs are not a beautiful symbol of success grown on lush trees in some secret chamber of expensive department stores.

The point is, much of humanity now sees the reality behind what fur coats are about. Seeing this, they are speaking out. This is a right we all have, and as a tool of education could be most effective. When, however, this knowledge is not used to educate and enlighten but to taunt and attack, it not only proves destructive but also generates anger. The entire message, which could have been compassionately conveyed to the less enlightened, is lost in abusive verbal attack. The verbal attacks eventually turn physical, resulting in a group of activists who use the law and amendment guaranteeing free speech to attack. Freedom of speech must be blended with the spiritual law of unconditional love.

The need for discernment can be easily seen. Man's law must be integrated with God's law. The soul and mighty I Am Presence must be consulted about how to use the freedom of speech amendment so that its highest properties are brought forth. Instead, people are running rampant with this law. In so doing, the very intent behind it has been totally subjugated to the more negative qualities in humans rather than the glorious spiritual qualities that the freedom of speech amendment was meant to encourage.

The law was created to enable humanity to voice its opinion and open the lines of communication. It was given for the advancement of humanity through dialogue and shared discoveries. It is vital for all lightworkers to see how this divine amendment is being grossly misused, currently functioning as a scapegoat for the voice of the negative ego.

As the masters urge me, I thus urge you, my beloved readers, to use your discernment regarding all things, this amendment in particular. As lightworkers we must keep vigilant and hold this gift in holy sanctity, using it only in the highest sense. If we are to help bring others into the divine truths that we ourselves have found within and around us, we must do this by education and example. Our words must ever be guided by soul and/or monad and never forced upon another. We can and indeed have the responsibility to lead thusly, but by divine design each must take the inner journey him/herself. Our words can be of utmost value in inspiring those we reach by written or spoken word, but the desire and willingness must always come from within each individual if the journey into his divine nature is ever to bear fruit.

We who are spiritual leaders must never misuse the freedom of speech in such a way that it causes fear, guilt or shame to our younger brothers and sisters. We have earned the right to encourage them by our own efforts and advancements, but never are we to try to force through manipulation anything that they themselves are not either seeking or ready for. This final injunction is given forth directly from Saint Germain. I have personally pledged myself to this law in the past and I encourage you, my beloved readers, to pledge yourselves as leaders to it as well. Much has been given and much is now expected, and what we give must be given as a sacred offering from the highest within us. Only in this way are we to teach and guide these who are in our charge.

Challenging Authority

Because laws are operative on many different levels, we as lightworkers must ask ourselves when or if it is appropriate to actively challenge authority. In the case of the bus seating law that forced all black people to the back of the bus, had not Rosa Parks actively challenged it, one might wonder how long it would have taken to make inroads against such discrimination.

This could not have been an easy decision on her part, as this was the law of the land and violating it was considered a crime. Yet following her own inner-soul attunement and guidance, she took this risk and in so doing, began a profound change in society.

I was discussing with the masters the matter of an appropriate challenge of authority and said, "This is a most delicate issue, as one could easily end up in jail."

To my amazement, there before me stood beloved master Jesus/Sananda, and in a most direct yet bemused fashion he responded by stating, "Yes, this is indeed true; you could also end up crucified." He then vanished within the soft light from whence he came and I at once understood his message.

Just as the drama of his life was played out at the time of a new dispensation, which required the massive cleansing and overhauling of one civilization in order to usher in the Piscean era, so we likewise stand at the threshold of a new civilization and the era of Aquarius. This too is a time period that demands an overhauling of civilization as we now know it, a time for the Christ within each of us to stand and walk with the light so we can help usher in this next millennium. He was certainly not saying that we should offer ourselves up for physical crucifixion, because this age is transforming in a different manner and his holy mission was unique. What I understood him to mean is that during this period the negative ego and lower aspects of both self and society were to be crucified so that the Christ might arise within us individually and globally.

In order to effectuate this transformation there will be times when our souls and/or monads will guide us directly to follow the higher law within us, such as was the case with Jesus, and on a more earthly level Rosa Parks. As humanity evolves, so do the governing laws, and humanity must help bring about this shift. As stated so eloquently in Ecclesiastes, "To every thing there is a season and a time for every purpose under heaven."

I was guided to make it clear that neither I nor the masters are by any means suggesting that we ignore the basic laws of the society in which we live. They say to try and live harmoniously within the structure of civilization, always operating from the highest aspect of any given law. They also say, however, that the great planetary shift now upon us calls for us to be open to the very highest within ourselves. This spiritual attunement will guide some of us to at times stand up to a given law, as the need of spirit will impress the necessity for change so indelibly upon us that as lightworkers of the spirit we will be able to do naught but respond to it.

Time and the Shifting of Spiritual Law

The above is a most delicate issue for some, yet it must be diligently explored. Certain laws were given forth from spirit, or God, if you will, at a certain time in history to help propel the people (our former incarnated selves) forward upon the path that leads toward initiation and ascension. These laws were brought forth through the Hierarchy of the day and were the highest expression of God's will for humanity at the time.

That these laws were brought forth by God and his messengers, otherwise known as disciples, initiates and masters attuned to the will of God, there is not the least doubt. Shifts in civilization accompany shifts in these laws. The basic truths of many of these laws still stand intact, yet the impact on the lives of the advanced initiates and embodied ascended masters will be quite different than when they functioned through a civilization, many of whose people were at the very early stages of initiation and most of whom had not yet begun the path.

Today most of us—indeed, all of us who are advanced lightworkers—have the commandment "thou shalt not kill" resonating to the core of our being. The people of the period when this commandment was given needed to be told directly that killing was *not* okay. Even today there are, unfortunately, many among us who need direct orders from God Himself not to kill, and so for these slumbering masses the law must yet be laid from without. To those of us who have seen the clear light of initiation, this law is part and parcel of our very selves.

What about self-defense and war? I again use the example of the Nazi regime to make a point. If pure evil is running amuck and striving to take over our planet, is it not our spiritual duty to stand up against it? Many beings of light were specifically guided to put themselves in this war and in other wars in order to help make the Earth a place reflective of the pure love and goodness of God. In this case the choice to fight a righteous battle for the greater good of the whole was indeed the highest choice. Those who were guided by their souls to refrain from fighting the outer battle of war formed, and still do, the ranks of the conscientious objector. If their motives were/are indeed pure and do not stem from the negative ego, then are they not likewise engaged in a battle for the good? The difference between them and those actively engaged in physical battle is that theirs becomes a spiritual battle and they work more on the subtle levels, resonating frequencies of love and brotherhood.

Each law and each individual's response to that law is a specific and unique case. That is why I say along with beloved master Jesus, "Judge not lest ye be judged." It is only God and the masters who know the true heart of man, and it is to that discernment alone that I leave the actions or nonactions of everyone. All I ask is that as lightworkers we weigh our decisions by the light of the most high and see what is the need of the hour, then have the courage to follow that need and the dictates of our own souls and spirits. It is thus that the lesser law will yield to the greater and the highest law of the new millennium will come to pass.

One very interesting aspect of spiritual law is that the meaning and application tends to change and shift along with the evolution of humanity. It is not so much that certain of the laws given forth at an earlier period are no longer applicable as that the application of those laws are taken up the spiral with evolving humankind.

For example, the commandment to honor thy father and mother has a variety of meanings and levels. The most obvious of these is to obey and honor one's parents. It was given during a certain phase of humanity's evolution when tribe and family were the means by which the civilization of the day functioned. As evolution progressed and new dispensations were given from spirit, we find Jesus in the New Testament proclaiming, "Who is my mother and who are my brethren? They that doeth the will of my Father, they are my mother and sisters and brethren." This was in direct response to being told that his mother and siblings were worried about him and that he should therefore stop his teaching to go see them.

If we then bounce forward in time to the present dispensation and consider the fact that humanity is evolving with astounding rapidity, taking initiation after initiation to complete its planetary ascension, one can see that sometimes in order to honor God one often has to act out of alignment with the desires of one's physical father and mother. This by no means implies that we should ever deliberately act with disrespect toward those who brought us into physical manifestation or try to cause them any discomfort whatsoever. In fact, we as initiates and masters should go out of our way to keep as much harmony as we can between our earthly families and ourselves. This, however, is not always possible.

If the respect you give to your earthly father and mother is answered with disrespect to you whose life is devoted to the journey of the spirit, what then can you do but to stay in integrity with self and continue on toward the beckoning spiritual heights? The ideal would be if parents would likewise honor the souls who came into the world through their vehicles to fulfill a specific mission. But for many of us, this is not always achievable. In cases such as this we must take the highest road possible with our earthly parents, but likewise take the stance of Jesus, honoring the divine Father and Mother, seeking integration with these divine aspects within ourselves.

During this particular age of change this is vital, for many are being called and many are being chosen, for many are choosing God first. This sometimes does not bode well with certain of our relatives who might have preconceived ideas about the path our lives should take, but we cannot tarry in our work because of it.

Sometimes it manifests in reverse, where the soul of the parent is more eagerly seeking God union than that of the child. This, as with all else, is based on certain karmic influences. In these instances those who are called to proceed with their initiations and ascension must also stick to their course, knowing God to be the ultimate Father and Mother. I am not in the least suggesting abandonment of the child in any way, shape or form. All I am saying is that we are now living in times of great acceleration, and all those who feel the stirrings within their souls should guiltlessly and freely follow their call to God.

Every day more and more people are connecting with Father/Mother God, thus elevating this commandment to incorporate a much higher level than it initially did for the civilization to whom it was first revealed. In truth, the commandments have not changed, but the level of our attunement to them is getting ever more refined as we are becoming closer to spirit. In the light of this awareness, law takes on nuances and color that hitherto could not be perceived. Yet the commandment to honor one's father and mother still has a literal applicability. The spiritual path is the path of balance and integration, and the literal honoring of one's father and mother and earthly extended family is still important.

Civil Law and the Awakened Soul/Spirit

There are certain specific instances of civil law that make even the half-awakened soul shudder and wonder what to do. There are certain laws held up to the population as necessary, as law invariably pulls at the heartstrings of lightworkers everywhere, often leaving us bereft and confused.

As I wrote this section I called in El Morya and Saint Germain to give further guidance and explanation on this subject. They made it clear to me that we of the light should stick to the light, and while we do our best to follow the law of the day and comply with the basic tenets of our society, where there is a blatant wrong in evidence we must fearlessly stand for the right and for the love/wisdom of God. Each person's puzzle piece is unique, as each individual is comprised of various ray structures, astrological configurations and so forth, so not everyone will feel inwardly summoned to the front lines. All who have even glimpsed the higher vision within themselves should therefore constantly strive to maintain that higher vision until it transforms their very aura and subsumes all lower aspects of self. For those who do spiritual battle from behind the scenes, there is likewise great power and great importance. It is everyone's responsibility to maintain and become the highest and noblest we can.

Comparing the Gandhi method versus the violent method of societal transformation, I asked El Morya and Saint Germain what they had to add to this discussion. As I expected, they were in favor of the Gandhi method. My two friends went on to explain that when standing for the right, even in the most passive way, risk is involved. The ending of the incarnations of both Gandhi and Martin Luther King then flashed before my inner vision. History, they said, had a place for aggression, and the soul learns much as the soldier. Then the image of Lord Krishna and Arjuna flashed before my inner vision and I recalled how much a soul who stands up to battle selflessly can learn. This phase of history would usher in the new age by means of spiritual light and love and the direct and selfless service of humanity to God. Although humanity learned much in fighting for family and country, now the battle is one of heart. The warrior is now the peacemaker; the only true war that is encouraged is fought within, between the negative ego, lower self, the soul/spirit and Christ consciousness. It is a method that advocates change and transformation, but by using the force of spirit rather than the force of arms.

Summation

I have only touched the surface of this subject with my friends El Morya, Saint Germain and Sananda. I could write a whole book, if not many, on this most fascinating subject. All Ten Commandments, all amendments to the Bill of Rights, as well as a great many of the state and federal laws could be examined. This subject could be broadened still further by examining all the different countries of the globe to see how man's laws related to the laws of spirit. I have only touched the tip of the iceberg to provide a lens through which you, my beloved readers, could begin to examine this vast subject. I trust that this chapter has provided this lens and I encourage my readers who feel drawn to the subject to explore and expand upon what has been written.

Conclusion by the Mahatma

I come forth in channel to speak to you directly, oh beloveds of my heart. You have in the reading of this most important book shown the courage to desire to know me fully and embrace me in the totality of my beingness. Lightworkers, truth seekers, devotees of God everywhere most often seek to know me only on the highest levels of my being. This type of knowing awaits the initiate, for reaching the godhead, or Source, is the call to which every soul and monad truly responds. Yet to know me thusly you must know me upon every level of my divine beingness. The realms to which this book has called you to explore and incorporate within your own wholeness are in truth the very realms you must traverse to reach me at the pinnacle of my absolute beingness.

Why do you think you are here upon this hallowed Earth? To deny your oneness with the Earth and all that lives and breathes therein? Certainly not! You believe that you are here to transcend the Earth; I tell you that this is truth, but only half the truth and half of that which is not understood by most of you except in fragments.

I Am the Mahatma. I embrace within myself all 352 levels of existence. You are yourselves an aspect of me and therefore you also embrace within your very selves all 352 levels of existence. By denying or trying to circumvent any aspect of self and therefore of the planet, which is part of your very self, how can you ever expect to truly and completely know me and join in full consciousness with me?

This book is but a step toward the understanding of the true nature of my being and therefore of your own. We already are one, oh my beloveds, oh you who are my very substance and self. I await to take you all into the fullness of that which I Am. In order to do this you must be willing to take responsibility and accept your own oneness with all of your planetary life. Although it is rightly your preference as well as your divine calling to function from above downward (that is to say, be who you truly are in your mighty I Am Presence and from that place divine do the needed work on the more materialistic spheres), yet it is by no means your calling to ignore these material spheres.

While your feet yet walk the Earth, let your heart and light also embrace her and tend to her welfare with all you have garnered from the loftier spheres. This is how I too function, my beloveds, as do all the planetary and cosmic masters. We remain centered and fixed upon that which for each of us is the highest, yet we actively participate in all that comes within the radiance of our being.

Therefore, when material such as that which you have read is set before you with its pure intent, know that it is in truth my prod to help you remember the world of which you are a part. Earth—a difficult lesson for all who have undertaken her challenges—is not always easy to look upon or act upon. Yet by the very nature of your being, here you are so called to both look and act upon her.

I am not speaking to you to tell you what part to play within and upon this globe, for that is a revelation each must bring forth from his/her own depths. What I do wish to tell you is that you are an intrinsic part of the planet itself, as you have aspects of your own essential nature upon all of her varied spheres. I marvel how like me you are, yet how much time you spend in seeking me. To know me best, just pause and recognize the fact that we are and ever have been one.

I ask you, then, as divine beings not to fear embracing any part of the whole of which you are a part. Of course, do this from the highest possible vantage point, claiming the divine fire within that in truth is your very self, but do it. You know the work that needs to be done, and many are the ways in which you can do the needed work. The way is certainly not the same for all, as each person is by God's own design meant to express his/her own aspect of the divine whole. The work you are meant to do, however, already thrills within your hearts and spiritual essences. All you need do is bring forth that work called right action by he who is now the Logos of your world and make it a tangible reality. Let the wisdom of your calling stream forth into your minds and infuse the whole of you that functions on this hallowed soil, then go ye forward and do the necessary work.

I applaud the courage of all of you who are willing to work with the material in this book as well as those of you who have long been working for the upliftment of humanity itself. Countless are the ways in which to serve—many more than could ever be written about in a three-dimensional book. Yet this book can set you on the path to find your true call to action, for this is indeed the need of the hour.

I call you all home. I call you unto the 352d level of godhead. I tell you likewise that in order to make the journey home, you must embrace the place, the world upon which you have chosen to journey, and pay attention to the needs of this world. I Am part of this world even as I Am part of each and every one of you. Make the journey complete, oh my beloveds, and take your stand even as you propel forward upon your journey unto Source.

It is my true and heartfelt prayer that this book has served to inspire you to follow whatever is your calling. It is likewise my prayer that you have come to see in greater light how God, how I, how the whole that you so dearly seek, is manifesting within the spheres of your daily civilization. When you work to heal the ills, you are thereby laboring to make that which is perfect even more perfect, for you are polishing one of the many faces and facets of God.

Know that I encourage you all unto ever greater heights and levels within my beingness. Even so, I encourage you to tend to the work at hand, for as I have said, my beingness pervades all. Keep moving through your initiations, keep reaching for the heights, but never forget that the higher you go, the more inclusive and grounded you become in your spiritual focus and the more fully is the whole revealed to exist in ultimate unity with the highest aspect of your being. Thus keep climbing upward, ever upward, oh ye pilgrims of the most high, but remember that the higher also holds within its spheres the less evolved. So do not forget to tend to the parts of the whole that are yet struggling to awaken.

I celebrate within each of you the inclusion of the whole of which you are a part into the auric sphere of your recognition and work. You are thus, as I Am, one centered in the height, the depth and breadth of your beingness, the calm at the center of life's ever-changing currents. Also are you the loving solution to the other parts within the whole that cry out for healing and attention. Invite me to continue to raise you up, ye who seek the pinnacle of my being, and I will do so. In return all I ask of you is to help uplift and upraise the part of you that struggles to see its way clear from the miasma of maya, illusion and delusion. I ask only that you do this in the way that your spirit so guides, as all within the cosmos must fulfill their one unique destiny as they continue to expand ever more fully, ever more deeply and ever more into the glorious being that is God Itself.

A Special Thank-You

I would like to give a special thank you to Zandria Fossa for her wonderful help in putting my books on computer and helping out with the editing. Her dedicated and devoted service in this area has allowed me to continue my creative flow of writing new books rather than getting bogged down in the time-consuming details of authorship.

I would also like to give a special thank-you to Rev. Janna Shelley Parker, Dr. Mikio Sankey and Wistancia for their help and editing in certain sections of this book.

About the Author

Dr. Joshua David Stone has a Ph.D. in transpersonal psychology and is also a licensed marriage, family and child counselor in Los Angeles, California. On a spiritual level he anchors what is called the Melchizedek Synthesis Light Academy & Ashram, which is an integrated inner- and outer-plane ashram representing all paths to God. Serving as a spokesperson for the planetary ascension movement, Dr. Stone's spiritual lineage is directly linked to Djwhal Khul, Kuthumi, Sananda, Lord Maitreya, Lord Melchizedek, the Mahatma and Metatron. He also feels a very close connection with the divine Mother, Lord Buddha as well as a deep devotion to Sathya Sai Baba.

Dr. Joshua David Stone
Melchizedek Synthesis Light Academy & Ashram
5252 Coldwater Canyon Ave., #112
Van Nuys, CA 91401
Tel. (818) 769-1181
Fax (818) 766-1782
http://www.rainstar.com/DrJoshuaDavidStone

Volumes in the series
The Easy-to-Read Encyclopedia of the Spiritual Path
by Joshua David Stone, Ph.D.
published by Light Technology

1. THE COMPLETE ASCENSION MANUAL
   How to Achieve Ascension in This Lifetime

2. SOUL PSYCHOLOGY
   Keys to Ascension

3. BEYOND ASCENSION
   How to Complete the Seven Levels of Initiation

4. HIDDEN MYSTERIES
   ETs, Ancient Mystery Schools and Ascension

5. THE ASCENDED MASTERS LIGHT THE WAY
   Beacons of Ascension

6. COSMIC ASCENSION
   Your Cosmic Map Home

7. A BEGINNER'S GUIDE TO THE PATH OF ASCENSION

8. GOLDEN KEYS TO ASCENSION AND HEALING
   Revelations of Sai Baba and the Ascended Masters

9. MANUAL FOR PLANETARY LEADERSHIP

10. REVELATIONS OF A MELCHIZEDEK INITIATE

11. YOUR ASCENSION MISSION
    Embracing Your Puzzle Piece

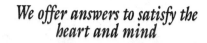

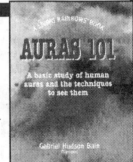

Former U.S. Naval Intelligence Briefing Team Member reveals information kept secret by our government since the 1940s. UFOs, the J.F.K. assassination, the Secret Government, the war on drugs and more by the world's leading expert on UFOs.

Behold A Pale Horse

About the Author

Bill Cooper, former United States Naval Intelligence Briefing Team member, reveals information that remains hidden from the public eye. This information has been kept in top-secret government files since the 1940s.

In 1988 Bill decided to "talk" due to events then taking place worldwide. Since Bill has been "talking," he has correctly predicted the lowering of the Iron Curtain, the fall of the Berlin Wall and the invasion of Panama, all of record well before the events occurred. His information comes from top-secret documents that he read while with the Intelligence Briefing Team and from over 17 years of thorough research.

by
William Cooper

$25⁰⁰

Softcover 500p
ISBN 0-929385-22-5

Excerpt from pg. 94

"I read while in Naval Intelligence that at least once a year, maybe more, two nuclear submarines meet beneath the polar icecap and mate together at an airlock. Representatives of the Soviet Union meet with the Policy Committee of the Bilderberg Group. The Russians are given the script for their next performance. Items on the agenda include the combined efforts in the secret space program governing Alternative 3. I now have in my possession official NASA photographs of a moon base in the crater Copernicus."

Table of Contents

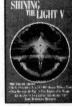

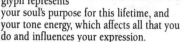